D1521604

Milton's Eve

Diane Kelsey McColley

MILTON'S EVE

UNIVERSITY OF ILLINOIS PRESS

Urbana Chicago London

Frontispiece: The creation of Eve, engraving from the *Biblia Maxima* (Paris, 1660)

© 1983 by the Board of Trustees of the University of Illinois
Manufactured in the United States of America

This book is printed on acid-free paper.

Library of Congress Cataloging in Publication Data

McColley, Diane Kelsey, 1934–
Milton's Eve.

Includes index.
1. Milton, John, 1608–1674. Paradise lost.
2. Milton, John, 1608–1674 — Characters — Eve. 3. Eve
(Biblical figure) in literature. 4. Women in literature. 5. Fall of man in literature. I. Title.
PR3562.M34   1983   821'.4   83–1313
ISBN 0-252-00980-0

For

Arthur E. Barker
Robert M. McColley
Lauren and Lelah Kelsey:

to whom the faithful
shepherd's art belongs.

Acknowledgments

Reading *Paradise Lost* is a form of communion. We may do it separately, but not alone. Our delightful task stirs up what Milton called a gust for Paradise, not only by making us desire the life of active goodness his poem figures forth with such beauty and interest, but also by creating a community of readers for whom its radiant cosmos is a deeply shared experience. Students of Milton can always say with pleasure, "This enterprise, many partake with me."

It is a pleasure to thank those who have partaken in this reading. Arthur E. Barker, Fellow of the Royal Society of Canada, first posed the problem that is the crux of my argument, that of the implications of unfallen Eve's separation from Adam, and has with truly Miltonic magnanimity provided light after light. Irene Samuel gave the manuscript a scrupulous reading and made valuable suggestions for revision of both structure and detail. Stella Perse Revard, Virginia Ramey Mollenkott, Carol Thomas Neely, Joan Larsen Klein, J. Max Patrick, Roy C. Flannagan, and an anonymous reader for the University of Illinois Press gave helpful evaluations and advice. Philipp Fehl, Barbara K. Lewalski, and Philip J. Gallagher commented expertly on certain sections, and Fay Porter Nowell, Susan Westbury, Cheryl Clark, and James L. Sanderson gave aid and encouragement. I am grateful to innumerable others, including scholars whose work I have mentioned primarily for the purpose of disagreeing with it, but who have contributed manifestly to the enterprise, and to my students at the University of Illinois and at Rutgers University, Camden College of Arts and Sciences.

The thesis of this study was first published in *Studies in English Literature* 12 (1972); and portions of it have been published in *Modern Philology* 74 © 1977 by The University of Chicago, *Sixteenth Century Jour-*

nal 9 (1978), *Milton Studies* 12 (1978), and *Familiar Colloquy: Essays Presented to Arthur Edward Barker,* ed. Patricia Brückmann (Ottawa: Oberon Press, 1977). I thank the publishers for permission to use these essays in *Milton's Eve.* N. Frederick Nash and the staff of the Rare Book Room of the University of Illinois Library provided a place to work and a peerless collection to work in. The Research Council of Rutgers, The State University of New Jersey, helped defray expenses of preparing the manuscript.

My husband, Robert McColley, has been a constant source of "meet conversation" and more-than-mutual help of every kind; and our children, Rebecca, Susanna, Teresa, Margaret, Carolyn, and Rob, contributed "more hands" and a cheerful and affectionate independence. I thank my parents, Lauren and Lelah Morris Kelsey, for their sense of beauty and of stewardship.

Contents

I

"Native Innocence": God's Ways toward Eve

On the last morning of their unfallen lives, according to John Milton, Eve suggests to Adam, "Let us divide our labours," for

> till more hands
> Aid us, the work under our labour grows,
> Luxurious by restraint; what we by day
> Lop overgrown, or prune, or prop, or bind,
> One night or two with wanton growth derides
> Tending to wilde.
>
> [9.205–12][1]

The ensuing dialogue explores the pith of Milton's thought about freedom and right action and issues in Adam's consent:

> Go in thy native innocence, relie
> On what thou hast of vertue, summon all,
> For God towards thee hath done his part, do thine.
>
> [9.373–75]

Probably no other writer, certainly no genre or topos, shows Adam and Eve responding to their calling to dress and keep the Garden; and no other interpretation of Genesis explains Eve's presumed separation from Adam at the time of her temptation by endowing Eve with a sense of responsibility.[2] Painters and poets usually depict prelapsarian life, if at all, as idle, sumptuous, and brief, and the first woman as inherently deficient in virtuous enterprise; the mother of mankind in art and verse is weak, vain, useless, mindless, trifling, grasping, vacillating, wanton, obstinate, presumptuous, and (none-theless) fatally seductive. At her most appealing, she embodies passion subjugating reason; at her worst she is the apt and willing instrument of evil. So great is the weight of misogynous tradition, in fact, that few readers of *Paradise Lost* have made bold to say with Adam that God has done his part.

Milton's predecessors offered two prevailing attitudes toward Eve's role in the Fall of Man. One was to blame the world's woes on Woman and regard her as a *malum necessarium* shaped for procreation and otherwise a briefly honeyed snare: an explanation that casts grave doubt on the providence of her Maker. The other was to agree that Eve was a "fair defect of nature" but to vindicate God by averring that the Fall was fortunate: sin entered the world through Eve that God might more perfectly manifest his glory through the process of redemption.[3] More recent interpreters have thought the Fall not only fortunate in the theological sense but also a forward leap in the moral and artistic development of mankind. If Adam and Eve had not fallen, the theory goes, they would have languished in an insipid reverie destitute of adventure and challenge. Without doing evil, they would not have known how to do good; without conflict, they would not have known courage, compassion, and triumph; without pain and death, they would not have known love and joy. Contrary to the laws of God and nature, it would seem, Adam and Eve fell upward.

For the Christian poet setting out to assert eternal Providence and human dignity, such a state of thought about God's ways, and especially about God's ways to women, could not accord with either faith or reason. If human love and accomplishment depended on faithlessness and failure, or God's grace depended on disobedience to God's word, or Paradise did not offer unlimited possibility for every sort of achievement and delight, God would not be God and Eden would be, as Eve avows, "no Eden" (9.341). Milton's response was to invite a renewal of the imagination by recreating a paradisal life so filled by God's creating hand with interest, opportunity, choice, and bliss that every human faculty and capacity could enjoy, free from the hindrances of sin, misery, and death, its fullest exercise, and to engage the reader in a mimetic experience of unfallen virtue that exercises, even in "all our woe," those faculties and capacities for fullest use in the process of regeneration.[4]

Given such a God and such a poetic program, how was Milton to cope with the eternal feminine in the shape of a notoriously obstreperous Eve?

The idea of Eve that Milton's age inherited resulted from a dualistic habit of mind that he strove in all his works to reform: the supposition that nature and spirit, body and soul, passion and reason, and art and truth are inherently antithetical and that woman, the primordial temptress, represents the dark and dangerous (or rebellious and thrilling) side of each antithesis. If this were so, then the God who made Eve and gave her to be "meet help" for Adam would be, as fallen Adam claims, baiting a trap. To incline man, through woman, to sin and thence to pain and death would be unjust; to create for Adam's meet help a mate unmeet and helpless would be improvident. Moreover, if passion and imagination are opposed to truth, the production of poetry is itself an impious enterprise. If Milton was to obey his own calling to "assert Eternal Providence, / And justifie the wayes of God to men"[5] in sacred song, his crucial task was, in the face of an overwhelmingly antifeminine tradition, to create poetically such an Eve as a just and provident God must be supposed to have created actually. That is, he had to create an Eve who is imaginative and rational, sensuous and intelligent, passionate and chaste, and free and responsible, and to show her fruitfully tempering the ingredients of virtue in everything she does until the moment when Satan's lies "into her heart too easie entrance won" (9.734): an Eve, in sum, who answers, and who might even at the moment of "too easie entrance" have continued to answer, to Adam's words of faith, which are also Milton's summons to his reader, "God towards thee hath done his part, do thine."

Most critics of *Paradise Lost,* however, find Eve fatally frail or innately perverse before the temptation begins. Many think her vain and obstinate, and Adam weak and uxorious, throughout the prelapsarian scenes.[6] Some who have taken care to exonerate her in earlier scenes nevertheless find her already corrupted in the separation scene, well before the narrator calls her "yet sinless" (9.659) and just at the point when Adam assures her that God has done his part.[7] I believe that readings of *Paradise Lost* in which Eve appears to be inclined toward sin before the Fall have been colored by expectations that Milton hoped to reform, and that his portrayal of her stands in radiant contrast to the sly or naive temptresses who bore her name in

the works of Milton's predecessors and contemporaries. Her prelapsarian words and acts, including those represented in the separation
scene, are not foreshadowings of necessary sin, but illustrations of
actual and potential virtue; they prefigure not only a possible fall,
but the work of regeneration, in which a fall is always possible but
never inevitable. All of Eve's speeches and actions, except the Fall itself and its direct results, body forth talents, virtues, and graces developing freely through the inspiriting and refining joys, liabilities,
perplexities, hazards, and opportunities of experience; and all are
applicable to the lives of the "fit audience" that Milton was addressing and creating.

This study is an effort to extricate Eve from a reductive critical
tradition, as Milton sought to redeem her from a reductive literary
and iconographic tradition, and to establish a regenerative reading
of her role: that is, to show that Milton has fashioned an Eve who in
all the prelapsarian scenes is not only sufficient to stand and able to
grow, but who while standing and growing, however vulnerably, is a
pattern and composition of active goodness and a speaking picture of
the recreative power of poetry itself.

The following brief account of the iconographic and literary milieu
from which Milton's Eve emerges, to be supplemented in subsequent
chapters, should assist her to emerge more fully to our present view.

The Iconographic Tradition

The *Earthly Paradise** of Jan Brueghel the Elder represents a wooded
landscape of glowing tranquillity, rich with lustrous fruits and delicate flowers and teeming with delightful birds and beasts, most of
them two by two, in alert repose or gentle play. From this entrancing
foreground, the eye is led by lights of stream and sky to two distant,
pale human figures. One reaches toward the other with one hand
and, with the other, toward a tree. Vaguely entwined around the
tree is what might be — or might not be — a vine. Nearer, two monkeys, the apes of human form,[8] take golden fruit, while a parrot, the
ape of human speech, looks knowingly on. In a clearing under the
barren reaches of the bough on which they sit, two cats intently
watching two mice hold innocence and premonition in similar poise.

*See the illustration section at the end of this chapter.

What might the human pair be doing? Several interpretations are possible, and our responses will reveal our assumptions about "native innocence." The reaching figure may be offering fruit from one of those trees of which God has said they may freely eat. Adam may be explaining to Eve that this (despite the nearer barren bough) is the one tree from which they may not eat. Adam and Eve might be discussing how best to prune "Fruit-trees [that] overwoodie reachd too farr / Thir pampered boughes" or to lead the vine "to wed her Elm" (5.213–16). But one would probably need to have read *Paradise Lost,* produced a half-century later, to make any of these responses, certainly the third. For most viewers, I suspect, the delayed discovery of the small, reaching human forms provides the experience of being "surprised by sin."[9] The beasts may seem to stir; the lion lifts his head and glares, and the young stag, an emblem of contemplation and purity of life,[10] pricks up his ears and prepares to bolt, if need be, out of the frame. The scene transmits a tremor of apprehension that lends poignancy to the peaceable.kingdom about to be lost.[11]

The iconographic tradition that shaped the Renaissance image of the first man and the first woman offered almost no representations that suggest what Milton makes the heart of his poem: the prelapsarian lives of Adam and Eve. Pictures of Adam and Eve in innocence, after God has married and instructed them, are extremely rare. Brueghel's is unusual even in its transient ambiguity. Most of the few I have found that do not foreshadow an immediate fall are book illustrations by northern artists: these include an illustration in the Junius Manuscript of the unusual lines, "and evermore, performing Heaven's behests / They dwelt in holy joy, nor sorrow knew"; an illumination in *Die sieben Zeitalter der Welt* (c. 1460) in which God blesses from above an innocently conversing human pair among tranquil animals; the illustration of Genesis attributed to Lucas Cranach in Luther's Bible of 1534; the frontispiece to John Parkinson's treatise on gardening, *Paradisi in Sole Paradisus Terrestris* (1629) — which, however, shows Eve in the ambiguous act of picking a strawberry, an emblem both of innocence and (in Bosch, for example) of lust; and the amorous engravings of Adriaen van de Venne and other Dutch artists for the works of Jacob Cats.[12] Even these few wistful exceptions do not suggest that life before the Fall was active, productive, or dramatic. Few artists imagined Adam and Eve setting about to increase and multiply, and perhaps none showed them obeying the injunction to dress and keep the Garden, despite the rich allegorical and metaphorical meanings of that commandment in homily and commentary and the abundant implications of the trope of cultivation in essay and verse. The pictorial tradition makes the Garden a place of idle pleasure, Adam muscular but ineffectual, and Eve either dangerously innocent or attractively wicked. Worse, by lavishing its greatest imaginative power on the moment of disobedience it suggests that all really interesting human activity began with the Fall. The Renaissance eye had little preparation for the entrance of Adam and Eve into Milton's poem as "Lords of all" in whose "looks Divine / The image of thir glorious Maker shon" (4.290–92), and the Renaissance imagination was poorly stocked with such images as Milton invents to embody his faith that a rich, vital, efflorescent and joyous life could be lived — indeed could only be lived — in responsive obedience to God.

Throughout the centuries of Christian art, representations of the first three chapters of Genesis have focused on the topos of temptation: Adam, Eve, Serpent, and Tree. Pictorial narratives regularly proceed from either the creation of Eve, the marriage, or the prohibition directly to the first sin, with no depiction of original righteousness in between. Since the text of Genesis does not offer an actual demonstration of original righteousness (though it rather suggests than denies its possibility), Bible illustrations follow this program, as do ancient sarcophagi, medieval church and book decorations, and Renaissance cycles such as Ghiberti's bronze doors, Cranach's narrative painting, and Michelangelo's Sistine frescoes. Usually, as J. B. Trapp points out, the Genesis cycle appears in surroundings that emphasize the process of redemption.[13] Michelangelo's is atypical in stressing, along with the offer of redemption, powerful conclusions of agony and woe. More often, the climax of an iconographic program is the Incarnation or the Celestial Paradise, and the sequence contrasts, often by visual parallels or oppositions, Eve as the instrument of evil with Mary as the vessel of grace — a contrast summed up in the recurrent topos of the Annunciation with the Expulsion. Whether or not the effects of the Fall are regarded as remediable, or even fortunate, however, the mother of mankind is primarily a temptress.

Those artists who, increasingly in the Renaissance, concentrated the story in a single scene almost invariably selected the moment of Adam's choice. In a few versions, such as Mabuse's, Raphael's, and the frontispiece to Genesis in the Geneva Bible, Adam and Eve both fall at once.[14] In others, such as Dürer's 1504 engraving or Titian's painting, a seductive Eve takes the fruit while an anxious Adam looks on perplexed or tries to restrain her. But most often, as in the paintings of Rubens, Tintoretto, Salviati, Dürer, and Cranach, the Medici tapestries, and van Linge's chapel window at Oxford, Eve tempts Adam, commonly taking the fruit from the Serpent's mouth with one hand and offering it to Adam with the other.

Within this tradition one finds a rich variety of Eves, ranging in predominant attributes from wanton frailty to superb and tragic dignity, but none that emphasizes, as Milton's does, her present and potential virtues. Above all, for the Renaissance artist, she embodies an overpowering physical beauty that is both a glory and a snare, uniting the Paradise she loses with the source of the loss. Often the temptation is implicitly sexual, and sometimes, as in the versions of Tintoretto and Floris, it is explicitly so. By linking beauty and sexuality directly to an immediate Fall, these works suggest to the unreflecting viewer either that beauty and passion are inherently corrupting, and therefore to be avoided, or else that the Fall produced erotic love and was therefore to be desired. These implications are among the misapprehensions Milton addresses in *Paradise Lost* by linking divinely created beauty and a chaste and ardent sexuality directly to "native innocence" and distinguishing their fallen parodies by a glitter and a greed that quickly pall. Whether or not it is primarily sexual, Eve's temptation of Adam conventionally represents human pride, self-love, and concupiscence overcoming reason. Self-love and concupiscence are allegorically associated with Eve and hence with womankind, and are often symbolized by making the Serpent's head Eve's mirror image.[15] The composite of these views is the antithesis of the goodness Milton forms her for.

A reader of *Paradise Lost* who wishes to remember the poles of interpretation Milton found in the iconography of Eve, and so be alert to the differences in his characterization of her, might use as touchstones two radically different sixteenth-century paintings: Hieronymus Bosch's marriage of Adam and Eve in the altar triptych known as *The Garden of Earthly Delights* and Raphael's fresco *Adam and Eve* in the Stanza della Segnatura.

In Bosch's painting, a benign though wary Creator presents a winsomely innocent, modest, simple, and pliant Eve to a naively delighted Adam. But at their feet, misjoined creatures struggle, and a haughty cat dispatches a paralyzed mouse in an unmistakable prefiguration of the Fall. The rabbit, a symbol of procreation, turns his back. The rest of the triptych fulfills the prolepsis: in the center, proliferations of echoingly lithe and golden-tressed Eves cavort in a fountain, like Spenser's "naked damsels,"[16] among emblems of lasciviousness and seduction, and in the third panel the occupants of hell display the perversities of lust. It is not clear whether the blameless-looking rabbit in panel one is tainted or merely defeated by the corrupt sexuality of panels two and three, but the parodies of Eve redound to shed a certain irony on their modest prototype.

Raphael's Cytherean Eve, on the other hand, is open, knowing, dominant, and intense. She and Adam reach toward the Serpent open-palmed. Not only is the Serpent half woman; it is a shadowed Eve: the same half-turned face, straight nose, bowed mouth, and rounded breasts, the same hair (the Serpent's darkened by shade) waved back over the left shoulder and hanging loose on the right, each grasping a limb of the tree, their heads nearly touching, and each bending on Adam the same provocative gaze. The Serpent is the dark side of Eve herself. The context of the fresco is the Stanza's magnificent tribute to divine and humane learning; it is architecturally linked to the *Allegory of Theology* and *The Glorification of the Holy Eucharist* and more remotely to *The School of Athens, Parnassus,* and all the virtues, arts, and sciences the Stanza celebrates.

Both paintings suggest a connection between the Fall and sexuality that Milton, asserting the essential goodness of creation, could not accept. Within their respective contexts, Bosch's modestly yielding Eve and Raphael's openly seductive one suggest opposed implications that Milton was moved to revise. Bosch's Eve, juxtaposed to vice and damnation, seems the innocent—perhaps deceptively innocent—source of sin and death; Raphael's, surrounded by monuments to humanity and divinity, seems the wanton portress at the gates of divine mercy and human achievement. The challenge for Milton, in the face of almost universal assertion that frailty's name is woman, was to create an Eve who might have been Adam's meet companion and help in all the spheres of grace and merit that the Stanza praises without ushering in the frenzied dissolution that Bosch's triptych decries: an Eve who combines the winning innocence of Bosch's Eve and the sensuous beauty of Raphael's with a mind "fit to participate / All rational delight" (8.390–91) and the talent, spirit, wit, and vitality to embody the lively conceptions of original righteousness, replete with accomplishment and joy, that Milton brings mimetically to birth.

The Literary Tradition

Until Milton undertook "things unattempted yet in Prose or Rhime," verbal accounts of the Fall displayed discursively what visual ones suggested graphically: a dualism reflected in the conflicting roles of primal man and woman. Typically, the story is interpreted literally as male virtue undone by female concupiscence and figuratively as passion subjugating reason or the soul made thrall to the body's rebel powers. In prose, both allegorical Fathers and literal-minded reformers saw the beauty, passion, and imagination Eve embodies as perils to avoid. In rhyme, poets linked Eden with Arcadia and made Eve a lovely nymph without distinct personality, responsibility, or moral sense, too mindless or too vain to help Adam except (for some) in procreation and, perhaps by that one merit, suited to effect his ruin. The result of patristic, Protestant, and humanist interpretations alike, and of their entwining, is what J. M. Evans, in his valuable account of the backgrounds of *Paradise Lost,* shows to be a minimizing view of Eve.[17]

In current usage, the word *dualism* may mean a belief that God created things visible and invisible; or that good and evil have different and perhaps equal eternal sources; or that matter and spirit are separate and opposed. For many of Milton's predecessors and contemporaries, the natural and the spiritual worlds seemed polar opposites and the visible world so corrupt that the only assurance of salvation lay in repudiating it altogether. Milton was a monist. For him, the distinction between things unseen by human eyes, such as the "millions of spiritual Creatures" who "walk the Earth / Unseen" (4.677–78), and things visible to them is one of degree, not of kind. All created beings derive from "one first matter" proceeding from God (5.469–72). The substance of angels is more refined and subtle than that of men's bodies and is single rather than compounded, but it is still "matter." Heaven has its times and latitudes and materials. Spiritual beings are in some sense "visible" to each other and, when they wish to be, to men. Presumably men, using light after light, will be able to see more and more. The Son of God, in whose "conspicuous count'nance, without cloud / Made visible, th'Almighty Father shines" (3.385–86), makes himself visible on occasion to Adam and Eve and, in the Incarnation, to their descendents. Nature and supernature, things seen and unseen, are a continuum. Evil is not the opposite but the perversion of good. Although visible nature lies under the curse of death by Adam's sin, to the regenerate all things are instrumental for goodness, since the Son's redemptive action has made possible both natural and supernatural renovation and the gradual sanctification of those responsive to it. Nor has anything in nature been abandoned by God's Spirit. In spite of the Fall, Michael tells Adam, "his Omnipresence fills / Land, Sea, and Aire, and every kinde that lives, / Fomented by his virtual power and warmd" (11.335–37).

For those to whom matter itself seemed hopelessly corrupt, sanctification seemed to require total renunciation of the things of this world. Richard Baxter could say with complete sincerity that ill health and a fearful conscience in youth were benefits from God, since they "made me vile and loathsome to myself . . . made the World seem to me as a Carkass that had neither Life nor Loveliness: And . . . destroyed those Ambitius desires after *Literate Fame,* which was the Sin of my Childhood!"[18] But Milton is writing about God's new creation, and about that unfallen world as an image of the goodness that can be found and practiced even in the fallen world by regenerate persons whose actions can help restore it, or parts of it, to something nearer its primitive brightness. The material world is the art of God, created in beauty and plenitude, animated by his Spirit and sustained by his providence, who saw that it was good and blessed it and bade it be fruitful. The forbidden tree might be thought of as God's signature on his work, his *Deus fecit* to remind Adam and Eve that "it is he that hath made us and not we ourselves," and so to free them from the pride that diminishes and breaks faith with the harmony of creation. That Sign is the one limit that frees them from all other limits. As the art of God, the natural world is wholly good. It can be depraved from good if the limit is crossed and the harmony broken. But if not, if God and each creature are held in love, it is all delight, beauty after beauty on every hand, and an inexhaustible cause to rejoice.

In contrast to the sense of wholeness, connectedness, and blessedness that composes the felicity of Milton's Garden, some interpreters of Genesis have supposed that matter, flesh, sexuality, and woman have something intrinsically wrong with them and that the story of our first parents shows woman as flesh, passions, nature, and sexuality seducing man as soul, reason, spiritual virtue, and contemplation from his proper relation to God. This kind of dualism has roots in classical, rabbinical, and patristic sources. That females lack the higher faculties and virtues seems implied by Aristotle's statement that the female is "a deformity . . . of nature . . . perhaps rather bad than good," lacking valor, and Plato's that men are reborn as women if they have been "cowards or led unrighteous lives."[19] According to Philo Judaeus, Eve fell first because "it was fitting that man should rule over immortality and everything good, but woman over death and everything vile. In the allegorical sense, however, woman is a symbol of the senses and man, of the mind."[20] Among the Fathers, Ambrose too explains, "Adam exists [in Paradise] as νοῦς [mind] and Eve as 'sense,'" though he also distinguishes between pure and impure emotions and says that if Eve had kept hers pure she would not have fallen.[21] Augustine sums up ways of allegorizing Adam and Eve but cautions against them, pointing out that although their relation may have spiritual signification, "they were created male and female . . . for the very purpose of begetting offspring," so that the Scriptures speak preeminently "of the matrimonial union by which the sexes are bound together."[22] Nevertheless, he appropriates the allegory himself when he observes, "Our flesh is an Eve within us."[23]

In Renaissance England, Juan Luis Vives applies the allegory to marriage, alleging that "in wedlocke the man resembleth the reason, and the woman the body: Nowe, reason ought to rule and the body to obey";[24] and a century later, in spite of the Reformation and the reign of Elizabeth, an undistinguished writer named Thomas Tuke could still state that "the Man and his Wife are a matrimonial creature: the Man is as the soule, and the Woman is as the body. The Man (as Soule) is to animate and rule, the Woman (as body) is to be animated and ruled of the Man."[25] But English Protestants generally resisted the allegorization of Scripture, and to that extent mitigated these misogynous connotations. In his *History of the World,* Sir Walter

Ralegh reports the "strange opinion" that "by the place or garden of *Paradise,* was meant the soule or mind; by *Adam, Mens,* or vnderstanding; by *Eue,* the sense; by the Serpent, Delectation"; though he reflects the still prevalent dualism by citing the "vnquiet vanity" of women as the Devil's means to mischief.[26] Sir Thomas Browne dismisses the allegory with tongue in cheek: "Whether the whole relation be not Allegorical, that is whether the temptation of the Man by the Woman, be not the seduction of the rational and higher parts by the inferiour and feminine faculties; or whether the tree in the midst of the Garden, were not that part in the Center of the body, in which was afterward the appointment of Circumcision in Males, we leave it to the *Talmudist.*"[27]

Meanwhile, on the Continent, some writers were pushing allegorical exegesis to its extreme. Troilo Lancetta, for example, allegorizes even God—as "ragione"—and mitigates Eve's inferiority only by a diminution of Adam that gives even less credit than usual to God's craftsmanship:

> Adam . . . signifies the frailty of human nature in its earliest form, untaught and inexperienced, with free will for both good and evil. Eve is a part of the same nature, and therefore Moses says that she is formed from the rib-cage, where reside the affections of concupiscence and ire [that is, the concupiscible and irascible parts into which moral theologians divided the wayward emotions] from which derive endless pleasures, which when ill-governed by reason are called, because of their ugliness, Belials, Satans, and similar horrid forms.[28]

Here, the implications of Raphael's Eve-like Serpent are inescapable. As a Protestant reformer, Milton drew from a large body of commentary and controversy that held, in opposition to the *contemptus mundi* of some of the Fathers, many medieval writers, and a number of Jacobean playwrights, the conviction that men and women are called to serve God and mankind by their work in this world, that women as well as men are created in God's image and endowed with reason, and that marriage was instituted by God before the Fall for mutual help, companionship, and delight as well as procreation.[29] However, puritan thought too was sometimes blighted by dualism. The more extreme Calvinists dwelt upon the depravity of matter and the helplessness of man as a way of stressing the glory and sovereignty of God, and their descriptions of original righteousness were often intended not to provide a model for regeneration but to show how far we have fallen. As a result, women and sexuality are suspect except when submitted to the strictest yoke of shamefastness and industry, and beauty's appeal to the senses is regarded with dismay. Thus even the Reformers did little to encourage exemplary, rather than merely cautionary, artistic representations of Eve.

In addition to pictorial and literary versions of Genesis itself, the Renaissance idea of unfallen Eve gathers imagery and insinuation from the long line of temptresses in earthly paradises that springs from such classical figures as Circe and Calypso, reemerges in Alcina and Armida, and finds its English culmination in Acrasia in Spenser's Bower of Bliss. This tradition is so pervasive, and Milton's imagery is often so close to its conventions, that readers are invited to see comparisons; but they are also challenged (preeminently, I believe) to make distinctions. The comparisons have been learnedly adduced by A. B. Giamatti in *The Earthly Paradise and the Renaissance Epic*. Regarding *Paradise Lost* as the sum of all the classical and Christian renderings of the tale of the hero who lays down his arms in an illusory garden to languish in the lap of a beautiful and debilitating seductress, Giamatti sees sinister shadows cast on Milton's Garden, in spite of its "higher Truth," by other epics and redoubled by allusions to fallen women that link Eve to them and to the "softening, even corrupting effect" of Nature. Selecting for attention those allusions that associate Eve with whatever is potentially deceptive in the beauty of nature or of women, Giamatti concludes that in the Fall "the 'old' story of a man who in spite of his better judgment yields to sensuality is told again."[30]

These three traditions, patristic, puritan, and humanist, form the body of opinion from which, or from parts of which, most Renaissance depictions of Eve derive, and many scholars have perceived traces of them in *Paradise Lost*. What needs further consideration is the habit of careful distinction between his Eve and her literary forebears by which Milton induces his audience to amend their assumptions in ways that bear vitally on the whole question of what it means to live a regenerate life. If we regard the Fall as the central act of the poem and conviction of sin in the reader as its primary purpose, we will of course see and stress the dark and sinister side of each image and allusion. But if we regard creation and regeneration as the poem's central process and the furtherance of this process in the reader as its

primary purpose, we will see in Milton's representation of original
righteousness and of Eve not only foreshadowings of original sin (re-
trospectively perceived) but also, and predominantly, patterns and
prolepses of regeneration. From this point of view, instead of being
tainted by previous gardens and previous women, this Garden and
this Eve may be seen as an artist's act of redeeming nature and wom-
anhood from the dualistic distortions his predecessors purvey. Or, to
put it the other way around, Milton is figuring forth the true Garden
and the true Eve, complete with the liabilities of liberty, of which all
corrupted gardens and women are travesties. To do this, he must
show Eve as meet help in a Garden given by the Sovereign Planter
not to corrupt and soften but to be dressed and kept by all the means
of cultivation, both literal and metaphorical, that the commandment
can imply.

Habits of Mind: Some Principles of Interpretation

"Reason," John Donne wrote to the Countess of Bedford, "is our
Soules left hand, Faith her right, / By these we reach divinity."[31] For
English Christian humanists, reason rectified and illuminated by
faith, embodied in words, and animated in action promotes ascent to
God by beings made and regenerated in God's image; though faith is
pre-eminent, right reason is co-operative. Viewed from these twin
premises of the dignity of man and the providence of God, human
history could not begin with an inevitable decline and fall. Indeed,
the concept of a fall implies an upright condition to fall from, and
original sin and separation from God imply original righteousness
and communion. Medieval poets may have been satisfied with a pre-
ordained *felix culpa,* but Milton's Renaissance humanism and Reformation theology required an explanation of the Fall that took free
will and human responsibility into account.

Although the concept of original righteousness was not new, it received renewed attention and speculation during the Reformation,
when commentaries on the Scriptures, newly translated for the common reader, began to proliferate. While their commentaries often
stress mankind's miserable condition in contrast to the glorious one
from which Adam fell, many Protestant expositors, including Calvin,
Luther, Perkins, Ainsworth, Ralegh, and Purchas, also reconsidered
what it might mean to be made in God's image and how the unfallen

condition of Adam and Eve might be applied to a regenerate person, to the reformed church and commonwealth, and to Christian marriage.

The core of Milton's belief about the potential virtues of human beings made and regenerated in the image of God is found in his definition of regeneration in *De Doctrine Christiana:*

> REGENERATION IS THAT CHANGE OPERATED BY THE WORD AND THE SPIRIT, WHEREBY THE OLD MAN BEING DESTROYED, THE INWARD MAN IS REGENERATED BY GOD AFTER HIS OWN IMAGE, IN ALL THE FACULTIES OF HIS MIND, INSOMUCH THAT HE BECOMES AS IT WERE A NEW CREATURE, AND THE WHOLE MAN IS SANCTIFIED BOTH IN BODY AND SOUL, FOR THE SERVICE OF GOD, AND THE PERFORMANCE OF GOOD WORKS.
>
> . . . .
>
> IN ALL THE FACULTIES OF HIS MIND; that is to say, in understanding and in will. This renewal of the will can mean nothing, but a restoration to its former liberty. [15:367]

For Milton, the Fall is not a matter of one part of man—the feminine, passible, and concupiscible part—perverting the rest, nor regeneration a matter of the redeemed soul transcending the corrupt body. He was not a dualist who opposed matter and spirit but an integrationist. If Adam and Eve had not fallen, Heaven and Earth would have become "One Kingdom" (7.161). The whole man (which means also the whole woman) was created good; the whole man fell; regenerated "in all the faculties of his mind, . . . the whole man is sanctified both in body and soul"; in death there is no separation of body and soul, but "the whole man dies"; in resurrection, mortality is "'swallowed up in life,' . . . not for the separation of the soul from the body, but for the perfecting of both" (*De Doctrina Christiana,* 15: 219 and 247); so also in daily life, "Wherefore did [God] creat passions within us, pleasures round about us, but that these rightly temper'd are the very ingredients of vertu?" (*Areopagitica,* 4:319). Milton's poem, too, presents not a lost idyll, much less creatures compelled by their own double nature to fall, but a drama of the first man and the first woman spiritedly engaging all the faculties of their minds to do, until their fall and after their repentance, what every redeemed and responsive man and woman is freed by regeneration to begin doing again.

Two generative principles elucidated by the work of Arthur E. Barker form the interpretive core of a regenerative reading of the

poem and of the character of Eve. The first, richly substantiated in
Milton and the Puritan Dilemma, is that, far from reflecting the endemic
dualism of his time, Milton's poetry represents and performs "the
integration of the natural and the spiritual . . . and the perfecting of
the first by the second with the increase not the loss of its peculiar
glory."[32] The second is that, far from leading to an inevitable fall, the
prelapsarian scenes in *Paradise Lost* lead to, and lead the reader in,
the process of regeneration, since the work of both prelapsarian and
regenerate life is a process of developing response to God's ways.

> Every prelapsarian incident in the poem involves for Adam and Eve
> (as for all its other creatures) a "calling," and every prelapsarian in-
> cident illustrates the possibility of a refusal. But what is significant
> about these incidents is not that they forebode the Fall but that they
> illustrate the kind of active response that is according to the norm of
> right. Milton's Creator does not punish his creatures for the limita-
> tions and even degrees of impercipience he has given them, even *un-*
> fallen, to use instrumentally in the development of the potentialities
> they have as his image, only for wilfully not so using them. It is pur-
> poseful growth towards completing that is implied, not only by the
> Orphic Raphael, but by every prelapsarian incident; and what this
> implies is the renovation, despite sin through woe, of the fallen but
> responsive and the infusing of new faculties and dimensions of percep-
> tion.

Paradise Lost, Barker continues, shows through the "rhythm of responsive individual experience, thrown into relief by irresponsible
contrast" that the continuity of God's ways "demands a continuously
developing response from men."[33] This work of response is not only
represented in the poem but evoked by it.

The cure for the reductive and disintegrative readings of *Paradise
Lost* produced by our own incoherent and friable age resides in these
principles of integration and regeneration inherent in the poem's
substance. They depend upon certain habits of mind and articles of
faith expressed alike in Milton's theology and in Renaissance poetics.
Though complex in application, these may be briefly stated. First,
God creates nothing that is not good. Second, every rational creature has freedom to become either better or worse; everything in nature can be either well used or abused; and evil is not the opposite
but the perversion of good. Thus, the passions and pleasures that

Jan Brueghel the Elder, *The Earthly Paradise*

Engraving attributed to Lucas Cranach from the 1534 Luther Bible

Illustrated title page from John Parkinson's *Paradisi in Sole Paradisus Terrestris* (second edition, 1656)

Engraving by Andriaen van de Venne from Jacob Cats, 's Werelts Begin, Midden, Eynde, Besloten in den Trou-Ringh (Amsterdam, 1643)

Illustration from Joseph Fletcher, *The Historie of the Perfect-Cursed-Blessed Man* (London, 1628)

Lorenzo Ghiberti, "The Gates of Paradise." Gilded bronze doors of the
Baptistry, Florence: upper left panel, Creation, Fall, and Expulsion

Hieronymus Bosch, Detail of panel from *The Garden of Earthly Delights*
(Prado, Madrid)

Raphael, Ceiling fresco, Stanza della Segnatura (Vatican, Rome)

dualists who contemn the flesh would banish become, when "rightly temper'd," "the very ingredients of vertu"; and right tempering requires right use of "all the faculties of the mind." Third, everything lost with Paradise has been by "one greater Man" restored and, through the reciprocal action of divine grace and human effort, and through purgative woe, can be regained.

The fashion of asserting that Milton's Christian doctrine is at war with his humanist art is happily passing from the critical scene, with renewed recognition that never has the stuff of life in all its dimensions and varieties been more consciously and conscionably woven than in Milton's epic poems. This integration is not a matter of shuttling the warp of drama through the woof of doctrine. Milton wrestles purposefully with each problem posed by the confrontation of Scripture with the claims of creative freedom for the greater glory of both, and in doing so he tackles every duality his predecessors — and indeed his critics — have invented. Whatever in creation dualists, be they puritans, libertines, mystics, prelates, politicians, or poets, put in opposition, Milton remarries in a design so entirely one flesh that it is difficult to talk about its parts without doing the violence to the poem of divorcing them again: nature and grace, matter and spirit, body and soul, action and contemplation, passion and reason, pleasure and virtue, liberty and obedience, creativity and responsibility, doctrine and poetry are united each to each and all to all.

The concept that the poem is a mimesis, simultaneously, of the processes of prelapsarian and regenerate response to calling — because, in fact, the processes are the same, as God's ways are consistent though progressively revealed as they are responded to — is of incalculable significance to the way we read and respond to the poem. If Adam, through Eve, was predestined to sin, then all are helpless and will fall again and again. If both were sufficient, free, and capable of responsive growth, and those qualities subject to renewal and increase, then there is hope for human goodness after all.

The chapters that follow deal with the cruxes of characterization most often invoked as proof that Eve was "fallen" before the Fall: Adam's diatribes, Eve's subordination, her relation to myth, her attraction to her own reflection, her dream, the work that takes her from Adam's side, and the separation colloquy; with the Fall itself; and with the regenerate responses that all the prelapsarian scenes prefigure.

Notes

1. All quotations from Milton's poetry and prose, unless otherwise specified, are from *The Works of John Milton,* gen. ed. Frank Allen Patterson (New York, 1931).

2. Studies of literary and expository treatments of Genesis include J. M. Evans, *"Paradise Lost" and the Genesis Tradition* (Oxford, 1968); A. B. Giamatti, *The Earthly Paradise and the Renaissance Epic* (Princeton, 1966); Watson Kirkconnell, *The Celestial Cycle* (Toronto, 1952); Arnold Williams, *The Common Expositor* (Chapel Hill, 1948); Sister Mary Corcoran, *Milton's Paradise with Reference to the Hexameral Background* (Washington, D.C., 1945); Grant McColley, *"Paradise Lost": An Account of Its Growth and Major Origins*... (Chicago, 1940); Harris Fletcher, *Milton's Rabbinical Readings* (Urbana, Ill., 1930); Frank Egleston Robbins, *The Hexameral Literature: A Study of the Greek and Latin Commentaries on Genesis* (Chicago, 1912); William Hayley, *The Life of John Milton, In Three Parts, to which are added Conjectures on the Origin of "Paradise Lost"* (Dublin, 1797).

Studies of the iconographic tradition include Roland Mushat Frye, *Milton's Imagery and the Visual Arts: Iconographic Tradition in the Epic Poems* (Princeton, 1978); Joanne Lewis Cocklereas, "Much Deceiv'd, Much Failing, Hapless Eve: Iconography and Eve in Milton's *Paradise Lost*" (Ph.D. dissertation, University of New Mexico, 1973); Francois Bucher, *The Pamplona Bibles* (New Haven and London, 1970); J. B. Trapp, "The Iconography of the Fall of Man," in C. A. Patrides, ed., *Approaches to "Paradise Lost": The York Centenary Lectures* (London, 1968), pp. 223–65; Jean-Dominique Rey, Andree Mazure, and Jean-Marie Lacroix, *Le Theme d'Adam et Eve dans L'Art* (Paris, 1967); Sigrid Esche, *Adam und Eva: Sundenfall und Erlösung* (Düsseldorf, 1957); J. J. Tikkanen, "Die Genesismosaiken von S. Marco in Venedig . . . ," *Acta Societatis Scientarium Fennicae* 17 (1891): 207–357.

3. A. O. Lovejoy traces the sources, ramifications, and pitfalls of this tradition in "Milton and the Paradox of the Fortunate Fall," *ELH* 4 (1937): 161–79, concluding that "the unhappy episodes in the story appear as instrumental to [its] consummation and, indeed, as its necessary conditions" (p. 179). J. B. Trapp finds that in the iconographic tradition "the Fall is the essential, even the happy, preliminary to salvation and eternal bliss" ("Iconography of the Fall," p. 231). Virginia R. Mollenkott disputes the application of the *felix culpa* to Milton's poem in "Milton's Rejection of the Fortunate Fall," *MiltonQ* 6 (1972): 1–5, as do Irene Samuel in "The Dialogue in Heaven: A Reconsideration of *Paradise Lost* III, 1–417" in *PMLA* 72 (1957): 601–11, reprinted in *Milton: Modern Essays in Criticism,* ed. Arthur E. Barker (Oxford, 1965), pp. 233–45; and Earl Miner, "Felix Culpa in the Redemptive Order of *Paradise Lost,*" *PQ* 47 (1968): 43–44. Peter A. Fiore, O.F.M., in "'Account Mee Man': The Incarnation of *Paradise Lost,*" *HLQ* 39 (1975): 51–56, documents the tradition that the Incarnation could have taken place without the Fall but argues that Milton regards it, rather, as a response to a foreseen Fall. I do not think that the idea of a *felix culpa* can properly be applied to Milton's view of the Fall, since Milton attributes freedom of the will both to Adam and Eve, who had the opportunity "by degrees of merit rais'd" to "open to themselves at length the way" to Heaven (7.157–58), and to the Son of God, whose glory has infinite opportunity to manifest itself in the goodness of creation and might have continued to do so in response to man's obedience rather than his Fall.

4. Arthur E. Barker, Fellow of the Royal Society of Canada, establishes the principle that *Paradise Lost* mimetically involves the reader in the process of regeneration in the prelapsarian scenes, in "Structural and Doctrinal Pattern in Milton's Later

Poems," in *Essays in English Literature from the Renaissance to the Victorian Age Presented to A. S. P. Woodhouse,* ed. Millar MacLure and F. W. Watts (Toronto, 1964), and *"Paradise Lost:* The Relevance of Regeneration," in *"Paradise Lost": A Tercentenary Tribute,* ed. Balachandra Rajan (Toronto, 1969).

5. Milton follows the usage defined by Sir Thomas Elyot in his *Defence of Good Women* (1540) when he says, "This worde *Man,* vnto whom reason perteyneth, doth imply in it both man and woman" (Diii). On the use of "man" and "men" to include woman by Milton and others see Elaine B. Safer, "'Sufficient to Have Stood': Eve's Responsibility in Book IX," *MiltonQ* 6 (1972): 10–14.

6. Critics who have found Eve weak and vain and Adam fatally uxorious before the Fall include Maurice Kelley, *This Great Argument* (Princeton, 1941), p. 149 n. 21; A. J. A. Waldock, *"Paradise Lost" and Its Critics* (Cambridge, England, 1947), pp. 34 and 61; Balachandra Rajan, *"Paradise Lost" and the Seventeenth-Century Reader* (London, 1947), p. 66; E. M. W. Tillyard, *Studies in Milton* (London, 1951), p. 13; Millicent Bell, "The Fallacy of the Fall in *Paradise Lost,*" *PMLA* 68 (1953): 874–75 and passim; Douglas A. Day, "Adam and Eve in *Paradise Lost* IV," *TSLL* 3 (1961): 378; B. E. Gross, "Free Will and Free Love in *Paradise Lost,*" *SEL* 7 (1967): 106 and passim; Fredson Bowers, "Adam, Eve, and the Fall in *Paradise Lost,*" *PMLA* 84 (1969): 266 and 271; Lawrence Babb, *The Moral Cosmos of "Paradise Lost"* (East Lansing, Mich., 1970). Babb sums up a standard view when he states that since Eve, representing passion in opposition to Adam's reason, is "a second class human being," it is doubtful that she is sufficiently responsible to be blamed for eating the apple: "Her sin, if she is guilty of any, occurs earlier at the time when she willfully overrules her husband and goes out alone" (pp. 49–50).

Recently, feminist critics have based readings of *Paradise Lost* on similar assumptions. Marcia Landy attributes to Milton a belief that women must be limited and submissive for the sake of authority and order in "Kinship and the Role of Women in *Paradise Lost,*" *MiltonS* 4 (1972): 3–18, to which Barbara K. Lewalski replies in "Milton on Women—Yet Once More," *MiltonS* 6 (1974): 4–20. Sandra M. Gilbert's account of feminist readings and misreadings of Milton in "Patriarchal Poetry and Women Readers: Reflections on Milton's Bogey," *PMLA* 93 (1978): 368–82, supposes that "Milton's myth of origins" sums up "a long misogynistic tradition" (p. 368). Since these readings focus on matters outside the poem, they tend to be partial in both senses of the word. Some of Landy's statements ignore Milton's vital distinctions; she thinks, for example, that "sexual pleasure apart from procreation is associated with sin" (p. 11) even though Milton's depiction of sexual pleasure without conception in Paradise is one of his most daring assertions. (It is true of course that the two could not have been unnaturally separated, and that Adam and Eve look happily forward to procreation as a source of further bonds of love.) Gilbert's use of evidence ignores the dramatic decorum of the bits she chooses, taking speeches clearly meant to be parodic, impercipient, or fallen as if they were Milton's own opinions and omitting his radical emendations of dualistic and misogynist assumptions.

7. For citations see Ch. V, n. 4 and 5.

8. H. W. Janson, in *Apes and Ape Lore in the Middle Ages and the Renaissance* (London, 1952), discusses monkeys as "a visual metaphor for the Fall" and "a projection of man's own weakness" with what were regarded as the specifically "female qualities" of "wiliness, an unstable temper, and sensuality" (pp. 116, 109, 133).

9. I am indebted for this observation to Philipp and Maria Raina Fehl.

10. George Ferguson, *Signs and Symbols in Christian Art* (Oxford, 1976), p. 25.

11. Frye reproduces three other versions by Brueghel that provide the sequel, culminating in his collaboration with Rubens (Frye, figs. 158 and 159 and plate VII). In them, one clearly sees the serpent in the tree and the fruit in Eve's hand, and the animals become progressively restive and hostile; dogs bark, the tigers' play grows fierce, and the peacock of pride centrally displays his tail.

12. The illustration from the Junius Manuscript (*Genesis B*) is reproduced in S. Humphries Gurteen, *The Epic of the Fall of Man: A Comparative Study of Caedmon, Dante, and Milton* (New York, 1896), p. 164 (Gurteen's translation); and the illumination in L. M. Delaissé, H. Liebers, and F. Masai, *Mittelalterliche Miniaturen* (Cologne, 1959), plate 35. The engraving in Joseph Fletcher's *History of the Perfect-Cursed-Blessed Man* (1628) appears at first glance to be a depiction of innocence, but Eve's gesture, according to a contemporary handbook on the "Langvage of the Hand," betrays "a close inclination to vice" (John Bulwer, *Chirologia* [London, 1644], p. 172), and most representations of Adam and Eve before the Fall similarly contain allusions to disobedience. The few that do usually show Adam and Eve in passive poses. The only exceptions I have found, which clearly celebrate a lively life before the Fall, are the engravings for the works of Jacob Cats, including *'s Werelts Begin, Midden, Eynde, Besloten in den Trou-Ringh*...(Amsterdam, 1643); "Paradisvs, sive Nuptiae primorum parentum, Adami & Evae," in *Faces Augustae, sive Poemata, Quibus Illustriores Nvptiae*...trans. Caspare Barlaeus and Cornelius Boyo (Dordrecht, 1643); and *Alle de Wercken van den Heere Jacob Cats* (Amsterdam, 1712); and similar engravings by Nicolaes de Bruyn and J. Th. de Bry after Martin de Vos, in the Printenkabinet of the Rijksmuseum, Amsterdam, which show Adam and Eve kneeling in prayer on the seventh day. Frye reproduces a further example, *The Paradise of the Senses in Eden* (ca. 1600) in *Milton's Imagery and the Visual Arts*, fig. 170; this and a few other examples may be seen in the Kitto Bible at the Huntington Library.

13. Trapp, "Iconography of the Fall," pp. 226 ff.

14. Reproductions of these and many other works mentioned in this chapter may be found in Frye, *Milton's Imagery and the Visual Arts.*

15. Works in which the Serpent resembles Eve in detail include illuminations in the Bedford Book of the Hours, the Grimani Breviary, and the *Très Riches Heures du Duc de Berry;* paintings by Salviati, Cranach, Michelangelo, and Masolino; and the statue of Cristoforo Solario. Titian's horned putto and Van der Goes's pigtailed urchin are exceptional in their lack of similarity to Eve. The motif of the woman-headed serpent is traced and discussed by John K. Bonnell in "The Serpent with a Human Head in Art and Mystery Play," *AJA*, second series, 21 (1917) and by Frye in *Milton's Imagery*, pp. 102–4. It is the subject of a dissertation written by Nona Flores at the University of Illinois, Urbana-Champaign.

16. Edmund Spenser, *The Faerie Queene*, 2.12.63–68. All quotations from this work are from *The Faerie Queene: A Variorum Edition*, ed. Edwin Greenlaw, Charles Grosvenor Osgood, and Frederick Morgan Padelford (Baltimore, 1966, 1932–57).

17. In *"Paradise Lost" and the Genesis Tradition*, II-VII, Evans provides a comprehensive survey of the Jewish, early Christian, neoclassical, and medieval treatments of Genesis and finds that "any thoroughgoing attempt to make the Fall seem plausible ultimately involves a reduction of Adam and Eve's intellectual or moral stature" (p. 97)—especially Eve's.

18. *Reliquae Baxterianae* (London, 1696), p. 5.

19. Aristotle, *Generation of Animals*, trans. A. L. Peck (Cambridge, Mass., 1943), p. 461; and *Poetics*, trans. Thomas Twining (London, 1812), pp. 143–44; Plato, *Timaeus*, in *The Dialogues of Plato*, trans. B. Jowett (Oxford, 1892), 3.461.

20. Philo, *Questions and Answers on Genesis,* trans. Ralph Marcus (Cambridge, Mass., 1961), p. 22.

21. *Saint Ambrose: Hexameron, Paradise, and Cain and Abel,* trans. John J. Savage, in *The Fathers of the Church* (Washington, D.C. 1947–) 42: 292.

22. Augustine, *The City of God,* Bk. 14, ch. 22, trans. Marcus Dods, in *A Select Library of the Nicene and Post-Nicene Fathers of the Christian Church,* First Series, gen. ed. Philip Schaff (Grand Rapids, Michigan, 1956; a reprint of the 1886–1889 ed.), 2: 278. Hereafter cited as *SLNPNF.*

23. Augustine, *On the Psalms,* Oxford translation, ed. A. Cleveland Coxe, *SLNPNF,* First Series, 8: 170.

24. Juan Luis Vives, *A very frutefull and pleasant boke called the Instruction of a Christian Woman,* trans. Richard Hyde (London, 1529 [?]), sig. Yiii^r.

25. Thomas Tuke, *New Essays, Meditations, and Vows* (London, 1614), p. 264.

26. Sir Walter Ralegh, *The History of the World* (1614), pp. 34 and 70.

27. Sir Thomas Browne, *Pseudodoxia Epidemica* (London, 1669), p. 4.

28. Troilo Lancetta, *La Scena tragica d'Adamo e d'Eva* (Venice, 1644), "Morale Espositionc."

29. On the changing definition of marriage during the Reformation see John G. Halkett, *Milton and the Idea of Matrimony: A Study of the Divorce Tracts and "Paradise Lost"* (New Haven, 1970).

30. A. B. Giamatti, *The Earthly Paradise and the Renaissance Epic,* pp. 300, 303, 343, and ch. 6 passim.

31. John T. Shawcross, ed., *The Complete Poems of John Donne* (Garden City, N.Y., 1967), p. 220. All quotations from Donne's poems are from this edition.

32. Barker (Toronto, 1942), p. 8.

33. Barker, "Structural and Doctrinal Pattern," pp. 189, 174, and 192.

II

"Rational Delight": The Marriage of Adam and Eve

W hen Adam asks God for "fellowship . . . fit to participate / All rational delight" (8.389–91), he explains his need for an equal partner, not satisfied with the companionship of "Man with Beast":

> Among unequals what societie
> Can sort, what harmonie or true delight?
> Which must be mutual, in proportion due
> Giv'n and receiv'd.
>
> [8.383–86]

"Rational delight" means at least three things: the delight of the mutual exercise of reason ("meet conversation"); delight grounded in reason ("rightly tempered"); and delight in the kind of interaction made possible by "proportion due" (*ratio*). This relationship, it turns out, will not provide equality in the sense of sameness, for Adam and Eve have different talents and their sex is "not equal" (4.296), but in the sense of mutual completion: not unison but "harmonie." Adam's words, and his later wrestling with the problem of Eve's "inferiority" and his own admiration of her, may be compared with Richard Hooker's explanation of the "subalternation" between them: woman, he says, "was even in her first estate framed by Nature, not only after in time, but inferiour in excellency also unto man, howbeit in so due and sweet proportion, as being presented before our eyes, might be sooner perceived then defined. And even herein doth lie the reason, why that kind of love which is the perfectest ground of

Wedlock is seldome able to yeild any reason of it self."[1] "Due and sweet proportion" is something like the third meaning of "rational delight," but Milton reverses the terms to emphasize the delight and de-emphasize the "inferiority." "Subalternation" is a problem for Adam even before the Fall, but a fruitful one that challenges his understanding by its unexpected opportunities. It does not become a problem for Eve until the moment of her fall. It is such a difficulty for the modern reader from the moment when the narrator introduces Adam and Eve as "Not equal, as thir sex not equal seemd; / ... Hee for God only, shee for God in Him" (4.96–99) that some suppose Adam's angry denunciation of Eve as a "fair defect / Of Nature" after the Fall to be Milton's own opinion of her from the start. By beginning at the bottom, with fallen Adam, by steps we may ascend to comprehension of what was really a revolutionary idea: that Eve was made not just for Adam, much less for his bane, but for "God in him."

Crooked by Nature?

Out of the depths of his ruin, after the Fall and before the process of regeneration has begun, Milton's Adam utters three complaints which demonstrate the effects of the Fall on a mind "once ... full of Peace, now tost and turbulent: / For Understanding rul'd not" (9.1125–27). In the first he rebukes Eve, not for disobeying God but for parting from his own side. In the second he implies that God designed Eve to tempt him. In the third he denounces Eve as "crooked by Nature" and marriage as a source of inescapable woe. These are salient speeches, for they lay bare the ruins to be repaired, and they do so by denying the fundamental pattern of experience which Milton represents in unfallen and in regenerate life: the continual reciprocity of divine providence and human responsibility.

Nevertheless, distinguished critics have treated these diatribes as if they expressed Milton's personal opinion. Samuel Johnson states that Milton had "something like a Turkish contempt for females"; James Holly Hanford that "the poet bears a grudge against woman as the perverse occasion of man's entanglement"; E. M. W. Tillyard that Adam's worst invective "is of course Milton's own voice ... uttering his ancient grievance"; and Harris Fletcher that it is "one of the most vividly personal utterances in all of Milton's works."[2] Innu-

merable others have agreed with fallen Adam's distorted view of unfallen Eve and allowed it to color their readings of the scenes before
the Fall. These interpretations obscure both the symptoms of original sin revealed in Adam's invective and the nature of original righteousness represented in the marriage of Adam and Eve.

There is no need to look outside the drama for an explanation of
Adam's tone. Its bitterness is no more vehement than the occasion
requires. But the content of his tirades is thoroughly perverse: he
attributes the Fall to Eve's original nature and to her liberty, and
therefore to God's ways to men. Far from being Milton's "own voice,"
Adam's diatribes give tongue to the voice of "our Destroyer" (4.749).
They epitomize stale antifeminine commonplaces still lingering in
Milton's lifetime, they are based on a dualistic *contemptus mundi*
which Milton thought blasphemous, and they contradict his firm belief that true obedience requires freedom. In sum, Adam's diatribes
illustrate Milton's contention that "nothing now adayes is more de-
generately forgott'n, then the true dignity of man, almost in every
respect, but especially in this prime institution of Matrimony";[3] and
he refutes them both in the reasoning voice of his prose and in his
representation of original and regenerate righteousness in *Paradise
Lost.*

Adam's first complaint (9.1134–42) attributes their plight, not to
their disobedience, but to Eve's "strange desire of wandering"[4] and to
a foolish attempt to prove her faith. Eve's rejoinder questions his
own invulnerability and defends her desire for a measure of freedom: "Was I to have never parted from thy side? / As good have
grown there still a liveless Rib." But then she capitulates to Adam's
false logic and turns the blame on him: "why didst not thou the Head
Command me absolutely not to go . . . ? / . . . Hadst thou bin firm
and fixt in thy dissent / Neither had I transgress'd, nor thou with
me." In short, both imagine that the Fall could have been prevented
only by a form of government Milton spent his life denouncing and
reforming.

There are seeds of truth in these recriminations, but they are sterile
ones. Adam was indeed the stronger, but that does not prove Eve insufficient. Eve's departure is defensible, but not on the grounds she
gives here; she had never thought her relation to Adam lifeless
before the Fall, and indeed one of her reasons for a brief separation
was that their mutual delight needed to be "rightly tempered."[5]

Adam is right that one need not seek tests of faith, but that is because the materials of obedience are always at hand, and Eve's desire to work for a while in her own way had sprung from a healthy desire to dress the Garden in obedience to the commandment and to preserve the liberty on which their obedience and their mutual love depend— that is, to cultivate freely the God-given opportunities of Paradise.

The seeds of evil in their recriminations, on the other hand, are fertile. Both Adam and Eve evade responsibility and deflect attention from the real disobedience. Each fixes the blame for their misery on the other. Worst of all, both suppose Eve a flawed creation, unable to act responsibly, and thus they dispute God's providence.

The commonplace attitude toward women from which these speeches derive their seeming authority made them wholly dependent on their male guardians. It is analogous to the attitude toward human nature which made the obedience of Christians dependent on monarchy and prelacy. Nearly every Renaissance writer on the duties of women instructs them that their first obligation is to preserve their chastity, prescribing close confinement, censored reading, industry, and silence. A favorite piece of advice is Jerome's to the parents of a young girl that "all her pleasure should be in her chamber."[6] Juan Luis Vives, advising Catherine of Aragon on the education of Mary Tudor, finds that "a woman hath no charge to se to, but her honestie and chastyte"; if she must venture from her chamber "let fewe se her, and none at al here her." He defends her right to literacy, since proper studies strengthen virtue, but if she misuses it to read of love and war—Ovid and Homer, for example— she should be "kept from all redynge"; and of course she should never teach, "because a woman is a fraile thynge, and of weake discretion, and they may lightly be deceyued: whiche thynge our fyrst mother Eue sheweth, whom the deuyll caught with a light argument."[7]

Although the Reformation did much to ease patristic restrictions on women's liberty, both puritan and moderate Anglican writers, while generally improving the lot of women by affirming the dignity and sanctity of marriage, continued to echo the old assumptions. The homily "Of the State of Matrimony" authorized by Queen Elizabeth reminded every parishioner that "the woman is a weak creature, not endued with like strength, and constancy of mind . . . prone to all weak affections, and dispositions of mind, more then men be, and lighter they be, and more vain in their fantasies and

opinions," and therefore "must be spared, and borne with."[8] Richard
Hooker commends the custom of having women given to their husbands in the marriage rite because "it putteth women in mind of a
duty, whereunto the very imbecility of their nature and sex doth
bind them, namely, to be always directed, guided, and ordered by
others.[9] John Donne, whose praises of love and marriage have rarely
been equaled, warns women to remember "that *they are the weaker
vessell, and that Adam was not deceived,* but *the woman was;* For . . . it implies a weakness in the woman, and an occasion of soupling her to
that just estimation of herself, *That she will be content to learn in silence
with all subjection.*"[10] Samuel Purchas warns that since women's passions are "more eager, vehement, violent, vnbridled," they should
"fortifie . . . their Hands with painfull working, their Feet with home-
keeping";[11] and William Perkins feels that husband and wife should
cleave to one another "as two bords are ioyned together with glue,"[12]
a description of marriage wholly at odds with the apt and lively conversation Milton sought in domestic life and the graceful and responsive harmonies which distinguish the dialogues of unfallen Adam
and Eve.

These examples represent the background against which Milton
displays the joyous activity and growth of an Eve who was obedient
but "not subjected," as Chrysostom observes,[13] before the Fall. Milton did not, of course, dispute the importance of chastity and obedience, but he consistently opposed the notion that restriction is a
means to virtue. When applied to the education of women, it is likely
to produce what he called "the uncovering inability of mind, so defective to the purest and most sacred end of matrimony" and to bind
a man "to an image of earthe and fleam" instead of "the co-partner of
a sweet and gladsome society."[14] Such society is illustrated in the
eager learning, the varied and poetic speech, and the responsive creativity of Eve. Throughout their unfallen lives, both Adam and Eve
are trying to achieve a more positive and fruitful kind of chastity: the
active exercise of free obedience in spite of doubt and danger which
Milton urges in *Areopagitica,* shows fulfilled "by one mans firm obedience fully tri'd" in *Paradise Regained,* and reaffirms in Samson's active
obedience, like his own, "in darkness and with dangers compast
round." That fallen Adam and Eve should repudiate this endeavor
in their recriminations is not a proof that it was wrong, but an effect
of their Fall.

Adam's second complaint is his defensive answer to the question-ing of the divine judge: "This Woman whom thou mad'st to be my help, / And gav'st me as thy perfet gift, so good, / So fit, so accept-able, so Divine, / That from her hand I could suspect no ill / . . . Shee gave me of the Tree, and I did eat" (10.137–43). The impli-cation that he was tricked is simply false, since Adam was "not de-ceav'd" (9.998 and 1 Tim. 2:4) and knew before he ate that Eve had succumbed to "cursed fraud" (9.904). More insidiously, Adam sug-gests that God is the author of sin—a blasphemy Milton warns against throughout his doctrinal prose. By blaming God for making Eve "so good," Adam falls into the kind of dualism that attributes evil to good things because they can be misused, an error which Milton combated in both mysticism and puritanism.[15] Milton's own voice again provides the rejoinder to Adam's perversity: "God . . . saith, because it is not good for man to be alone, I make him therefore a meet help. God supplies the privation of not good, with the perfect gift of a reall and positive good; it is mans pervers cooking who hath turn'd this bounty of God into a Scorpion."[16]

Adam's excuse resembles his earlier words to Raphael: "so ab-solute she seems / . . . All higher knowledge in her presence falls / Degraded" (8.547–52). However, in the earlier conversation love is in the process of tempering, and Eve's beauties are blessings as long as they "subject not" (8.607). Here Adam expresses the revulsion that follows distempered passion and regards Eve's good qualities as mere bait. He perverts the truth that her loveliness is the work of her Creator and that in the well-tempered breast beauty nurtures love of God.

The stern reply of the Son echoes Saint Paul on the subordination of wives,[17] but it does not suggest that Eve was in any way a defective creation. Here, as throughout the poem, Milton interprets subordi-nation as an opportunity for the exercise of special virtues, among them the arts of just government and glad service practiced in the Kingdom of Heaven. The Son's affirmation that Eve was "Adorn'd . . . indeed, and lovely to attract / Thy Love" and that "her Gifts / Were such as under Government well seem'd" confirms the impor-tant principle in *Areopagitica* that all created things, including those that dualism regards as temptations to be avoided, should be regarded as opportunities for obedience: "Wherefore did [God] creat passions within us, pleasures round about us, but that these rightly temper'd are the very ingredients of vertu?"[18] What Eve's seemly gifts were, and what kind of government best promoted their temperate development, were among the central concerns of Adam and Eve throughout their unfallen life, especially in their last unfallen dialogue.

In his third diatribe Adam continues to denounce Eve and adds a despairing prophecy of the miseries of marriage. Observing in agony the new hostilities of nature, he feels that all fertility and nurture have become "propagated curse." When Eve tries to soothe his "fierce passions" with "soft words" he cries,

> Out of my sight, thou Serpent, that name best
> Befits thee with him leagu'd, thyself as false
> And hateful; nothing wants, but that thy shape,
> Like his, and colour Serpentine may shew
> Thy inward fraud, to warn all Creatures from thee
> Henceforth; least that too heav'nly form, pretended
> To hellish falsehood, snare them.[19]
>
> [10.867–73]

Adam is not wholly wrong, of course. Eve has played the Serpent's part. Her beauty has moved him, and she has enticed him to disobey God. But, again, he supposes a discrepancy between outward form and inward substance and has thereby denied God's providence in creating Eve. Again, instead of repudiating Eve's sin, he repudiates Eve herself, and in doing so he rejects the process of regeneration provided by the judgment.

Adam's tirade continues (10.873–88) with an elaborate recapitulation of the common view of woman as *apta author malis* found in nearly every portrait of Eve except Milton's: she is, Adam claims, "crooked by nature."[20] In spite of the blasphemy implied, chronicle and drama before and during Milton's time regularly put Eve on Satan's side before the temptation. According to the *Cursor Mundi*, "Bitwene satan & his wyf / Adam is sett in mychel strif / Bothe thei be on o party / To ouercome man with trichery."[21] In the Chester *Creation* Satan assumes that the intrinsic lightness of woman will make Eve an easy target: "That woman is forbyd to doe, / for anything therto will shooe . . . / for women are full liccoris,"[22] and Du Bartas, after praising Eve and marriage, nevertheless states that Satan attacked "the part he finds in euident defaults: / Namely, poor Woman, wauering, weake, and vnwise, / Light, credulous, news-louer giuen to lies."[23]

Hugo Grotius's *Adamus Exul* continues this tradition into the seventeenth century, as Satan speculates, "The female mind is light; / Prone to neglect commands, fickle in undertakings, / She varies willingly. . . . / What is not new displeases, / Her blest lot's tedium, her frail inconstancy, / Vain hope . . . all these assure me my desire. / Woman, apt source of ill, is sure without the rest."[24] And Sir Walter Ralegh sums up popular opinion when he comments, "But what meanes did the Deuill find out, or what instruments did his owne subtletie present him, as fittest and aptest to work this mischiefe by? euen the vnquiet vanitie of the woman; . . . what was the motiue of her disobedience? euen a desire to know what was most vnfitting her knowledge, an affection which had euer since remained in all the posteritie of her sexe."[25]

In *Paradise Lost*, the only character who speaks of Eve's liabilities before the Fall is Eve herself, reflecting on states gladly outgrown and temptations fervently rejected. No one supposes her naturally wayward, and Satan — at the point where, in other dramas, he is already savoring his presumed success — is so awed by her "graceful Innocence" that he is at first "of enmitie disarmed" (9.459–64). Even more significantly, Milton thoroughly refutes the imputations summed up by Grotius, by showing in the prelapsarian scenes Eve's strong sense of responsibility and her growing understanding of the abundant opportunities of her calling. Her mind is not light; her conversation mingles careful questioning, sober reflection, wit, and gentle gaiety. Her lot is not tedious; it is full of challenge, perplexity, and bliss. Each prelapsarian scene, from her choice of love for Adam over self-love at the lake to her faithful attention to the Garden as Satan approaches, reveals in Eve virtues directly opposed to the weaknesses usually cited. By shifting these commonplaces from their usual position in drama and commentary — that is, in descriptions of Eve before the Fall — to the speeches of fallen and despairing Adam, Milton exposes their distortions.

Adam completes his repudiation of Eve by asking, "O why did God . . . create at last . . . this fair defect / Of Nature, and not fill the world at once / With Men as Angels without Feminine, / Or find some other way to generate mankind?" (10.888–95). The phrase "this fair defect / Of Nature" sums up Adam's impious dualism: God's creation, it claims, is naturally defective but temptingly fair.[26] The whole question is inapposite to his experience of Eve, in whom he has

found "fellowship . . . fit to participate / All rational delight" (8.389–
91). What it does echo—in thorough opposition to Milton's "own
voice"—is the voice of the anonymous adversary who answered Milton's first divorce tract by ridiculing his high standards for women
and marriage. Assuming, like Adam's question, that women were
made solely for procreation, the *Answer* argues that the main purpose
of marriage is not "the solace and content in the gifts of the mind
only" (a reduction of Milton's argument to its most unusual point),
for then "it would have been every wayes as much, yea more content
and solace to *Adam;* and so consequently to every man, to have had
another man made to him of his Rib instead of Eve: this is apparent
by experience, which shews, the man ordinarily exceeds women in
naturall gifts of the minde, and in the delectablensse [*sic*] of converse."[27] Milton explicitly refutes this view in *Tetrachordon:* "*Austin*
contests that manly friendship in all other regards [except procreation]
had bin a more becoming solace for Adam. . . . But our Writers [the
English Reformers] deservedly reject this crabbed opinion; and defend that there is a peculiar comfort in the maried state besides the
genial bed, which no other society affords."[28]

Thus far, Adam's diatribe has been misogynous. Its conclusion
(10.896–908) is misogamous: the whole institution of marriage, he
predicts, will prove to be a curse, for either a man will never find a fit
mate or else he will be prevented from marrying her; marriage will
be at once a battlefield and a prison.

The grain of truth in this passage is that it is miserable to find oneself "Wedlock-bound / To a fell Adversary"; the degradation such a
calamity can cause is a motive for Milton's divorce tracts. But his
argument for divorce is not based on a denunciation of marriage. It
is based on his firm Protestant belief that marriage is a holy institution, ordained by God at the creation of the world for the good of all
men, and that it provides "the neerest resemblance of our Union
with Christ";[29] his purpose is to show that this great good should not
be denied to those who are bound by error in a conjunction which is
so spiritually destructive that instead of resembling that "Union" it
divorces it.

Adam's repudiation of marriage suggests again the recurrent *contemptus mundi* that Milton protested against in both patristic and puritan thought. Many of the Fathers supposed that God instituted
marriage and procreation not in Genesis 1:27–28 and 2:22–24,

which they interpreted allegorically, but in Genesis 3:16, the judgment of Eve, and that the first sexual union is reported in Genesis
4:1, "Adam knew his wife and she conceived." Jerome states that "in
Paradise Eve was a virgin, and it was only after the coats of skins
that she began her married life," and urges converts not to "seek the
coat of marriage given to Adam on his expulsion from the Paradise of
virginity."[30] Tertullian recommends that "such as shall wish to be received in Paradise, ought . . . to begin to cease from that thing from
which Paradise is intact."[31] Even in Milton's day it was commonly
assumed that "Adam knew not Eve, till he knew sin."[32] According to
this view, before the Fall Adam and Eve were virgins wholly devoted
to contemplation; after the Fall marriage was permitted for the discipline of desires now carnal and the perpetuation of a race now mortal, but virginity was still the condition most conducive to the service
of God. And although most Puritans insisted that marriage and procreation were instituted before the Fall, and thus were commanded
to some and allowed to all, Richard Baxter sounds curiously like the
Fathers when he complains that "the business of a married state doth
commonly devour almost *all your time,* so that little is left for holy con-
contemplations, or serious thought of the life to come."[33]

For Milton, in contrast, these writers whom fallen Adam imitates
were rejecting opportunities and responsibilities provided by God in
the first two chapters of Genesis and reestablished through the Judgment in the third. For him, as for many puritan writers, the family
was the seminary of piety and civility through which God might best
be served. The joining of Adam and Eve as "one flesh" and the commandment to "increase and multiply" were first principles of obedience, grounded in the right use of the things of this world. Milton
goes further than most, however, in declaring the goodness not only
of companionship and procreation but also of delight, citing "wisest
Salomon" in support of "a kinde of ravishment . . . in the entertain-
ment of wedded leisures."[34] In *Paradise Lost* he places "the Rites /
Mysterious of connubial Love" among the joys of Paradise and explicitly attributes to Satan the notion that virginity is superior to
wedded love: "Our Maker bids increase, who bids abstain / But our
Destroyer, foe to God and Man?" (4.742–43, 748–49).[35]

Of the many early treatises on virginity, that of Gregory of Nyssa
is particularly illuminating, because in *Paradise Lost* Milton presents
the exact reverse of the process of restoration Gregory prescribes.

Urging that we "restore the divine image from the foulness which the flesh wraps around it," Gregory states:

> We . . . are allowed to return to our earliest state of blessedness by the very same stages by which we lost Paradise. What are they? Pleasure, craftily offered, began the Fall, and there followed after pleasure shame, and fear . . . ; and after that they covered themselves with the skins of dead animals; and then they were sent forth into this pestilential and exacting land where, as the compensation for having to die, marriage was instituted. Now if we are destined "to depart hence, and be with Christ," we must begin at the end of the route of departure. . . . Marriage, then . . . is the first thing to be left.[36]

In *Paradise Lost,* marriage is the first thing to be repaired. The first gesture toward reparation is Eve's plea, "Forsake me not thus, *Adam.* . . . Between us two let there be peace," and Adam's reply, "Let us no more contend . . . but strive / In offices of Love, how we may light'n / Each others burden in our share of woe" (10.914–36, 946–65).[37] A step backward occurs when Eve in her turn slips into a despairing *contemptus mundi* with its attendant renunciation of procreation; aware that their sharpest sorrow will be seeing their children born to misery they have caused, she suggests wilful barrenness or suicide. Adam replies that her contempt of this life, though it indicates "something . . . sublime" in her, betrays a desire "to evade / The penalty pronounc't" (10.1021–22); and as he reasons, in response to Eve, he begins to perceive the identity of their foe and to realize that obedience to the conditions of the Judgment is essential to the plan of redemption. Far from repudiating Eve and renouncing marriage and procreation, as he has done in his fallen diatribes, he now sees that the very means of salvation will come through fulfillment of these providential responsibilities: both Adam and Eve are called to their parts in preparing for the salvation of the world by the promised "Seed of Woman" (10.1028–46).

The passages that follow continue to reverse Gregory's prescription. Gregory's second step in the process of restoration is to "retire from all anxious toil upon the land, such as man was bound to after his sin." Adam's is to recognize that "Idleness had bin worse; my labour will sustain me" (10.1055–56). Gregory's third step is to "divest ourselves of those coverings of our nakedness, namely the wisdom of the flesh" and "all illusions of taste and sight." Adam's is to recall that their Judge had "Cloath'd us unworthie, pitying while he judg'd," and to trust that in answer to prayer he would teach them knowledge of the operations of nature sufficient to supply their bodily needs and "remedie or cure / [The] evils which our own misdeeds have wrought . . . so as we need not fear / To pass commodiously this life, sustain'd / By him with many comforts . . ." (10.1059 ff.). For Gregory, the blessed life is "to enjoy the Good in its purity, unmixed with one particle of evil"; for Milton, "what wisdome can there be to choose, what continence to forbeare without the knowledge of evill? . . . Assuredly we bring not innocence into the world, we bring impurity much rather: that which purifies us is triall, and triall is by what is contrary";[38] and Michael's revelations to Adam educate him in the effects of evil by which he may know and choose the good.

The speeches in which Adam and Eve gradually recognize and accept their responsibilities in a difficult, frustrating, but still providential world thoroughly repudiate the *contemptus mundi* recommended by the Fathers, summed up by Gregory, and angrily adopted by Adam in his diatribes. They affirm Milton's view that in regenerate as well as unfallen life, every part of God's creation, including every faculty of men and women, is made for goodness and should be well used. Milton does not deny the patristic ideal that the greatest good is the knowledge and love of God. But for him both the means and the effect of contemplation is the imitation of God's ways, and knowledge, love, and imitation of God do not transcend but rather redeem all of nature and of human experience. He represents in his poem a process of education that "cannot in this body found itself but on sensible things" and that teaches us to use all the opportunities of both divine and humane wisdom "to repair the ruines of our first Parents by regaining to know God aright, and out of that knowledge to love him, to imitate him, to be like him, as we may the neerest by possessing our souls of true vertue, which being united to the heavenly grace of faith makes up the highest perfection."[39]

The scenes before the Fall in *Paradise Lost* represent in the process of development the "true vertue" to be repaired. The Fall and Adam's dualistic and antifeminine diatribes show its perversion. The dialogue in which Adam and Eve, thanks to prevenient grace, accept again with humility and hope the responsibilities of marriage, procreation, and cultivation presents the pattern of renovation. In studying Milton's model for the obedience of regenerate men and women,

Adam's unregenerate diatribes against Eve and marriage are a useful guide to the perverse response we are not to make. Milton's Eve
is not, as Adam asserts in his first complaint, a vain creature who
made the Fall inevitable; she is a free creature of God who fell, yet
who might, even separately, have stood—as Adam in his turn, individually, should have stood—had she continued to do her part. God
does not, as Adam implies in his second complaint, create beauty
and pleasure to tempt men; they are, rightly tempered, potential ingredients of virtue. Marriage is not, as he claims in his third complaint, a hindrance to human happiness; it is a "mutuall help to piety" and to "civill fellowship of love and amity."[40]

Although Adam's recriminations are resonant, not with Milton's
own voice but with the voice of "our Destroyer," they also provide an
example of God's power to bring good out of evil, for they have a
much-needed purgative effect on Eve, and she immediately repents.
The fact that fallen Adam is wrong about unfallen Eve does not min-
imize the grievousness of Eve's sin or the extent of their loss; on the
contrary, it allows the reader to see that both are greater than Adam
in the heat of anger is able to grasp. But, for that very reason, the
opportunities of regeneration are also greater. They involve not the
repudiation but the redemption of the earth God has made and all
that therein is, beginning, for Milton, with "Marriage, which is the
neerest resemblance of our union with Christ."

"Eccentricall Equation"

Probably the feature of Milton's treatment of Eve that is most unpalatable to modern readers is her subordination to Adam. Since the
assumptions on which it rests are foreign to our thought, its operations elude us; and the abuses that the Genesis story has been misread
to support may blind us to the fact that Milton does not condone
those abuses. On the one hand, we think of subordination as a negative state and ask, like fallen Eve, "Inferior who is free?" On the
other hand, if we believe that Milton accepts ancient assumptions
about the hierarchical order of creation and its functions, we may
think that she is not submissive enough.[41] Since, we suppose, she is
an inferior being, however much we may lament that predicament,
she ought to behave like one. These contradictory impulses deny to

Eve the benefit of Milton's principles of prelapsarian and Christian liberty and impede our responses to the whole poem.

The decorum of Eve's relation to Adam requires that we set aside both assumptions and, grasping the nettle of Eve's subordination firmly, consider what wholesome uses and reconsiderations the responsible libertarian poet finds for it.

First, we need to observe that in *Paradise Lost* subordination is not inferiority, and that Milton's Eve is equal to Adam in sanctitude while remaining, as the Vulgate has it, *adjutorium*—one who by helping gives delight—in allegiance. Like the Garden itself, this condition is an unfettered opportunity, to be well used though capable of being abused. Modern readers have come to understand the Bible in ways that divest it of antifeminine rabbinical and patristic accretions, and this is the direction in which Milton, with his Reformation fervor for such divestment, is already moving.[42] At the same time he is committed to preserving the harmony and coherence of an ordered cosmos and the typology of marriage as a resemblance of Christ and the church. He therefore portrays Adam and Eve in mutual service and freedom, but Adam's "perfection" as excelling in wisdom and Eve's in complaisance, and Adam as fitter to rule than to subject himself to his wife when such a choice becomes necessary (10.144–56). But while retaining some degree of subordination for Eve, he purges that state of all suggestion of weakness or wickedness, inferiority or limitation, carnal precedence or unequal responsibility, and avoids the radically false dichotomy of opposing freedom and service. This man and this woman have different gifts, so that Eve has particular pleasure in helping and learning from a husband she admires, and Adam has particular pleasure in attending to the peace and liberty of a wife he cherishes. But each also increasingly participates in the other's particular virtues, and both are responsible to obey God and to serve and govern the creatures subordinate to them. The whole order is linked together by a process of calling and response in which growth proceeds and liberty increases in proportion to the hearkening to God's voice and the voices of God-in-others with which each being exercises liberty and responsibility, and by which each knows the happiness of both magnanimity and gratitude. Like all opportunities, the harmonious order in which Eve's relation to Adam participates has as its maker and (for the reader) its model the Son of God,

whose ardent obedience exalts him and will exalt with him all who
respond to his call.

An application of the principle of subordination to the relations of
men and women that is more startling than Milton's occurs in *The
Faerie Queene* when Britomart, Spenser's "warlike Maide," having rescued Artegall in a thoroughly knightly way and liberated him and his
fellows from the "womanish attire" the Amazons have garbed them
in, reigns as princess over the Amazons and calmly

> changing all that forme of common weale,
> The liberty of women did repeale,
> Which they had long vsurpt; and them restoring
> To mens subiection, did true Iustice deale:
> That all they as a Goddesse her adoring,
> Her wisedome did admire, and hearkned to her loring.
>
> [7.7.42]

This action on the part of a reigning woman is comprehensible only
in the context Spenser provides: in Britomart's ethos, the subjection
of men to women debases men and thereby robs women of fit husbands, whereas if there is "true Iustice" the subjection of women to
men exalts them both—at least in "Faerie lond." But it is a woman
who converts the bellicose Amazons by this strenuous advice; and
we need to understand that Spenser means to dignify women, not
debase them. One of the innovations of Milton's unfallen world,
however, is that Adam can be preeminent (though most so in the
eyes of Eve) without Eve's "subjection." All things are moving toward perfection, and no one depends for his promotion on the demo-
tion of another.

The idea of order that Milton modifies to achieve freedom within
coherence is the classical concept of the chain of being in which all
creatures are hierarchically linked. Even in the seventeenth century,
these relations were schematized according to the Ptolemaic model
of a concentric universe, sphere within sphere, in charts that often
show how different species, parts of the body, and arts and sciences
correspond to the spheres. Since these cosmic maps are circular, the
hierarchies are arranged not upward and downward but inward
(toward Earth) and outward (toward Heaven). Milton sometimes
retains this perspective, at least metaphorically, for the sake of its
coherence, but he radically modifies it by his sense of process, his

esteem for Earth both as good in itself and as a means toward Heaven, and his scriptural view of mutual help between partners who are "heirs together of the grace of life" (1 Peter 3:7). Thus Milton relieves the microcosm-macrocosm metaphor of its fixity while retaining its coherence much as by discarding rhyme while retaining a flexible meter he insures that no word must be forcibly yoked to another, but that all join in a harmonic "concent" responsive to the whole sense. And what he does with metaphor and verse form he does also with marriage.

Although the views of Copernicus and Kepler had begun to alter the astronomical model passed down from antiquity, seventeenth-century imagery and metaphor retained many of its features.[43] In brief, the Greek philosophers had taught that since God would not deny being to anything capable of being, everything that can exist does exist; that there are no gaps in the chain of being; and that everything in nature is distinguished from the species or kinds to which it is linked by fine gradations or degrees of "perfection" defined by the powers of the soul. Thus Adam, using the Ptolemaic model, speaks of "the scale of Nature set / From center to circumference, whereon / In contemplation of created things / By steps we may ascend to God" (5.509-12). "Created things" include angels, composing nine orders in three hierarchies (Raphael ranks them "Orb within Orb" [5.596]); the heavenly spheres and whoever inhabits them (Milton, in keeping with the ideas of continuity and plenitude, suggests that "middle Spirits . . . Betwixt th'Angelical and Human kinde" may dwell on the moon [3.461-62]); then man, the microcosm who encompasses in himself correspondences to all the rest; and animals, plants, and stones, each arranged in orders by kinds and each corresponding emblematically to its peers in the other orders. The body politic was similarly conceived, as was the mind of man in faculty psychology, with reason as governor over will, memory, fancy, and the passions and affections (that is, all the emotions). In both microcosm and body politic, the head as God's vicar was to do for the members what Milton said poetry should do for the affections: keep them in "right tune."

When considering Milton's use of this model one must divest one's imagination of its graphic schemata. The universe of *Paradise Lost* is not imaged by the static Ptolemaic chart and its "degrees" are not exactly "higher" and "lower." When Satan traverses the universe, whether he goes "up or downe / By center, or eccentric, hard to tell, / Or Longitude" (3.574–76); the worlds perform a "starry dance," and the earthly orders are similarly engaged. There is a functional system of authority and subordination, but in it, though "of Elements the grosser feeds the purer" (5.415–16) yet stars feed plants and, generally, the "higher" serves the "lower"; angels serve men, and Adam and Eve nurse the Garden and, as husband and wife, minister to each other. The function of this system is the delegation, not (as Satan imagines) the limitation, of powers and the exaltation, not the subjection, of subordinates, giving each angelic and human being the dignity of responsibility. Its purpose is the fullest possible diversity and development of persons combined with the fullest cooperation and mutual responsiveness between them, all kept in harmony by love of God. In it, each self is increasingly perfected through increasing participation in love.

For Milton, the "perfection of the soul" is not a state but a process. As Richard Hooker explains it,

> God alone excepted, who actually and everlastingly is whatsoever hee may be . . . all other things besides are somewhat in possibilitie, which as yet they are not in act. And for this cause there is in all things an appetite or desire, whereby they inclyne to something which they may be: and when they are it, they shall be perfecter then nowe they are. All which perfections are conteyned under the generall name of *Goodnesse*. And because there is not in the world any thing wherby another may not some way be made perfecter, therefore all things that are, are good. Againe sith there can be no goodnesse desired which proceedeth not from God himselfe . . . all things in the worlde are saide in some sort to seeke the highest, and to covet more or lesse the participation of God himselfe.[44]

Among beings endowed with reason and choice, one's place in the order does not limit one's degree of perfection, but rather gives it a sphere of unique action through the service which is perfect freedom.

Milton attributes a process of increasing individuation through increasing response to God whose law is love to every character in the poem except Satan and his crew. Its source and exemplar is the Son,[45] who after creating Adam greets him, "call'd by thee I come thy guide" (8.298) and whose willing obedience and propitiation, the Father says to him, will "exalt / With thee thy Manhood also to this Throne"

(3.313–14). Its perverse parody is Satan, whose "fixed mind" that is "not to be chang'd by Place or Time" (1.97, 253) isolates itself from the harmony of creation, so that he grows less distinct and less interesting the farther he falls from God. He almost grasps the principle of finding one's self through losing it when he first sees Adam and Eve and considers repentance, but he chooses to accept his identity not from God, whose image he once was, but from his fallen and deceived followers, who are the images of his fallen self, and his subsequent degeneration from archangel to feigned cherub to serpent to involuntary snake manifests dwindling personhood. In contrast to Satan's subservient file, the obedient warrior angels combine cooperation with individual initiative:

> . . . led in fight, yet Leader seemd
> Each warriour single as in Chief . . . ;
> As onely in his arm the moment lay
> Of victorie.
> [6.232–33, 238–40]

Raphael as Adam's teacher and guest both exemplifies such obedience and provides an explanation of it—"freely we serve, / Because we freely love" (5.538–39). Abdiel, independently choosing to obey God against huge odds, tells Satan that God in subordinating the angels to the Son is "farr from thought / To make us less, bent rather to exalt / Our happie state," while servitude is the lot of those who follow Satan, "Thy self not free, but to thy self enthrall'd" (5.828–30; 6.181). The memorable northern angel is Abdiel; Belial and Mammon we encounter every day.

All of these considerations apply to Eve's relation to Adam. Each serves the other, and both exercise all the faculties of mind and heart. But Adam's authority gives his special talents for vigilance and just government opportunity for full development and preserves Eve's freedom for the development of her own special talents of openheartedness and imaginative response, which in turn are among her helps to him. Eve's subordination does not impose "a Slavish approach to *Gods* behests" (*Of Reformation*, 3:3). Wherever beings are arranged in orders, the arrangement is made for the augmentation of each member, for greater individuation through manifold relations, and for the greater splendor of their mutual joy. Even angels, Milton points out in *The Reason of Church-Government*, "are distinguisht and quaterniond into their celestiall Princedoms, and Satrapies"; even "the state also of the blessed in Paradise, though never so perfect, is not therefore left without discipline. . . . Yet it is not to be conceiv'd that those eternal effluences of sanctity and love in the glorified Saints should by this meanes be confin'd and cloy'd with repetition of that which is prescrib'd, but that our happiness may orbe it selfe into a thousand vagancies of glory and delight, and with a kind of eccentri-call equation be as it were an invariable Planet of joy and felicitie" (3:185–86).

"Sanctitude Severe and Pure"

The passage most often cited by those who want to show Milton unfair to women is no doubt "Hee for God only, shee for God in him" (4.288). In order to understand its implications, it is important to recognize that Milton in this very phrase assigns more dignity to Eve than was usual, and to discern the implications of the passage within its context.

The narrative voice is at this point telling us what Satan saw. Satan, with his "fixt mind," is observing and defining Adam and Eve for his own purposes. The passage is by no means Satanic, but the narrator tells us only what even Satan, with his vestiges of heavenly percipience limited by his lost sense of process and response, is able to discern. And, as is often true, we the readers are expected to be more perceptive not only than Satan, to whom Adam and Eve are a "sight tormenting," but than the narrator also, who at this point has adopted his persona of the excellent conventional observer. His observations reflect the conventional expectations of his audience with some differences that will take root and grow. For the moment, the Renaissance audience hears almost what it expects; but since, unlike Satan's mind, the personae of Adam and Eve are not fixed but in process they are going to change, grow, and deepen in each other's company. The slight differences from expectation that the narrator infuses are predictions of growth.

The delight that torments the undelighted fiend is the sight of diverse living creatures, among whom

> Two of far nobler shape erect and tall,
> Godlike erect, with native Honour clad

> In naked Majestie, seemd Lords of all,
> And worthie seemd, for in thir looks Divine
> The image of thir glorious Maker shon,
> Truth, wisdome, Sanctitude severe and pure,
> Severe but in true filial freedom plac't;
> Whence true autoritie in men; though both
> Not equal, as thir sex not equal seemd;
> For contemplation hee and valour formd,
> For softness shee and sweet attractive Grace,
> Hee for God only, shee for God in him.
>   [4.288-99]

The passage continues by developing images of Adam's authority and Eve's subjection modified by his gentleness and her willingness, as they pass in "Simplicitie and spotless innocence . . . hand in hand . . . the lovliest pair / That ever since in loves imbraces met" (4.318, 321-22).

In the context of the literary and iconographic tradition, it is unusual for Milton to include Eve in all the qualities enumerated in the first eight lines. It would have been easy for him to apply those characteristics to Adam and relegate Eve to "sweet attractive Grace"; even the choice of "grace" rather than a more strictly physical kind of beauty suggests divine favor. Here, Eve is clearly a bearer of the divine image, participant in honor, majesty, truth, wisdom, sanctitude, freedom, and authority as one of the lords of all.

At this point the narrator produces one of those ambiguities which invite the reader to choose a meaning and thereby make him aware of his own opinions. "Though both / Not equal, as thir sex not equal seemd": is the "as" a conjunction of similitude or of explanation? Are Adam and Eve "not equal" in all ways or only in regard to sex? Does inequality imply disparity of merit, or only distinction of qualities? Do their bodily forms limit Adam to contemplation and valor and Eve to softness and grace, or are these talents to be shared? If he is for God only, is he not for God in her? These questions can be answered only by watching Adam and Eve unfold in response to experience and to each other. In the lines to follow we learn already that Eve's first gaze is the contemplation of a reflection of heaven, and Adam's hand is "gentle."

As A. B. Giamatti has noted, "Hee for God only, shee for God in him" echoes by its syntax Tasso's description of Rinaldo and Armida:

"L'uno di servitù, l'altra d'impero / si gloria, ella in se stessa ed egli in lei." ["One glories in slavery, the other in command, / She in herself and he in her."][46] In spite of the echoing syntax, and in addition to the reversed line of command, two thoughts could hardly be more different than "She [glories] in herself and he in her" and "He [is formed] for God only, shee for God in him." Further, the conclusion Renaissance ears are likely to have expected is not "shee for God in him" but simply "she for him." And this distinction is so vital that Milton's whole characterization of Eve may be referred to it. She is in the right as long as she serves not just Adam but "God in him," and much that she has been blamed for may be regarded as a way of avoiding a mutually narcissistic or enslaving condition of servitude to something less in him than God.

Milton's narrative affirmation that, in emphatic plural, "in thir looks Divine / The image of thir glorious Maker shon" is a radical statement. Later we learn that Eve is also Adam's image, but, lest there be any doubt that God's image shines in her, we learn so at her first entrance. The later hint that the divine image in Eve proceeds from the Father and (or through) Adam should not disconcert us. It is a part of the normal processes of creation and procreation by which God gives his creatures a share in the creation and in responsibility for it. As Charles Williams points out, God's responsive creatures, and the Creator-Son himself, take joy in being derived from another in this endless procession of love.[47]

The notion that woman may not have been created in the divine image at all was sufficiently current before the Reformation that Protestant expositors of Genesis almost always assure their readers that she was, sometimes excepting the attribute of dominion. It is notable that Milton's narrator includes that attribute and that Adam (in one of his more dualistic moments) describes that faculty not as missing from Eve but only as less expressed in her: a concept he grasps intellectually but not emotionally (8.544). Although most Protestants agreed about Eve's subordination to Adam and some thought God's image less bright in her, all thought her equal in possessing a soul capable of heavenly ends. An early and thoroughgoing defender of women, Henry Cornelius Agrippa of Nettesheim, states,

Almyghty God the maker & nourisher of all thynges . . . of hyse great bountyfulness, hath create mankynde lyke vnto hym selfe, he made them man and woman. The diuersitie of which two kyndes, standeth onely in the sondry situation of the bodily partes, in which the vse of generation requireth a necessary difference. He hath giuen but one similitude and lykenes of the sowle, to bothe male and female, betwene whose sowles there is no maner dyfference of kynd. The woman hathe that same mynd that a man hath, that same reason and speche, she gothe to the same ende of b[l]ysfulness, where shall be noo exception of kynde.[48]

John Swan says that "woman as well as man, was partaker of the same image,"[49] and John Yates, concerned like Milton lest God should be thought the author of sin, that "the Lord would not paine [Adam] in sending him a meete helper; as for their Soules they were equally inspired, that they might both be partakers of the same happiness."[50] William Whately argues, "Now a woman also hath a soule, an immortall spirit to make her a living and a reasonable creature," since otherwise Eve could not have known, and therefore could not have sinfully transgressed, God's law; and he indignantly adds that the belief that women had no souls must have been "the device of some brutish and sensuall man, that by instilling this most absurd conceit into that sexe, would faine draw them to commit all licentiousnesse with boldnesse, for if they have no soules it could be no fault in them."[51] John Salkeld affirms that "this word image doth equally signifie, and may be equally attributed both to man and woman: seeing that they both participate of reason, and vnderstanding, both bee indued with an immortal soule, both partakers of free will, both capable of supernaturall gifts, both of grace and glory."[52] Such is the image Milton figures forth in Eve, but (in both senses of the word) processively.

Meet Help

Protestant commentary on Genesis 2:18, God's creation of meet help for Adam, was, despite its insistence on the subjection of wives, a step in the liberalization of attitudes toward women because it increased their responsibilities as promoters of godly living. Milton goes a long step further: his definition of obedience specifically excludes the possibility of involuntary subjection, and his definition of marriage differs from others both in the way he orders its purposes and in his insistence that all of its responsibilities are mutual.[53]

Earlier interpreters and some of Milton's contemporaries limited woman's role to the one kind of work Adam could not do alone: procreation. The patristic exaltation of virginity and the medieval requirment of celibacy for the clergy afforded little honor even to that work. Reformation commentary used the verse not only as an opportunity to argue for allowing marriage to the clergy but also to teach that the family is the basis of a well-ordered commonwealth and the means of populating Heaven. William Gouge calls the family "a little Church, and a little commonwealth . . . a schoole wherein the first principles and grounds of gouernment and subjection are learned."[54] Donne comments on Genesis 2:18 that "both of *Civill* and of *Spirituall* societies, the first roote is a *family;* and of families, the first roote is *Mariage,* and of mariage the first roote . . . is in this Text."[55] Perkins advises that family life should include a daily "conference vpon the word of God" and "inuocation of the name of God, with giuing of thanks for his benefits"—both of which Adam and Eve observe in their discussions of God's commands and their morning and evening prayers—and states that "those families wherein this service of God is performed are, as it were, little Churches, yea euen a kind of Paradise vpon earth."[56] These analogies prepared Milton's audience to see in his dramatization of the first marriage implications for the church, the commonwealth, and the school as well as the family.

Protestant arguments for marriage ameliorated the status of women by enumerating ways in which a wife could provide meet help, not only as a vessel of procreation and a remedy of lust (the latter, as Donne pointed out, not a proper cause of love, "for so it is a love, *Quia mulier,* because she is a woman, and not *Quia uxor,* because she is my wife"[57]) but as a loving companion with a responsible role in the government of the family. This amelioration was a halting one, however, because of the tendency to oppose nature and grace and limit woman's work to the former realm. Milton frees Eve from this limitation by integrating nature and grace, by making her a "Spirituall" as well as a "Civill" help, by stressing that this help is mutual, and by revising common metaphors of the relations of the sexes.

Gervase Babington's exposition of Genesis 2:18, for example, expresses a regard for women that is intended for their good but not altogether consonant with their dignity.

That Woman is honoured with the title of a *Helper,* not onelie sheweth
the goodnesse of the institution, . . . but teacheth also how deere and
beloued shee should bee to her Husband, for whose good shee was ordained and giuen. Who will not cherrish, foster and loue what is giuen
him for a helpe, not by Man, but by God himselfe? Her helpe consisteth chieflie in three things, in bearing him Children, the comforts
of his life, and stayes of his age, which hee cannot haue without her.
In keeping his bodie holie to the Lorde, from filthie pollution which
the Lord abhoreth. The Apostle so teaching when he speaketh thus:
For the auoyding of Fornication, let euerie man haue his own wyfe; and thirdlie, in gouerning his house, Children, and Familie, and many wayes
tending his owne person, both in sickness and health. These all and
euerie one, are great helpes, and therefore the Woman iustlie to be regarded for them.

Milton, as we shall see, subordinated these three kinds of help to a
greater one and made them fully mutual. Further, Babington ampli-
fies his message with an archetypal metaphor that Milton used quite
differently in *Paradise Lost.* Babington continues, "In this last, man
also hath his care, to wit, so to furnish the woman with direction and
abilitie, that she may doo within dores what of her should be done.
Whereupon, the man is compared to the Sunne that giueth light,
and the Woman to the Moone, that receiueth light from the Sunne
. . . contrary with many idle Drones, that shine with the beames of
their wiues, that is, idlie liue by theyr Wiues sore labour."[58] Raphael's astronomical speculations modify the sexual metaphors of sun
and moon and of sun and earth to the advantage of moon and earth:

> consider first, that Great
> Or Bright inferrs not Excellence: the Earth
> Though, in comparison of Heav'n, so small,
> Nor glistering, may of solid good containe
> More plenty then the Sun that barren shines,
> Whose vertue on it self workes no effect,
> But in the fruitful Earth; there first receavd
> His beams, unactive else, thir vigour find.
> [8.90–97]

Further, the lighting of moon and earth may be "reciprocal," the
moon itself may be fertile and inhabited, and the whole universe
may be filled with life reciprocally nurtured, for

> other Suns perhaps
> With thir attendant Moons thou wilt descrie
> Communicating Male and Femal Light,
> Which two great Sexes animate the World,
> Stor'd in each Orb perhaps with some that live.
>   [8.146–50]

For Milton the whole cosmos is expressed in full reciprocity as an interinanimation of the sexes correponding to the microcosm of human marriage.

Perkins's list of purposes for marriage is similar to Babington's but adds the propagation of an Elect and stresses the callings of both parties rather than household comfort.

> The first is procreation of children, for the propagation and continuance of the seede and posterite of man vpon earth.
>
> The second is the procreation of an holy seed, whereby the Church of God may be kept holy and chaste, and there may alwaies be a holy company of men, that may worship and serue God in the Church from age to age.
>
> The third is, that after the fall of mankind, it might be a soueraigne meanes to auoid fornication, and consequently to subdue the burning lust of the flesh. . . .
>
> The fourth ende is, that the parties married may thereby performe the duties of their callings, in better and more comfortable manner.

In specifying the duties of the "Mistresse of the house," Perkins states that she assists "the Master of the family . . . not onely in office and authoritie, but also in aduise, and counsell vnto him"; but her duties still lie, as Babinston says, "within dores," where she is "to gouern the house . . . exercising her selfe in some profitable employments" and "ordering her children and servants in wisdome" and "to giue the portion of food vnto her family, or cause it to be giuen in due season."[59]

The commentary of Nicholas Gibbens is closer to Milton's marriage tracts in placing companionship before sexual and economic roles as the chief good of marriage and in affirming that woman was created both a "reasonable soule" and a "delight"; but he lacks Milton's sense that the benefits of marriage should be mutual.

> Her nature is *to be like vnto the man* in soule and in bodie, to differ in sex. The end of her creation was to be *a help to man* . . . : first, for the societie of life, to increase his joy, she was made to be alwaies his de-

light. Secondlie to obtaine the blessing: Increase and multiply, she
was made to be an help for procreation. Thirdlie, to help him in bringing up of children and gouerning the familie . . . . Herby wee conclude, first that the woman is of the same nature with man, of like
reasonable soule. 2. That she was made for man and ioyned vnto him
for his good. . . . [60]

Milton's "divorce" tracts belong to this vast literature in defense of
matrimony, but they radically reorient it.[61] "In matrimony," he states
in *Tetrachordon,* "there must be first a mutuall help to piety; next, to
civill fellowship of love and amity, then to generation, so to household affairs, lastly, the remedy of incontinence" (4:88). Thus he
gives first place among helps to the love of God and second to love of
each other, so that his definition corresponds to the summary of the
law, which is to love God and one's neighbor. The main premise of
the divorce tracts is that the first end of marriage is service of God
and "fellowship of love" while its secondary purposes are generation
and chastity, yet the divorce laws allow a remedy for the frustration
of the second but not the first. (In *Paradise Lost* he removes any umbrage this subordination may seem to cast on the "genial bed"; again,
subordination is not devaluation.) Further, all of the helps he mentions are "mutuall," as he stresses again in his discussion of marriage
as a covenant, "the essence whereof, as of all other Covnants, is in
relation to another, the making and maintaining causes thereof are
all mutual, and must be a communion of spiritual and temporal
comforts." Like all covenants, marriage requires liberty of conscience,
for it is "a solemn thing, some say a holy, the resemblance of Christ
and his Church; and wee know all Sacred things, not perform'd sin-
cerely as they ought, are no way acceptable to God in their outward
formality" (4:126). This liberty should be extended to both men and
women, for "the Gospel seems to make the wife more equal to her
husband in these conjugal respects then the law of *Moses* doth"
(4:215). Defining marriage as "a divine institution joyning man and
woman in a love fitly dispos'd to the helps and comforts of domestic
life," Milton adds the unusual comment, "If any shall ask, why *domestic* in the definition? I answer, that because both in the Scriptures, and in the gravest Poets and Philosophers, I finde the proper-
ties and excellencies of a wife set out only from domestic vertues; if
they extend furder, it diffuses them into the notion of some more

common duty then matrimonial" (4:105–6). That a woman might develop virtues beyond the domestic sphere had rarely occurred to generations who advised women to train their tongues to silence and their feet to home-keeping.

Reformation commentary on the roles of wives gave women an active and realistic calling and a fragment of dignity on which Milton could build his appreciations of Eve's accomplishments, including her work in the Garden, in ways consistent with his belief that liberty is essential to obedience and with his own calling as an artist. Milton's Eve fulfills the puritan requirements with grace and gaiety; but she has lights and powers of her own that are not mere reflections of Adam's, and she was not created simply to make his life easy. Both are placed in the Garden to achieve Heaven by degrees of merit, and the good for which Eve is joined to Adam includes not only delight but all the offices of piety and civil fellowship. In her responsible and creative use of liberty and talent in all the scenes before the Fall, Eve provides a pattern not only for wives newly dignified by Reformation defenses of matrimony but for all who endeavor to walk with God under the dispensation of Gospel freedom.

Two further considerations, one political and the other theological, may help clear up the difficulties of perceiving Eve's liberty in relation to Adam.

Civil Obedience: The Body Politic

The political principle may be distinguished from the theological one only for the sake of argument, since for Milton piety and civility, or love of God and love of neighbor, are as inseparable as body and soul. The common assumption was that a clear line of authority, headed by a ruler who is himself ruled by reason, is necessary for concord, since among equals every decision is open to dispute. Milton, who ultimately decided that the government of one is unsuitable to a Christian commonwealth, adopted this assumption only insofar as it corresponds to his vision of the transmission of charity and adapted it to his idea of Christian liberty by applying his views on the limits of prelatical and civil authority to the "little church and little state" of the family. If marriage is to resemble the union of Christ with the members of his church, it will resemble "that Feast of love and heavenly-admitted fellowship" to which "*Christ* invited his Disciples to sit as Brethren, and coheirs of the happy Covenant, which at that Table was to be Seal'd to them" (3:4). Before he had rejected monarchy, Milton clarified his view of the right and wrong uses of authority by an analogy of monarchy to marriage: "We know that *Monarchy* is made of two parts, the Liberty of the Subject, and the Supremacie of the King. . . . Yet these devout prelates . . . set at nought . . . the holy Cov'nant of Union and Marriage, betweene the King and his Realme, by proscribing and confiscating from us all the right we have to our owne bodies, goods and liberties" (3:56–57). Even if Eden were a monarchy, marriage would be made of the supremacy of the husband and the liberty of the wife: but in fact, it is governed by counsel — or council, as Milton had hoped England would be.

Expositors of Genesis frequently pondered the question of whether Eve's subjection to Adam took place before or after the Fall; that is to say, whether headship and subordination are intrinsically necessary for a harmonious society or whether authority became necessary only after the Fall introduced inordinate and conflicting desires. The question is a basic one for the controversies of Milton's time because it asks what a commonwealth would have been like if it could have developed without sin, if there had been no Fall, and therefore what it should be like for those regenerated in God's image.

Chrysostom believed that the subjection of women occurred after the Fall and was both prescribed and implanted in human nature as an act of mercy.

> . . . with us indeed the woman is reasonably subjected to the man: since equality of honor causeth contention. And not for this cause only, but by reason also of the deceit (1 Tim. ii 14) which happened at the beginning. Wherefore you see, she was not subjected as soon as she was made; nor, when He brought her to the man, did either she hear any such thing from God, nor did the man say any such word to her: he said indeed that she was "bone of his bone, and flesh of his flesh:" (Gen. ii 23) but of the rule of subjection he made no mention to her. But when she made an ill use of her privilege and she who had been made a helper was found to be an ensnarer and ruined all, then she is justly told for the future, "Thy turning shall be to thy husband." (Gen. iii 16)
>
> To account for which: it was likely that this sin would have thrown our race into a state of warfare; (for her having been made out of him would not have contributed any thing to peace, when this had hap-

pened, nay, rather this very thing would have made the man even the harsher, that she made as she was out of him should not have spared even him who was a member of herself:) wherefore God, considering the malice of the Devil, raised up the bulwark of this word; and what enmity was likely to arise from this evil device, he took away by means of this sentence and by the desire implanted in us: thus pulling down the partition-wall, i.e., the resentment caused by that sin of hers.[62]

Adam's rib does indeed become a bone of contention after the Fall in *Paradise Lost.* Before it, Milton observes as Chrysostom does that Eve is not subjected to Adam by God or man; the only person who speaks of Adam's pre-eminence is Eve herself (4.444–48).

A more widespread view in Milton's time was that Eve was subject to Adam before the Fall and that a civil hierarchy would have evolved even if the Fall had not occurred. In the words of its bluntest advocate, "You wives be content to be subject to your husbands, as it is sure *Evah* was before the fall at least, and probable after too, for we read of no brawles betwixt them."[63] An exception to the general rule was the attitude of the Levellers, who do not take the Fall into account at all in their belief that "man had domination given him over the beasts, birds, and fishes. But not one word was spoken in the beginning, that one branch of mankind should rule over other," for "every single man, male and female, is a perfect creature of himself."[64] For the most part, however, the reformers upheld civil authority by comparing the governed with Eve. Perkins answers those "anabaptists" who "despise gouernment" by distinguishing two kinds of subjection:

> the first, *Seruile:* the second, *Ciuill.* The former is the subiection of a slaue or vassall, who is onely to seeke the proper good of his Lord and Master. The latter whereby one man is subiect to another for the common good. The former came in by sinne: the latter was before sin, in innocencie: thus the Apostle reasoneth, I. Tim. 2. 12. *Let the woman be subiect to the man: for she was taken out of the man.*[65]

Submission for Donne is a mutual assistance, based on Pauline doctrine, no less required of the person in authority than of his subordinate:

> The wife is to submit herselfe; and so is the husband too: They have a burden both. There is a greater subjection lies upon her, then upon the *Man,* in respect of her transgression towards her husband at

first. . . . But if she had not committed that fault, yet there would have
been a mutuall subjection between them; . . . for if *Man* had continued
in innocency, yet it is most probably thought, that as there would certainly have been *Mariage,* and so *children, so also there would have been
Magistry,* and *propriety,* and *authority,* and so a mutuall assisting of one
another. . . . [66]

Although Greek Father, puritan, and Anglican differ as to the
probability and degree of Eve's subordination to Adam in the state
of innocence, all agree that a more mutual and voluntary relation
would have developed than in a society subject to prescriptive law.
Milton goes farther. In *Paradise Lost* he accords to Eve in innocence
the freedom that he thought necessary for true obedience and called
upon church and commonwealth to provide the regenerate; and he
gives Eve the simplest and most gracious of responses:

> "For wee to [God] indeed all praises owe,
> And daily thanks, I chiefly who enjoy
> So farr the happier lot, enjoying thee
> Praeeminent by so much odds, while thou
> Like consort to thyself canst no where find."
> [4.444–48]

"Daughter of God and Man"

The theological principle involves subtle but steady suggestion
that the relation of Adam and Eve, though human, vulnerable, and
fraught with challenge, is potentially and increasingly the image of
the Son's relation to the Father within the Godhead.[67] For both Eve
and the Son, obedience is a response to goodness inseparable from
an unhampered creativity to which nature in turn responds. When
the Son rides forth to rout the rebel angels, "Heav'n his wonted face
renew'd, / And with fresh Flow'rets Hill and Valley smil'd" (6.781–
84); when Eve goes forth "among her Fruits and Flours," which the
Son has created and called her to nurture, "they at her coming
sprung / And toucht by her fair tendance gladlier grew" (8.44–47).

Twice in addressing Eve, once at the beginning and once at the
end of what we see of their unfallen life, Adam calls her "Daughter of
God and Man": she is "Daughter of God and Man, accomplisht *Eve*"
(4.660) and "Daughter of God and Man, immortal *Eve*" (9.291). In
one way the designation is a gentle reminder of her subordination;

he is a creature of God only, she of God and him. In another and more important way, however, it is a bold comparison, for it echoes the names "Son of God" and "Son of Man," which are the names of the incarnate Christ.

The analogy between the role of Eve and that of the Son derives its authority from several passages in St. Paul's Epistles, of which the most pertinent is in I Corinthians II.3: "But I would have you know, that the head of every man is Christ; and the head of the woman is the man; and the head of Christ is God." The first parts of this three-fold relation are echoed unceasingly by contemporary commentators on the duties of marriage, more often with reference to Ephesians 5.23: "For the husband is the head of the wife, even as Christ is the head of the church." But the third part, "the head of Christ is God," involves a concept of the relation of the Father and the Son drama-tized by Milton in ways some readers have thought heretical, since the Son is apparently not regarded as being omniscient and omni-present, but which scholars have recently shown to be, if slightly heterodox, still within the main stream of Christian doctrine. This concept is called "subordinationism," and Milton's dramatization of it is resonant with implications for all Christian covenants, including marriage.

Since the publication of *De Doctrina Christiana* in 1825, many schol-ars have supposed that Milton was not a Trinitarian but an Arian; that is, that he believed the Son created *ex nihilo,* neither co-eternal nor co-equal nor even consubstantial with the Father. Recently W. B. Hunter, J. A. Adamson and C. A. Patrides have opposed this view and shown that Milton's subordination of the Son to the Father has support from both the Greek Fathers and the Cambridge Platonists and agrees with the rich tradition, shared in part by Christian, Greek and Jewish thought, of the Logos, regarded as the intermedia-ry through whom the unknowable God accommodates himself to the understanding of rational creatures.[68] The principal features of Mil-ton's subordinationism, as elucidated by Hunter, Adamson and Pat-rides, seem to be these: he believes, in agreement with the authors of the Nicene Creed, that the Son is "begotten of his Father" and "of one substance with the Father"; but he also argues that numerically and thus essentially the Son is a distinct person, one in substance but not one in personal essence with the Father; and that his sonship, at least in his act of submission in the process of atonement, includes a subordination to the Father that implies a distinction of wills. If, as Stella Revard has pointed out, the Son were co-essential as well as consubstantial with the Father, their unity of will would be a matter of necessity; but by distinguishing and subordinating the volition of the Son, Milton can show his obedience to consist in acts of free choice, so that "the foundation of Milton's Trinity is not identity of origin but unanimity of Heart—the bond of love."[69] It is this distinction of persons that enables Milton's God to call the Son "By Merit more then Birthright Son of God" (3.309), a commendation not Arian but centrally Christian in its assertion of the dignity of obedience.

Milton is not alone in recognizing a distinction of wills within the Godhead. Chrysostom, responding to critics of his own day who thought St. Paul's comparison contrary to the doctrine of the Trinity, and warning that its proportions should not be regarded as equal or as applicable to all particulars, makes a statement pertinent both to Milton's subordinationism and to his view of marriage:

> For had Paul meant to speak of rule and subjection . . . he would not have brought forward the instance of a wife, but rather of a slave and master. For what if the wife be under subjection to us? it is as a wife, as free, as equal in honor. And the Son also, though he did become obedient to the Father, it was as the Son of God, it was as God. For as the obedience of the Son is greater than we find in men towards the authors of their being, so also His liberty is greater.[70]

John Donne, also comparing the Trinity and the family, in a baptismal sermon on the text from Ephesians 5, combines orthodox Trinitarianism with a similar distinction of wills among the persons of the Godhead, and does so with a similar sense of the relation of freedom and obedience:

> The *father and I are one,* says Christ: one in *Essence,* and one in *Consent* . . . if we could consider severall wills in the severall Persons of the Trinity, we might be bold to say, *That the Father could not have given him, if he had not given himselfe.* . . . [T]he unexpressible and unconceivable love of Christ is in this, that there was in him a willingnesse, a propensnesse, a forwardnesse to give himselfe to make this great peace and reconciliation, between God and Man; It was he himselfe that gave himself; Nothing inclined him, nothing wrought upon him, but his own goodness.[71]

This is the Son's "immortal love / To mortal men, above which only shone / Filial obedience" (3.267–69), the source and example of all love, including "Mariage, which is the neerest resemblance of our union with Christ."

In *Tetrachordon* Milton affirms the Pauline analogy, not just as an apt similitude but as a chain of being by which the divine image is extended and responded to:

> Moreover, if man be the image of God, which consists in holines, and woman ought in the same respect to be the image and companion of man, in such wise to be loved as the Church is belov'd of Christ, and if, as God is the head of Christ, and Christ the head of man, so man is the head of woman; I cannot see by this golden dependence of headship and subjection, but that Piety and Religion is the main tye of Christian Matrimony. . . . [4:74]

Without presuming to rationalize the mystery of the Trinity, Milton makes it clear that when the Son in Book 3, in Chrysostom's words, "did become obedient to the Father," with, in Donne's words, "a forwardnesse to give himself" towards which "nothing wrought upon him, but his own goodness," he became the prototype of "a savory obedience" rooted and nurtured in "filial freedom" and conferring the dignity of merit. Chrysostom, Donne and Milton all have in mind the principle — no paradox to believers in a provident God — that a true obedience and a true freedom are proportionate and that each promotes the other. When newly fallen Eve asks, "Inferior who is free?" she perverts the meaning of that "golden dependence" headed by the Son's ardent obedience to the Father and exemplified, until the Fall, by Adam's to the Son and Eve's to Adam and so to "God in him."

The crucial act that both epitomizes this process of response and re-opens it to regenerate men is the Son's voluntary offering of himself in Book 3 in propitiation for men's foreseen enthrallment. The fact that this offer is made before the enthrallment does not mean that the Fall is fortunate — the Incarnation could have taken place and helped to raise mankind without it[72] — or that it is inevitable. No "least impulse or shadow of Fate" (3.120) touches either man's disobedience or the Son's obedience. That his sacrifice is voluntary is indicated by the dramatic moment when God the Father, declaring that justice requires "rigid satisfaction, death for death," asks,

"Where shall we find such love?" (3. 212–13) and waits while "all the Heavn'ly Quire [stand] mute, / And silence [is] in Heav'n" (3. 217–18). Into this awful silence the narrator interjects the comment,

> And now without redemption all mankind
> Must have bin lost, adjudg'd to Death and Hell
> By doom severe, had not the Son of God,
> In whom the fulness dwels of love divine,
> His dearest mediation thus renewed.
> [3.222–26]

Mankind might have been lost: it is not from necessity but from love that the Son replies,

> Account me man; I for his sake will leave
> Thy bosom, and his glorie next to thee
> Freely put off, and for him lastly dye . . .
> [3.238–40]

The two distinct voices in this exchange keep clear a basic article of faith: that lucid, unswerving justice and mercy at all costs are both essential to charity. The Father's dependable justice is necessary to the dignity and the liberty of rational beings, and the Son's mercy to their salvation. At the same time, the dialogue demonstrates the calling and response that is the rhythmic pattern of true obedience.

Two evocative explanations have been put forward for the Father's harsh manner. Irene Samuel hears in his speech "the toneless voice of the moral law," which the Father uses to encourage "the distinctive tones of a quite different voice . . . the Son's compassionate tone is made possible by the passionless logic of the Father."[73] Arthur Barker suggests that Milton's God purposely and ironically adopts the authoritarian role Satan attributes to him "in order to challenge the Son and induce from him a loving and sacrificial response."[74] The two suggestions have in common the essential perception that the Father elicits from the Son a voluntary and distinctively personal offering. His daring gift is not a result of perfect foreknowledge. It is made in trust that only good can come of obeying God. He "attends the will / Of his great Father" (3.270–71) and is in return exalted, through his very humility, and with him those he descends to save. The Father's reply expresses God's bounty to those who risk all for good: the Son shall be "in Adam's roome / The Head of all mankind," and those who respond shall "Receive new life" (3.285–86, 294):

> Nor shalt thou by descending to assume
> Mans Nature, less'n or degrade thine owne.
>   . . . because in thee
> Love hath abounded more than Glory abounds,
> Therefore thy Humiliation shall exalt
> With thee thy Manhood also to this Throne. . . .
>   [3.303–04, 311–13]

The Son has yielded himself unconditionally to the need for perfect love; the Father in turn declares that the Son will "be judg'd and die," but then will "dying rise, and rising with him raise / His Brethren" (3.295–97), becoming by his loving assent to lowliness the triumphant Christ.

Two applications to the second part of St. Paul's analogy, and to Milton's Eve, are immediately apparent: subordination is not demeaning, but is a means of promotion by unpredestined merit; and obedience is not a following of a set of instructions but a response to a divine calling, made in one's own distinctive way. The idea that service means loss of power, freedom, dignity, and opportunity is the central distortion of the Satanic mind. By assenting to it at the moment of her fall—but not before—Eve falls into real subjection and servitude, for subjection means having to serve something less than God or his image in what he creates, and servitude is labour that does not preserve or cultivate God's goodness in creation. The truth made manifest by the Son's willing and loving subordination is that such obedience empowers, frees, ennobles and opens the way to ever-increasing opportunity.

When he goes forth in response to the will of the Father, on creative and redemptive missions that are in every sense free and responsible acts, the Son offers a perfect pattern of answering love by which we are to measure all other choices—including the going forth of Eve in Book 9, the act on which unregenerate Adam and a host of critics blame the Fall. As Chrysostom cautions, the comparison of Adam and Eve to God the Father and God the Son must be taken in due proportion, and it cannot be applied to all particulars. Eve's sweet persistence and Adam's doubts fall on our own imperfect ears with warning notes and a foretaste of catastrophe. Adam and Eve are mutually discovering the process of calling and response, but for them the discovery is not yet complete. We know as we read the scene that Eve will not continue to do her part, and there is terror and pity in the knowledge. But the conversation and the departure are a part of their obedience, not of their disobedience. Eve's relation to Adam is meant to be, and is growing to be, as nearly as possible like the Son's to the Father. Both Eve in her going forth and Adam in his willingness to give her instruction, freedom and opportunity continue humanly to seek fulfilment of the pattern that the Father and the Son divinely shape; it is only Eve's failure to return still sinless and Adam's subsequent failure to turn to God, trusting in his providence, that break the pattern.

The Son demonstrates the service that is perfect freedom; and in the relation Milton attributes to Adam and Eve in the state of innocence and commends to regenerate men and women in the state of grace, the man is head of the woman, in as nearly as possible the same way that Christ is the head of the man and God is the head of Christ: not, of course, in proportion; only in the qualities of love each shows. This relation is exemplary for all the covenants of the regenerate, whom Milton calls to accept with faith their potentialities and responsibilities as restored images of God, and to go forth in the world using every faculty and talent in performing deeds answerable to God's ways.

Notes

1. *The Works of Mr. Richard Hooker . . . : In Eight Books of Ecclesiastical Polity* (London, 1662), p. 304.

2. Samuel Johnson, *The Lives of the English Poets* (Dublin, 1779), p. 199; James Holly Hanford, *A Milton Handbook* (New York, 1926), p. 213; E. M. W. Tillyard, *Milton* (London, 1930), p. 266; Harris Fletcher, ed., *The Complete Poetical Works of John Milton* (Cambridge, Mass., 1941), n. to 10.866, p. 349. Fletcher asks elsewhere, however, "Why is it that almost everyone who deals with Milton's statements about women begins with Adam's violent attacks on Eve after the Fall . . . and almost never mentions Adam's wistful appeal to Raphael in which Eve is so greatly lauded?" (*The Intellectual Development of John Milton* [Urbana, Ill., 1961], 2:177).

3. Milton, *Tetrachordon,* 4:47.

4. Critics' agreement with this assumption is challenged by Stella Revard in "Eve and the Doctrine of Responsibility in *Paradise Lost,*" *PMLA* 88 (1973): 72–73.

5. This awareness is implied in 9.205-25.

6. Jerome, "Letter to Gaudentius," trans. W. H. Fremantle, *SLNPNF,* Second Series, gen. ed. Philip Schaff and Henry Wace (Grand Rapids, Mich., 1957–69; a reprint of the 1890–1900 edition), 6:259.

58   *Milton's Eve*

7. Vives, *The Instruction of a Christian Woman,* trans. Richarde Hyrd (London, 1529 [?]), signatures Bii–Fii. Vives represents the patristic point of view; Reformer Heinrich Bullinger, on the other hand, warns that women should not be "euer shut vp, as it were in Cage . . . for to kepe them euer in mewe, is ynough ether to make them starke foles or els to make them naughtes, when they shall once come a brode into companye" (*The Christen State of Matrimony,* trans. Miles Coverdale [n.p., 1541], signature Kiiii). Ruth Kelso provides a good summary and an extensive bibliography of Renaissance attitudes toward the education of women in *Doctrine for the Lady of the Renaissance* (Urbana, Ill., 1956), and Pearl Hogrefe discusses those most compatible with Milton's in *The Sir Thomas More Circle* (Urbana, Ill., 1959).

8. *The Second Tome of Homilies . . . Set out by the Authority of the Late Queen's Majesty: and to Be Read in Every Parish Church Agreeably* (London, 1640), p. 241. One should observe that this homily is intended to be a defense of women against tyrannous husbands.

9. Richard Hooker, *Works . . . in Eight Books of Ecclesiastical Polity* (London, 1662), p. 304. "Imbecility" was of course closer than it is now to its Latin root, meaning "weakness."

10. *The Sermons of John Donne,* ed. George R. Potter and Evelyn M. Simpson (Berkeley, 1955), 2:344–45; quotations are from 1 Peter 3:7 and 1 Tim. 2:11 and 14.

11. Samuel Purchas, *Microcosmus, or the Historie of Man* (London, 1619), pp. 481 and 485. The whole chapter (pp. 472–87) sums up both sides of the question, "how and why Women are better or worse then Men," explaining that they are capable of more charity and piety if well governed and of more evil if left to their own devices.

12. William Perkins, *Christian Oeconomie,* in *Workes,* trans. Thomas Pickering (Cambridge, 1618), 3:671.

13. Chrysostom, *Homilies on First Corinthians* Homily 26, Oxford trans., revised by T. W. Chambers, *SLNPNF,* First Series, 12:150.

14. Milton, *The Doctrine and Discipline of Divorce: Restor'd to the Good of Both Sexes. . . ,* 3:393, 391, 400.

15. See Barker, *Milton and the Puritan Dilemma,* ch. 17 and passim.

16. Milton, *Tetrachordon,* 4:84.

17. Eph. 5:22–33, comparing the relation of husband and wife to that of Christ and the church, is cited by nearly every writer and preacher on matrimonial duties, including Milton. In interpreting Milton's views on marriage it is important to keep in mind his views on Christian liberty: if "the husband is the head of the wife, even as Christ is the head of the church," a wife's obedience to her husband shares the liberties and responsibilities Milton thought necessary for the obedience of Christians to Christ; see also Barker, ch. 7.

18. Milton, *Areopagitica,* 4:319.

19. Compare, for example, Jerome's "Letter to Gaudentius" and Tertullian, *On the Apparel of Women,* in *The Ante-Nicene Fathers,* ed. Alexander Roberts and James Donaldson (Grand Rapids, Mich., 1968), 4:15.

20. Kester Svendsen traces the "crooked rib" tradition and its misogynous implications in *Milton and Science* (Cambridge, Mass., 1956); J. M. Evans provides a comprehensive survey of the "minimizing view" of Eve in *"Paradise Lost" and the Genesis Tradition;* and C. L. Powell gives a history of antifeminism in *English Domestic Relations, 1487–1653* (New York, 1917). Herschel Baker discusses the traditional relation of sex and the *contemptus mundi* in *The Wars of Truth* (Cambridge, Mass., 1952); and A. B. Giamatti traces it through the illusory gardens of classical, medieval, and Renaissance literature in *The Earthly Paradise and the Renaissance Epic.*

21. *Cursor Mundi,* ed. Richard Morris, Early English Text Society (hereafter ab-

breviated *EETS*), nos. 57, 99, 101 (London, 1874 and 1893), Trinity ms., lines 725–28.

22. Chester II, *The Creation*, ed. Hermann Deimling, *EETS* Extra Series, no. 62 (London, 1893), pp. 27–28.

23. *DuBartas His Deuine Weekes and Workes,* trans. Joshua Sylvester (London, 1613), p. 243.

24. Watson Kirkconnell, trans. of Grotius in *The Celestial Cycle* (Toronto, 1952), pp. 109–11. See Vergil, "Varium et mutabile semper / femina" (*Aeneid,* 4.569–70).

25. Ralegh, *History,* p. 70.

26. Charles Clay Doyle has pointed out that "in giving such a speech to fallen Adam, Milton implicitly condemns this masculine attitude, not only anti-feminism *per se* but also the patronizing fondness which co-exists with contempt for the sex" ("Nature's Fair Defect: Milton and William Cartwright on the Paradox of Women," *ELN* 11 [1973]: 107–10).

27. *An Answer to a Book, Intituled The Doctrine and Discipline of Divorce* (London, 1644), p. 12.

28. Milton, *Tetrachordon,* 4:85.

29. Ibid., p. 98.

30. Jerome, "Letter to Eustochium," *SLNPNF,* Second Series, 6:29; see *Hali Meidenhad,* ed. F. S. Furnivall, *EETS* no. 18 (London, 1922), an early Christian exhortation to young women to shun the horrors of sex, childbearing, and house-keeping.

31. Tertullian, *An Exhortation to Chastity,* in *The Ante-Nicene Fathers,* 4:58. Tertullian argues that nothing but law makes a difference between marriage and fornication; most patristic statements on chastity take into account Paul's assurance that the marriage bed is undefiled. In spite of Reformation commendations of marriage, the notion that sexuality is intrinsically corrupt still reemerged in the seventeenth century, as in Purchas's characterization of the process of procreation as "base, abominable, viperous" (*Microcosmus,* pp. 156 ff.).

32. Wye Saltonstall, *Picturae Loquentes* (London, 1631), sig. A9.

33. Richard Baxter, *A Christian Directory* (London, 1678), 2:7–8.

34. Milton, *Tetrachordon,* 4:86.

35. Cf. John Calvin, *Commentarie vpon Genesis,* trans. Thomas Thymme (London, 1578), p. 72: "Let the wicked lerne to set against these wicked suggestions of Sathan, this sentence of God, wherwith he hath appointed man to a matrimoniall life, not to his destruction, but to his saluation."

36. Gregory of Nyssa, *Of Virginity,* trans. William Moore and Henry Austin Wilson, *SLNPNF,* Second Series, 5:358–59.

37. Eve's rehabilitation and her remedial role are discussed by A. H. Gilbert in "Milton on the Position of Women," *MLR* 15 (1920): 7–27 and 240–64, an early defense against the charge of misogyny; Mary Ann Nevins Radzinowicz in "Eve and Dalila: Renovation and Hardening of the Heart," in *Reason and Imagination: Studies in the History of Ideas, 1600–1800,* ed. J. A. Mazzeo (New York, 1962), pp. 155–81; and Joseph H. Summers, *The Muse's Method* (London, 1962), ch. VII: "The Voice of the Redeemer." In Loredano's *Life of Adam* Eve becomes "an incentive to good" (facs. of 1659 translation, intro. Roy C. Flannagan with John Arthos [Gainesville, Fla., 1967], p. 57).

38. Milton, *Areopagitica,* 4:311.

29. Milton, *Of Education,* 4:277.

40. Milton, *Tetrachordon,* 4:88.

41. Examples include the statements of Fredson Bowers and Lawrence Babb cited in ch. I, n. 6. At the other extreme, William Empson in *Milton's God* (London, 1961) applauds Eve's overturning of what he thinks God's tyrannous order.

42. Virginia Ramey Mollenkott gives a clear demonstration of the scriptural basis for "mutual and voluntary loving service" (p. 34) in *Women, Men, and the Bible* (Nashville, 1977). See also Phyllis Trible, *God and the Rhetoric of Sexuality* (Philadelphia, 1978), esp. ch. 4, a reading of Genesis 2-3 as a Hebrew celebration of Eros in which male and female sexuality are created simultaneously and God specifically refrains from giving the man dominion over the woman (pp. 97-98).

43. The idea of order as developed in Greek, medieval, and Renaissance thought is discussed in Arthur O. Lovejoy, *The Great Chain of Being: A Study of the History of an Idea* (Cambridge, Mass., 1936); C. S. Lewis, *The Discarded Image: An Introduction to Medieval and Renaissance Literature* (Cambridge, England, 1964); and E. M. W. Tillyard, *The Elizabethan World Picture* (London, 1960). Lewis discusses Milton's use of hierarchical order in *A Preface to "Paradise Lost"* (Oxford, 1942), ch. 11, and John G. Halkett applies it to domestic order in *Milton and the Idea of Matrimony* (New Haven, 1970).

Irene Samuel finds that "*Paradise Lost* cannot turn on a doctrine of hierarchy as the central ordering principle of a universe in which everyone has a natural superior whom he must obey and a natural inferior whom he must rule. If Raphael, explaining the chain of being, loosely describes the higher orders of creation as 'nearer to . . . [God] placed or nearer tending' and asserts that man and angel are more alike than different, if Milton himself assigns the sense of strict hierarchical superiority exclusively to Satan, the poem cannot hinge on just such a system as Milton's prose constantly denies. Abdiel is right to serve truth rather than his immediate overlord Satan" (*Six Critical Approaches*, p. 242). See also Professor Samuel's *Dante and Milton* (Ithaca, N.Y., 1966), esp. pp. 155-57 and 190-95. In "Milton on Women—Yet Once More" (*MiltonS* 6 [1974]), Barbara Kiefer Lewalski comments on Milton's "curiously fluid conception of hierarchy . . . according to which angels and men are seen to differ in degree only, . . . and human beings are encouraged to expect the gradual refinement of their own natures to virtually angelic condition (V, 470-505)." and adds, "How much more fluid, then, the hierarchical distinction between man and woman?" (p. 6).

44. Richard Hooker, *Of the Lawes of Ecclesiasticall Politie* (1593), ed. Georges Edelen, in *The Folger Library Edition of The Works of Richard Hooker*, gen. ed. W. Speed Hill (Cambridge, Mass., 1977) 1:72-73.

45. Arthur E. Barker shows that Milton's individuation of characters "should be seen also in the representation of the Son," and that this representation should be seen "as making the rest possible" ("Structural and Doctrinal Pattern," p. 186).

46. Giamatti's translation; in *The Earthly Paradise and the Renaissance Epic*, p. 314.

47. Charles Williams, Introduction to *The English Poems of John Milton* (London, 1940), reprinted in *Milton Criticism*, ed. James Thorpe (New York, 1969).

48. Henry Cornelius Agrippa, *A treatise of the nobilitie and excellencye of womenkynde*, trans. David Clapham (London, 1542), sig. Aii.

49. John Swan, *Speculum Mundi* (Cambridge, England, 1635), p. 500.

50. John Yates, *A Modell of Divinitie, Catechistically composed* (London, 1623), p. 162.

51. William Whately, *Prototypes, or, the Primarie Precedent Presidents Out of the Booke of Genesis. . . .* (London, 1640), p. 4.

52. Salkeld, *A Treatise of Paradise,* p. 105. See also John Calvin, *Commentarie vpon Genesis,* pp. 72–73; Andrew Willet, *Hexapla in Genesin,* p. 12; Nicholas Gibbens, *Questions and Dispvtations Concerning the Holy Scripture* (London, 1602), pp. 38–39; and Ralegh, *History,* pp. 19–20.

53. On definitions of marriage and orderings of priorities see John Halkett, *Milton and the Idea of Matrimony* (New Haven, 1970), chapter I.

54. William Gouge, *Of Domesticall Duties* (London, 1634), p. 17.

55. John Donne, *Sermons,* 2:336.

56. Perkins, *Workes,* 3:669–70.

57. Donne, *Sermons,* 5:120.

58. Gervase Babington, *Certaine Plaine, briefe, and comfortable Notes, vpon euery Chapter of Genesis* (London, 1596), pp. 24–25.

59. Perkins, *Workes,* 3:671 and 700.

60. Nicholas Gibbens, *Qvestions and Disputations Concerning the Holy Scripture,* pp. 93–94.

61. Early and representative examples of such defenses are Erasmus's *Encomium matrimonii* (Basel, 1518), translated by Richard Taverner in 1530[?] as *A ryghte frutefull Epystle . . . in laude and prayse of matrymony,* his *Christiani matrimonii institutio* (1526), written for Catherine of Aragon, and his marriage colloquys, two of which appeared as *A modest meane to mariage,* trans. N. L. (London, 1518); Agrippa's *The Commendation of Matrimony,* trans. David Clapham (London, 1540); and Bullinger's *The Christen State of Matrimony,* trans. Miles Coverdale (1541). Protestant commentaries on Genesis and guides to Christian conduct of the sixteenth and early seventeenth centuries almost invariably commend marriage. In general, Milton's view is closer to that of Erasmus, More, and their circle and of Anglicans like Donne and Jeremy Taylor, or of Puritans within the Anglican Church who, like them, preserved a sense of the relation of nature and grace as an interactive process and could therefore relate the natural family to the household of faith, than to that of Separatists whose extreme Calvinism polarized the state of nature and the state of grace. For a thoroughly documented discussion of Reformation views on the purposes of marriage and their order of importance, see Halkett, *Milton and the Idea of Matrimony,* ch. 1.

62. *Chrysostom, Homilies on First Corinthians,* Homily 26, *SLNPNF,* First Series, 12:150–51.

63. Whately, *Prototypes,* p. 9.

64. William Everard et al., *The True Levellers' Standard Advanced* (London, 1649); quoted in A. S. P. Woodhouse, *Puritanism and Liberty* (London, 1938), p. 379.

65. Perkins, *An Exposition vpon the Epistle of Jude,* in *Workes,* 3:536. See also Alexander Ross, *The First Book of Questions and Answers vpon Genesis,* pp. 25–26, and Whately's instruction that the husband's authority is for "the good of his wife, the encrease of vertue in her, and reformation of vice; the making her better and helping her to comfort here, and saluation hereafter euen in better manner than she could be helped without an husband. So all gouernours haue their power from God, rather for the benefit of them whom they gouerne, than for their owne ease, pleasure, profit, or for the fulfilling of their own desires. . . God ordained al gouerners, both priuate and publike, that by their meanes (who alwaies should be (as they are called) their betters) inferiours might the better be drawne to him, and so liue a peaceable and quiet life, with all godlinesse and honesty" (*A Bride Bush, or, A Direction for married Persons* [London, 1623], pp. 109–10.

66. Donne, *Sermons,* 5:114–15.

67. Similarities of role and speech between Eve and the Son have been pointed out by Mother Mary Christopher Pechcux in "The Second Adam and the Church in *Paradise Lost,*" *ELH* 34 (1967): 173; by Joseph H. Summers in "The Voice of the Redeemer in *Paradise Lost,*" *PMLA* 70 (1955): 1082–89; and by Charles Williams, *op. cit.*

68. W. B. Hunter, J. A. Adamson, and C. A. Patrides, *Bright Essence: Studies in Milton's Theology* (Salt Lake City, 1971). Patrides does not agree that the subordinationism of *De Doctrina Christiana* carries over into *Paradise Lost,* since the Father calls the Son "equal to God" (3.306). As the scene is dramatized, however, the Son subordinates himself to the Father, and his obedience comes from merit, not necessity. Adam also addresses Eve as an equal; only she and the Son acknowledge their subordination.

69. Stella Revard, "The Dramatic Function of the Son in *Paradise Lost:* A Commentary on Milton's 'Trinitarianism,'" *JEGP* 66 (1967): 58.

70. Chrysostom, *Homilies on First Corinthians,* p. 150.

71. Donne, *Sermons,* 5:113, 122.

72. "Indeed it is a Question among the School-men, whether Christ should have been incarnate, though *Adam* had not sinned; but it was never doubted, whether he should have been crucified without it": Thomas Tanner, *Primordia, or, the Rise and Growth of the First Church of God Described* (London, 1683), p. 12.

73. Irene Samuel, "The Dialogue in Heaven: A Reconsideration of *Paradise Lost,* III, 1–417," in Barker, *Modern Essays,* p. 235.

74. Barker, "The Relevance of Regeneration," pp. 68–69.

III

"Shapes of Things Divine": Eve, Myth, and Dream

One of the reasons often cited for agreeing with fallen Adam's complaint that Eve is "crooked by nature" is that Milton compares her, even unfallen, to archetypal temptresses from classical myth. William Empson, for example, thinks that the myths show that "all the beauty of nature, through Eve, is a covering, like hers, for moral deformity"; Jonathan Collett that they "implicate Eve by aligning her with Satan" and suggesting that she "may not be included in the bond of nature and grace"; and Davis Harding that they contribute to a "clandestine discrediting of Adam and Eve" that "begins almost with the first lines which describe them to us."[1] Since Milton thought that blaming God for sin by implying he made Eve wrong was the primal blasphemy, it will repay to us examine these mythical allusions for their regenerative connotations.[2] Providently, Milton supplies an interpretive key in his first direct similitude and a parallel but contrasting allusion after the Fall, both comparing Adam and Eve to Jupiter and Juno.

At the center of Book 4, in the midst of "all delight to human sense expos'd" in the "Blissful Paradise / of God," Adam and Eve lie "Imparadis't in one anothers arms / The happier *Eden.*" Satan, watching "with jealous leer maligne" half turns aside from envy and complains, "these two . . . shall enjoy thir fill / Of bliss on bliss, while I to Hell am thrust, / Where neither joy nor love, but fierce desire, /Among our other torments not the least, / Still unfulfill'd with pain of longing pines" (4:205, 208–9, 505–11). The lovemaking of Adam and

Eve, in all its pure and unabashed delight, is what Satan hates most. He does not see their love as his opportunity, but as bliss denied him and a torment to be destroyed. The love that is wholly and ever-increasingly fullfilled because it is in right tune with God and all creation is the essence of Paradise.

The sight that so torments Satan is presented with a classical simile. Having told the story of her awakening and first crucial choice, in a rhapsodic narrative that is a gift of love to Adam, Eve

> with eyes
> Of conjugal attraction unreprov'd,
> And meek surrender, half imbracing leand
> On our first Father, half her swelling Breast
> Naked met his under the flowing Gold
> Of her loose tresses hid: he in delight
> Both of her Beauty and submissive Charms
> Smil'd with superior Love, as *Jupiter*
> On Juno smiles, when he impregns the Clouds
> That shed *May* Flowers; and press'd her Matron lip
> With kisses pure.
>
> [4.492–502]

After Satan has succeeded in perverting their bliss so that they too have "neither joy nor love, but fierce desire," Adam leads Eve

> to a shadie bank,
> Thick overhead with verdant roof imbowr'd
> . . . . Flours were the Couch,
> Pansies, and Violets, and Asphodel,
> And Hyacinth, Earths freshest softest lap.
> There they fill of Love and Loves disport
> Took Largely, of thir mutual guilt the Seale,
> The solace of thir sin, till dewie sleep
> Oppress'd them, wearied with thir amorous play.
>
> [9.1037–45]

The "Love" in this passage is spurious. Once the intoxication of the "fallacious Fruit" has ebbed, they fall into "grosser sleep / Bred of unkindly fumes, with conscious dreams / Encumberd," wake with darkened minds naked of innocence and honor, and "destitute and bare / Of all thir vertue" fall to mutual recrimination and hatred bred of guilt (9.1046 ff.).

Both passages allude to an episode in the *Iliad* and, like many of Milton's classical allusions, invite the reader to see distinctions as well as relations. In Book XIV of Chapman's translation, while Jupiter and Juno embrace,

> Beneath them both fair Tellus strew'd the place
> With fresh-sprung herbs, so soft and thick that up aloft it bore
> Their heav'nly bodies; with his leaves, did dewy lotus store
> Th'Elysian mountain; saffron flow'rs and hyacinths help'd make
> The sacred bed; and there they slept. When suddenly there brake
> A golden vapour out of air, whence shining dews did fall,
> In which they wrapt them close, and slept till Jove was tam'd withall.
> [14.288–98][3]

The description of fallen sexuality in *Paradise Lost* is more like the passage in the *Iliad,* in its context as well as its imagery, than the description of unfallen love that the later passage parodies. In the *Iliad* Juno seduces Jove with the devious purpose of distracting him from the war, and Jove woos Juno by the doubtful persuasion that neither she nor the partners of his many adulteries (whom he names) ever before "did wound / My entrails to such depth as now with thirst of amorous ease." Fallen Adam woos Eve in an equally tactless way:

> Never did thy Beautie since the day
> I saw thee first and wedded thee, adorn'd
> With all perfections, so enflame my sense
> With ardor to enjoy thee, fairer now
> Then ever, bountie of this vertuous Tree.
> [9.1029–33]

Homer's Jove, after Juno's mock protest that Ida is too exposed for decency, says,

> I fear not if the eye
> Of either God or man observe, so thick a cloud of gold
> I'll cast about us that the sun, who furthest can behold,
> Shall never find us.

Milton's Adam, after "innocence, that as a veile / Had shadow'd them from knowing ill, was gon," seeks cover in a different way. "How shall I behold the face / Henceforth of God or Angel, earst with joy / And rapture so oft beheld? . . . Cover me ye Pines, Ye

Cedars, with innumerable boughs / Hide me, where I may never see them more" (9.1054-55, 1080-81, 1088-90).

Milton divides the implications of the Homeric passage between the two allusions. In Book 4, the lovemaking of Adam and Eve, like that of Jove and Juno, affects the harmony and fertility of the earth. Their concord in both love and work influences (in the astrological sense) and attunes the whole. After the Fall, flowers do not spring up in response to their sexual union, as they do for Jove and Juno, but are merely "the Couch." The veil of innocence (represented in the earlier passage by Eve's golden hair, which in turn echoes the "golden vapour . . . whence shining dews did fall,") is gone, and they are "naked left / To guiltie shame" (9.1057-58). Before the Fall, Adam smiles on Eve "as *Jupiter* / On *Juno* smiles, when he impregns the Clouds / That shed *May* Flowers"; after the fall Adam and Eve emerge from narcissistic sexual excess to the bitter conflict which is the real context of Juno's deceitful seduction of Jove.

By dividing the allusion into an unfallen and a fallen scene, Milton sorts out the devious sexuality of the pagan gods from the innocent sexuality of unfallen Adam and Eve. The kinship of the gods' embrace to the fertility of earth's progeny is assigned to unfallen Adam and Eve, and their conflicts and deceits to the guilt that attends fallen lust. By embedding the simile of Jupiter and Juno in his description of Adam and Eve, Milton, as is usual in his prelapsarian classical allusions, hints at trouble to come but "paints out" far more vividly the differences between fallen, exploitative, divisive forms of sexuality on the one hand and unfallen and regenerate love, in harmony with all creation, on the other. This distinction has special significance for an audience who still had doubts about the propriety of sexual bliss in God's Garden. It prepares for Eve's lyrical love song to Adam (4.639-56), Milton's encomium to wedded love (4.750-75), and Adam's epithalamion (8.510-20), in which chaste sexual love is frankly praised as the crowning pleasure of Paradise. At the same time, the distinction between the two allusions invites us to make similar discriminations in interpreting other uses of classical myth.

Most of the goddesses to whom Milton compares unfallen Eve are, in their innocent aspects, patronesses of natural fertility: Juno of childbirth, Delia of woodlands, Flora, Pales, Pomona and Ceres of flowers, flocks, fruits, and seed-crops.[4] Even Athena, remotely connected to Eve by their unusual births, is according to Sir Thomas

Elyot "found fyrste in Grecia, plantyng and settyng of trees."[5] In addition, however, there are five potentially damaging allusions: the comparisons of Eve to Proserpina, Pandora, Circe, and Venus on Ida, and implicitly to Narcissus. Knowing that Eve will fall and will tempt Adam, we see these comparisons as foreshadowings of sin. Yet Milton handles each of them in such a way that they do not taint unfallen Eve or declare her fall inevitable. On the contrary, for as long as she remains unfallen, Eve redeems the beauty, the richness of sensory experience, and the erotic delight that the pagan impersonations depict in their fallen and destructive forms.

Just before Eve enters the poem, an allusion to Proserpina raises doubts about her sufficiency to stand. This garden, the narrator says, is fairer than

> that fair field
> Of Enna, where Proserpin gathring flours
> Her self a fairer Flour by gloomie Dis
> Was gatherd, which cost Ceres all that pain
> To seek her through the world . . .
> [4.269-73]

Just before her fall, the passage is echoed when Satan finds Eve among her roses,

> oft stooping to support
> Each flower of slender stalk . . . them she upstaies
> Gently with Mirtle band, mindless the while,
> Her self, though fairest unsupported Flour,
> From her best prop so farr, and storm so nigh.
> [9.427-33]

When we come to the second passage, we should both hear the echo and be alert to the difference: Prosperina is gathering flowers, while Eve is supporting them.

The significance of this difference is both literal, stressing Eve's obedience to the commandment to dress and keep the Garden, and metaphorical, involving all the figurative meanings the commandment implies. Milton's Paradise, as many scholars have observed,[6] is not a place of static perfection but one of growth and accomplishment. In this new creation, as Raphael sings, all things have "their seeds within themselves"; and this universal procreativity applies to man the microcosm in all his faculties. "God gaue vnto man," as Ralegh explains, "all kinde of seedes and grafts of life . . . whereof which soeuer he tooke pleasure to plant and cultiue, the same should futurely grow in him, and bring forth fruit, agreable to his own choyce and plantation."[7] This process manifests the relation of providence and free will: God the "Sovran Planter" gives the seeds of all things and continually empowers those made in his image to cultivate them creatively and providently. Men and women are free to nuture (or neglect) the seeds and grafts of life within themselves by nurturing (or neglecting) them in the rest of the creation. Adam and Eve have within themselves seeds of thought, art, moral wisdom, worship, and love. Like the surging fertility of the Garden, these potentialities — and especially that sensuous vitality represented in classical myth — need, as Eve recognizes and says, to be lopped, pruned, propped, and bound in order to bear wholesome fruit. The *contrast* between Eve and Proserpina both stresses Eve's active virtue and assigns her greater responsibility for her fall. And although the comparison prefigures the Fall, it doubly prefigures the processes of resurrection and regeneration: Proserpina and harvest will return, and Eve's talents for nurturing the seeds of life will be restored.

This complex use of myth recurs frequently in Milton's thought. "Not with so much labour," he wrote to Charles Diodati, "is Ceres said to have sought her daughter Proserpina, as it is my habit day and night to seek for this *idea of the beautiful* . . . through all the forms and faces of things (for many are the shapes of things divine) and to follow it as it leads me on by some sure traces which I seem to recognize."[8] He uses pagan myth not only to contrast with Christian truth but for the traces of truth in myth itself, for its implications for the regenerative process in human lives, and in order to involve the reader in the search for the remnants of truth and beauty "through all the forms and faces of things."

A second perplexity is the description of Eve at her marriage as

> More lovely than Pandora, whom the Gods
> Endowed with all their gifts, and O too like
> In sad event, when to the unwiser Son
> Of Japhet brought by Hermes, she ensnar'd
> Mankind with her fair looks, to be aveng'd
> On him who had stole *Joves* authentic fire.
> [4.714–19]

Milton does not say that Eve is like Pandora now, nor that the "sad event" is inevitable. Rather, by calling Eve "too like" Pandora "in sad event" he foretells the wrong choice to come but implies that Eve might have chosen better. After the pivotal "when," where we might expect him to say something disagreeable about Eve, he develops the Pandora side of the simile and thus invites us to distinguish between the traces of truth and the parodies of truth in the myth. The truth is that the first woman was gifted by God. The parody is the notion that Jove sent Pandora for revenge. If we were to read the passage as a straightforward, rather than a parodic, prolepsis of the Fall, we would have to conclude that Eve was made by a capriciously malicious God both to cause the Fall and to punish Adam for falling. In other words, Milton elicits from us here any lurking suspicion we may have that God is the source of sin. If we believe, however, that Milton was writing to "assert Eternal Providence," we will notice ways in which the story of Pandora is a distorted version of the story of Eve, or the story of Eve is a rectified version of the story of Pandora.

In one of his marriage tracts, Milton provides a gloss in a passage which addresses exactly the question before us, whether God is the author of sin. Milton, of course, is arguing that he is not. Even the pagan philosophers, he says, were "able to justifie the counsels of God" by attributing sin to "mans own freewill self-corrupted," even though they "knew not what a consummat and most adorned *Pandora* was bestow'd upon *Adam* to be the nurse and guide of his arbitrary happiness and perseverance, I mean, his native innocence and perfection, which might have kept him from being our true *Epimetheus.*"[9] That is, the philosophers knew enough not to think God the author of sin even though they could not know from the story of Pandora what we should know from the story of Eve, that God made woman not to tempt man but to be the nurse and guide of the voluntary virtue on which his happiness depends. The blasphemy of supposing that God caused sin by making woman vain is implicit in most representations of Eve and indeed in most interpretations of *Paradise Lost;* but Milton so portrays Eve that she might have prevented Adam from becoming "our true Epimetheus" if she had continued in her calling.

Milton again tests our ability to distinguish the regenerative from the degenerative implications of myth in a superficially even more damning comparison, that of Eve with Circe. Obviously, the comparison prefigures the effects of the Fall, since both Adam and Eve will sink into the kind of sensuality Circe traditionally represents. But nothing in the passage explicitly taints unfallen Eve. As she works among her roses, Satan in the Serpent tries to "lure her Eye" by "many a wanton wreath";

> she busied heard the sound
> Of rusling Leaves, but minded not, as us'd
> To such disport before her through the Field,
> From every Beast, more duteous at her call,
> Then at Circean call the Herd disguis'd.
>   [9.517–23]

Again, the passage not only declares Eve superior but invites us to make distinctions. The beasts of Eden are not only more obedient than Circe's; they obey in the only way God's creatures can obey in an unfallen world—voluntarily. Circe's beasts are bewitched and debased men; Eve's are real beasts, those "Innumerous living creatures" God has called forth from the earth, has blessed, and has pronounced good. They disport themselves before Eve out of sheer desire to please, a natural response to a guardian whose dominion is gracious, temperate, and just. Further, while the situations are analogous, the roles are reversed. This time it is the tempter who is disguised as a beast and the lady who will be bewitched. Circe's beasts obey her only after they have fallen; Eve's obey her only before she falls. Figuratively, the appetites of the senses, which the animals represent in standard allegory,[10] are good gifts in those who obey God; after the Fall they will be enthralled by sin.

But again, while the contrasts between Circe and unfallen Eve predominate, even the similarities have implications for the regenerate life. Circe is not congenitally evil, but a perversion of good. She is, according to Homer, Vergil, Ovid, Boccaccio, and Alciati, a daugther of the Sun.[11] But, according to the influential mythographer known as Albricus, she has been prostituted by the fallen Venus of the adulterous episode with Mars, which he interprets as lust dishonoring virtue: "When the Sun unveils their guilty love, Venus revenges herself by leading astray the daughters of the Sun—

that is to say, the five senses: Pasiphaë, the sense of sight; Medea, hearing; Circe, touch; Phaedra, smell; Dirce, taste."[12]

In Paradise, of course, the senses are not yet fallen, and even in the fallen world Milton believes them redeemable. The pleasure of touch, however, is the one Adam finds it hardest to temper. Describing Eve to Raphael, he says, "I . . . must confess to find / In all things else delight indeed, but such . . . As us'd not, works in the mind no change, / Nor vehement desire . . . but here / Farr otherwise, transported I behold, Transported touch" (8.524–30). This difficulty, by the way, is one of the reasons Eve decides later on to leave Adam alone for a while. Raphael replies with due concern, but with a certain angelic impercipience regarding the human condition, "But if the sense of touch whereby mankind / Is propagated seem such dear delight / Beyond all other, think of the same voutsaf'd / To cattel and each Beast" (8.579–85): a clear warning of the Circean potential of sexual passion should Adam and Eve cease to temper that particular ingredient of virtue. Adam responds, however, by restoring the sense of touch to its proper place: he esteems the "genial bed" with a "mysterious reverence," yet subordinates its delights to "those graceful acts, / Those thousand decencies that daily flow / From all her words and actions, mixt with Love" and adds that even these "subject not," for he is "still free" to "Approve the best, and follow what I approve" (8.598–611).

Then, rightly assuming a continuity between earthly and celestial pleasures, Adam courteously asks whether angels also express their love by touch, and Raphael replies glowingly, though in a rather tactless way,

> Whatever pure thou in the body enjoy'st
> (and pure thou wert created) we enjoy
> In eminence, and obstacle find none
> Of membrane, joynt, or lim, exclusive barrs:
> Easier then Air with Air, if Spirits embrace,
> Total they mix, Union of Pure with Pure
> Desiring; nor restrain'd conveyance need
> As flesh to mix with flesh, or Soul with Soul.
>   ]8.622–29]

Raphael's words echo Adam's exclamation that husband and wife "shall be one Flesh, one Heart, one Soule" (8.499). But angelic embraces, though more thorough than human ones, are not procreative. Adam and Eve have "their seeds within themselves," and the pleasure of touch encourages them to "increase and multiply."

Circe, then, represents one of those natural pleasures we see in retrospect as temptations, but which for Milton were good if risky gifts of God that nurture virtue when rightly used and, if corrupted, need to be purged and restored.

The final disreputable goddess to whom Milton compares unfallen Eve is Venus. Of course there are many Venuses, representing everything from heavenly love to lust.[13] Milton does not contrast a transcendent, heavenly Venus to a dangerous earthly one before the Fall, since then there was no discord between heaven and earth or between charity and erotic love. Instead — and here's the rub — he specifically compares and contrasts Eve with the divisive Venus who bribed Paris and precipitated the Trojan War. Eve as she rises to greet Raphael is fairer than "the fairest Goddess feign'd / Of three that in Mount *Ida* Naked strove." Eve is naked, however, because "No vaile / Shee needed, Vertue-proof, no thought infirme Alterd her cheek"; and she is immediately compared with the Virgin of the Annunciation:

> On whom the Angel *Haile*
> Bestowd, the holy salutation us'd
> Long after to blest *Marie*, second *Eve*.
> [5.385–87]

Renaissance sculptors and painters regularly and intentionally conflated or juxtaposed Eve and Venus, Venus and Mary, or Mary and Eve, in order to compare Eve with Venus and contrast her with Mary.[14] Milton, I believe, is the only artist who does the reverse. Since Eve is almost always represented as a temptress, comparing her with Venus in a passage on *un*libidinous love ("no thought infirm") is highly irregular. The narrator stresses this difference when he concludes the passage with an Olympian description of Raphael and Adam feasting while Eve "Ministered naked" and exclaims,

> "O innocence deserving Paradise! if ever, then
> Then had the Sons of God excuse to have bin
> Enamour'd at the sight; but in those hearts
> Love unlibidinous reign'd."
> [5.444–48]

By showing that the same beauty that tempts fallen hearts is an innocent joy to virtuous ones, the comparison of Eve and Venus places
responsibility for temptation where it belongs and directs attention
to the state of our own hearts as we respond to naked Eve. On the
other hand, by comparing *un*fallen Eve with Mary, Milton focuses
attention on Eve's virtues: if she had continued in obedience, he implies, Eve might have done her part in the generation of souls as fully
as Mary was to do her part in the regeneration of souls. Although the
passage hints that Eve could become as divisive as Venus on Ida, it
stresses that she might become as responsive to her calling as Mary;
and at this point in the narrative she is still free to choose well.

But Milton does not simply contrast Venus with Eve. He compares them, too, in order to bring out those potentials of Venus
which are in fact applicable to unfallen Eve and to the lives of the regenerate, and in order to challenge us to re-integrate in our view of
primordial woman potentialities which centuries of dualism have led
us to fragment.

In neoplatonic allegory, the Judgment of Paris signifies the choice
among the Amorous Life, the Active Live, and the Contemplative
Life, or in Ficino's words, *voluptas, imperium,* and *sapientia,*[15] the contemplative life or wisdom being preferred. In Milton's Paradise,
however, Adam and Eve are learning to cultivate all three: their love
for each other, or the amorous life; their care of the Garden, or the
active life; and the love of God, or the contemplative life. Indeed,
Milton so portrays these callings that they are reciprocal and indivis-
ible. After the Fall, the three ways diverge and are perverted into
lust, faction, and folly. But Eve does not fall until she tries to snatch
the contemplative life by choosing a false Minerva — by eating what
she erroneously calls "this intellectual food . . . of operation blest to
Sapience" (9.768, 796–97), rather than continuing to cultivate wisdom by cultivating the Garden and the marriage.

For Milton, then, the Judgment of Paris is a false dilemma. As he
argues in his tracts on domestic, civil, and religious liberty — perhaps
another version of the three goddesses — we need to be free not to
choose one and repudiate the others but to choose all three. The
need for harmony among the sensuous, the active, and the contemplative ingredients of virtue, and for freedom to cultivate all the
seeds of life in all possible ways is one of many reasons why Eve de-
clines to have her liberty "straitn'd by a Foe." When she goes off

alone to do her work, and to temper the amorous life which Adam shows some inclination to pursue to excess, she is keeping the active life in balance with the rest. It is not until she accepts the apple of discord that she divorces the three kinds of virtue, leaving her sons and daughters to choose among them, like baffled Parises, and bring ruin, or to follow her example and seek renewed concord.

All of these thorny allusions to classical myth involve difficulty and choice: choice for the reader and choice for Eve. As long as Eve obeys God and Adam — whether they work together or apart — she is free to choose: not between Venus Pandemos and Venus Urania but between the union of divine and human love and the loss of both. If we read the drama in this way, the "sad event" remains suspended as long as Eve continues to choose well. Even though we know the outcome, Eve is so characterized that it need not have happened — our foreknowledge does not touch the freedom of her will. As temptress, Eve becomes what the mythical *figurae* represent in the fallen world. Until then, she is still developing gifts, graces, and virtues from which they also fell; and in the process of regeneration all of these ingredients of virtue can resume development, though now through pain and woe, and "not without dust and heat."

"Answering Looks"

The allusion to pagan fable that most haunts views of Milton's Eve is her Narcissus-like behavior when, fresh from her Creator's hand, she pauses at the verge of the mirror lake attracted by her own reflection and has to be called twice: first by God, who leads her to Adam, and then, as she starts back toward the softer beauty of the face in the lake, by Adam himself. Scholars have often noted echoes from Ovid's tale of Narcissus and attributed to Eve a native vanity that issues in the Fall, sometimes finding additional sinister implications in the scene's subterranean imagery and in parodic resemblances between the creation of Eve and the birth of Sin.[16] Others have argued that Eve's narcissism, since she quickly outgrows it, is an innocent stage of human development.[17] Recently, critics have exalted Eve's self-admiration either as a species of Platonic contemplation or as a preconscious unity with nature that her awakening consciousness of otherness shatters, so that her escape from immersion in the unconscious becomes a kind of fall and the official Fall a commendable re-

bellion against the oppressive forces of reason.[18] According to Don
Parry Norford, "There is a certain beauty, and even a sacred mystery, in Eve's narcissism" because it represents "the linking of above
and below, man and nature, in uroboric unity"; yet, paradoxically,
Eve's self-assertion in the Fall "generates human civilization," a feat
that Norford believes could not have been achieved in obedience to
God because "in *Paradise Lost,* as in Christianity in general, selfhood
is demonic"; and although this approach conflicts with Milton's conscious intentions, "if there were nothing in *Paradise Lost* but what
Milton intended, it would be a relatively superficial work."[19] In other
words, Norford reverts to the view that Milton was of Satan's party
without knowing it, and makes the poem itself a pool of Narcissus for
our own projections rather an invitation to drink of Siloa's brook.

The scene in which Eve is tempted to prefer her self to Adam is a
textual remedy for a narcissistic reading of the poem. It takes the
reader with Eve through a pattern of response that is a mimetic
model, both for the art of marriage and for the art of reading. Like
Eve, the reader pauses to see his own reflection, but that is not the
end of the interpretive process, nor of Eve's experience. The allusions to Ovid's Narcissus do not show either that Eve was primordi-
ally vain or that selfhood develops through sin. They dissociate Eve,
by careful attention to the differences in the two stories, from the fla-
grant narcissism habitually attributed to her in other representations
of Genesis; and they stress the unlikeness between the compulsive
and incestuous union of Satan and Sin to produce Death and the free
and awakened alliance of Adam and Eve to produce a multitude of
diverse lives. Like all good adventures, Eve's narrow escape from
narcissism is exigent and perilous, requiring her to lose herself in
order to find herself while leaving her full freedom to fail, and re-
warding her with new opportunities and powers; and the poem is
just such an adventure for the reader.

Renaissance apologists for poesie were well aware that any work
of art can be a pool of Narcissus or a wellspring of grace, in either of
which we can be sea-swallowed and cast again,[20] depending on our responses. Although, as Sidney concedes, "mans wit may make Poesie
. . . infect the fancie with unwoorthie objects, . . . whatsoever being
abused, doth most harm, being rightly used . . . doeth most good";
the right use of poesie is "figuring foorth good things" in order to
awaken "the inward light each mind hath in itself," to "take naughti-

nesse away, and plant goodnesse even in the secretest cabinet of our
soules"; while the right use of reading is to "take that goodnesse in
hande" with the aim of "well-doing."²¹ Spenser exercises the reader's
ability to choose between narcissistic delectation and wholesome action while he follows Guyon, as Milton says, through "the bowr of
earthly blisse that he might see and know, and yet abstain," and thus
performs "the scanning of error [so necessary] to the confirmation of
truth" (4.311). Shakespeare tells us that art holds "the mirror up to
nature, to show virtue her own feature, scorn her own image" (*Hamlet* III.ii); and Milton that poetry is a divine gift "of power . . . to in-
breed and cherish . . . the seeds of vertue, and publick civility, to
allay the perturbations of the mind, and set the affections in right
tune" (3.238). For these Renaissance poets, poetry illuminates those
chaotic depths we now call the unconscious and healthfully appropriates their energies not only for art's sake but also for life's sake;
they urge the reader to turn from art to life as Eve turns from her
"chrystal mirror" to Adam. The episode gives both Eve and the
reader an opportunity to distinguish themselves from Echo, who can
only repeat, and Narcissus, who sees only himself, and instead to
make instructive and delightful use of all the poem's living waters,
including but not stopping at those that reflect themselves.

Just as Eve's choice provides a model for a regenerate reading of
the poem, Satan's survey of the Garden, which precedes and prepares
for it, provides an image of a perverse reading, as, perched "like a
Cormorant" on the tree of life he

> not true Life
> Thereby regaind, but sat devising Death
> To them who liv'd; nor on the vertue thought
> Of that life-giving Plant, but only us'd
> For prospect, what well us'd had bin the pledge
> Of immortality. So little knows
> Any, but God alone, to value right
> The good before him, but perverts best things
> To worst abuse, or to thir meanest use.
> [4.196–204]

For Milton all materials, processes, and powers, like poetry, are the
stuff of virtue to those who love God and their neighbors and the
stuff of sin to those who do not.²² Satan, in his desire to pervert God's

works to "worst abuse," puts "to meanest use" what might have been a means of rebirth even for him. By reducing himself from archangel to bird of prey and brooding "like a Cormorant" over ways to blight the new creation and make it sterile, he parodies the Spirit who in the beginning "Dove-like [sat] brooding on the vast Abyss / And [made] it pregnant": the Spirit whom the poet asks to instruct him as he writes his poem (1.19–22). At the same time, Satan's misuse of the Tree prepares by proleptic parody for Eve's right use of the lake; for although she could have used her mirror as a pool of Narcissus, and trapped herself within herself, she uses it instead as a source of truth when, by a creative act of memory, she uses the experience to understand her calling and makes it into a poem (4.448–91) for her husband.

The lake into which Eve looks is one in which many waters unite their streams. Milton's "fit audience" was prepared to find figurative meanings in the waters of Eden by the similitude of the four rivers of Genesis as the four cardinal virtues.[23] His own best gloss for his description of them is the comment in *Areopagitica* that "truth is compar'd in Scripture to a streaming fountain; if her waters flow not in a perpetuall progression, they sick'n into a muddy pool of conformity and tradition" (4.333). It is this sense of process, and not dark hints of primordial deviousness, that accounts for the constant and varied motion of the divergent streams that spring from the great river which unchanging in its course, passes beneath the Mount of Paradise:

> for God had thrown
> That Mountain as his Garden mould high rais'd
> Upon the rapid current, which through veins
> Of porous Earth with kindly thirst up drawn,
> Rose a fresh Fountain, and with many a rill
> Waterd the Garden; thence united fell
> Down the steep glade, and met the neather Flood,
> Which from his darksom passage now appears,
> And now divided into four main Streams,
> Runs divers, wandring many a famous Realme
> And Country whereof here needs no account.

The ensuing lines, with their metatextual modesty and their glance at the Muse, are professedly among Milton's most artful, formally alluding to the topos of the *locus amoenus* in which art and nature are either at war in illusory groves or at peace in (mimetically) real ones; and it is full of ambiguous imagery that invites best or meanest use.

> But rather to tell how, if Art could tell,
> How from that Saphire Fount the crisped Brooks,
> Rowling on Orient Pearl and sands of Gold,
> With mazie error under pendant shades
> Ran Nectar, visiting each plant, and fed
> Flours worthy of Paradise which not nice Art
> In Beds and curious Knots, but Nature boon
> Powrd forth profuse on Hill and Dale and Plaine,
> Both where the morning Sun first warmly smote
> The open field, and where the unpierc't shade
> Imbround the noontide Bowrs: Thus was this place,
> A happy rural seat of various view. . . .

Milton's art pointedly calls attention to itself, to the poetic process and its purpose of nurture, distinguishing between "Art" and the "nice" and "curious" art-for-art's sake that he has rejected in renouncing rhyme. Onomatopoetically the passage continues,

> mean while murmuring waters fall
> Down the slope hills, disperst, or in a Lake,
> That to the fringed Bank with Myrtle crownd,
> Her chrystal mirror holds, unite thir streams.
> [4.236–42, 260–63]

This is the mirror in which Eve beholds herself.

Several features of Milton's imagery make these united waters a metaphor for poetry. The waters of poetic inspiration in Milton's invocations include "the Pierian Spring" of *Lycidas* (15–16), the springs the "Muses haunt" (3.27), but also, and pre-eminently, "Siloa's Brook" (1.11, 3.30). Milton reinforces the kinship of these tropological streams by crowning the "chrystal mirror" with myrtle, which, following Ovid,[24] he apostrophizes along with laurel and ivy at the beginning of *Lycidas* as emblems of his craft. Around the lake, "the Birds thir quire apply," and, punningly, "aires, vernal aires . . . attune / The trembling leaves," while Pan, the Graces, and the Hours knit earthly and divine influence in their dance. Opposed to the waters of sacred song and poetic truth are the rivers of Hell and the "Stygian pool" (3.14). The word "pool"—water that does not flow and is not fed — is associated with Satan (9.77) and the lust-god Chemos (1.411), never with Eve.

The myrtle-crowned bank, the union of streams, and the nuptial context also make Eve's mirror a marriage emblem that, by virtue of the allusion to Narcissus and other ambiguous imagery, provides a choice of interpretations. Words like "wandring," "mazie error," "darksome passage," and "mirror" contain warning notes. During her temptation and fall they will be explicitly associated with Eve, and here they are implicitly associated with her by their erotic resonances. But these are prelapsarian caves and streams. The diverse waters of the art of God are bountifully nourishing and ever fresh, "visiting each plant," and this image too will be associated with Eve, who visits "Each Flour" in "Her Nursurie" and brings them "water from th'ambrosial Fount" (8.44–47, 9.427–31, 11.275–79). Since to the pure all things are pure, the sinister implications afforded by a Satanic "prospect" do not taint the actual goodness of the fertile pleasures and opportunities, including passionate and procreative sexuality, offered for right use to Adam and Eve. The lake of potential narcissism and the wandering streams that form it rightly suggest to the postlapsarian mind a warning against self-love and the joint egoism that sometimes afflicts erotic love; but in Paradise, since erotic love is not yet blind and the very quality of selfhood is yet to be investigated, the mirror is innocently held up to the sky as a potential instrument of growth. And that is how Eve uses it: not at the moment of turning from the lake to Adam, but in the act of converting the experience into a poem.

In contrast, poets and painters before and during Milton's time regularly associate unambiguous images of vanity and self-love with Eve, which she never renounces. Commonly, other Eves see flowers as images and adornments of their own beauty, never as creatures to be nourished. Even more commonly, Eve's mirror is the woman-headed serpent, which often resembles Eve in detail, suggesting that she is tempted not by an external snake but by her own concupiscence, or by a narcissistic attraction to what is most like herself.[25] By relegating the bi-form serpent to the gates of Hell and giving Eve a mirror whose invitation to narcissism she can reform into an awakening of conscience and then a poem, Milton provides Eve with what he calls in *De Doctrina Christiana* a "good temptation," whereby "God tempts even the righteous for the purpose of proving them . . .

that both they may become wiser by experience, and others may profit by their example" (15:87). Eve uses her mirror to scan error and discern truth, and both she and Adam become wiser by it. Having chosen rightly between the image of herself in the lake and the image of God in Adam, she goes forth, as Milton would have us go forth from his poem, to acts of love and right uses of art: she waters flowers "from th'ambrosial Fount," and she tells her story "by a fresh Fountain side."

Eve narrates the episode (4.440–91) with far greater depth and perspicacity than she was capable of when it occurred. The poem she makes is a recollection in a tranquillity that is possible only because she has used the substance of the recollection to make herself what Milton says a poet must be, the pattern of a true poem. Its spirited honesty and stylistic variety remind us that conversing in a language able to annunciate truth felicitously is one of the lost pleasures of Paradise that inspired poets can regain. "That day I oft remember," she begins, indicating that she and Adam have been living sinlessly for some time; and she recalls her courtship with relief, gratitude, sobriety, amusement, gaiety, and wit. Her first awareness is onomatopoetic:

> a murmuring sound
> Of waters issu'd from a Cave and spread
> Into a liquid Plain, then stood unmov'd
> Pure as th' expanse of Heav'n.

Her first steps are almost stumblingly alliterative: "I thither went / With unexperienc't thought, and laid me downe"; and her proneness is elongated in double vowels: "to look into the cleer / Smooth Lake, that to me seemd another Skie." Whereas Adam first turns his eyes "strait toward Heav'n" (8.256), Eve, who is God's image through him, turns hers to a mirror of Heaven. To her surprise, as she relates in syntax that comically reflects the action,

> A Shape within the watry gleam appeerd
> Bending to look on me, I started back,
> It started back, but pleas'd I soon returnd,
> Pleas'd it returnd as soon with answering looks
> Of sympathie and love. . . .

The language of heavenly shapes is neoplatonic, suggesting the potential for narcissism in that form of love wherein, according to Pico, the lover worships in the beloved "the Image his [the lover's] soul has formed."[26] In his later conversation, Adam too will reveal a liability to detach contemplation from reality that needs to be (and is) corrected, and his potential for dualism as well as for contemplation is foreshadowed here when Eve first sees him "under a Platan," which is the tree, as Plato tells us at the beginning of the *Phaedrus,* under which Socrates taught. Both Adam and Eve have the inherent and enlivening need of incarnate beings to distinguish between their own images and the images God has made, and to integrate the workings of perception, imagination, and reason that produce understanding. And that is what Eve does in this scene. Although the Eve of the story does not yet know that the playful inhabitant of "that other Skie" is herself, Eve as narrator recognizes the risks of narcissism as she recounts her calling:

> there I had fixt
> Mine eyes till now, and pin'd with vain desire,
> Had not a voice thus warnd me, What thou seest,
> What there thou seest fair Creature is thy self,
> With thee it came and goes: but follow me,
> And I will bring thee where no shadow staies
> Thy coming, and thy soft imbraces, hee
> Whose image thou art, him thou shall enjoy
> Inseparablie thine, to him shalt beare
> Multitudes like thy self, and thence be call'd
> Mother of human Race: what could I doe,
> But follow strait, invisibly thus led?

What happens next is crucial. Seeing Adam, she tells him with a note of loving banter, she finds him "less faire, / Less winning soft, less amiablie milde, / Then that smooth watry image; back I turnd." All the well-known human liability to become immersed in self-absorption echoes in her self-mocking confession. But she never actually reaches the lake, as Ovid's Narcissus does, to admire her own reflection knowing what it is. Instead, she makes the choice on which all further choices depend: she returns to Adam in response to his own cry.

Why, if not merely to reveal vanity, does Eve need to be called twice? Several observations may be made.

First, the method of Eve's creation is a part of what Milton believes to be God's way of creating all things, and requires for its completion the free and deliberate choice that Eve's decision, after she knows whose face is in the lake, supplies. According to Milton's theory of creation *de deo,* rather than *ex nihilo* (15:21–25), God gave of his own substance to be the matter of creation, but withdrew his will from it, so that his reasoning creatures might be free and nature might be instrumental to their purposes. The risk of this freedom is isolation in self: and that is what Satan chooses. Its purpose is the possibility of love; the beloved must be perceived as other before he or she can be loved any way but narcissistically. As in God's creation of cosmos out of chaos in Book 7, separation precedes relation; and it is through relation, not immersion in self, that selfhood develops. Adam, having given of his own substance to make Eve, learns in this episode to respect her freedom; and Eve learns to take pleasure in her origin. Creating one being out of another, but assuring the freedom that is necessary to love, is God's normal method of bringing forth, in which Adam has shared; and Eve will share in it by bearing "multitudes like [her] self" whose freedom she too will need to respect.

Second, Eve's remark, "what could I doe, / But follow strait" raises the question of the woman's consent in the marriage that is to be the pattern of all marriages. Her moment of hesitation marks her discovery that her will is free. Her turning and returning recapitulate the rubrics of solemnization of marriage in the Book of Common Prayer, preserved from the Sarum Rite,[27] in which a deliberate loosening and refastening of hands before the bride makes her vows bear witness to the intent of the church that her consent should be voluntary. It is important to Milton's concept of domestic liberty that Eve should respond spontaneously yet preparedly to Adam, and not only to his appearance but to his speech and the clasp of his hand, in full knowledge of who she is.

Milton states in *De Doctrina Christiana* that "the love of a man towards himself consists in loving himself next to God," his care for his own salvation being a primary duty. This self-regard is opposed both to self-hatred, which produces sin, and "the extravagant self-love, whereby a man loves himself more than God, or despises his neighbor in comparison with himself." From "righteousness toward ourselves . . . as from a fountain, the special virtues in general derive their origin," since it includes pursuit of good, resistance to evil, and regulation of our affections, so that "our highest affections may be placed on the objects most worthy of them" (17:201–3). Eve's account of her first experience shows her growing understanding of this pattern. She does not marry what Raphael will call "an outside"— nor, since she clearly has a mind of her own, does Adam—and to do so would have been the psychological equivalent of marrying the wat'ry image. Instead, the marriage is a covenant of trust typologically prefiguring the New Covenant between Christ and the church.

Third, Adam's urgent speech is not without its own potentiality for narcissism: "Part of my soul I seek thee, and thee claim / My other half." Later, conversing with Raphael, Adam in attributing his own proper excellence to Eve and misevaluating hers reveals a capacity to confuse images, and in the Fall he will become disastrously possessive. Eve's turning back toward the lake, though she properly sees it as a childish gesture since outgrown, provides a valuable precept for Adam, and in his own account of Eve's creation, in his rectified version to Raphael of wedded love, and in the separation colloquy, Adam prizes the love of one who is free and "conscious of her worth."

Fourth, in order to be a "good temptation" for Eve, self-love has really to be a temptation, which it cannot be until she knows that the water-sprite is her own reflection and can compare her image with the reality of Adam. In addition to "exercising and manifesting" the "faith and patience" of the righteous, a "good temptation" can have the purpose of "lessening their self-confidence and reproving their weakness," to the benefit both of themselves and of others, and "is therefore rather to be desired" (15:87–89). A weakness, in the unfallen or the regenerate "righteous," is an opportunity for growth and in her narrative Eve not only acknowledges the weakness but manifests the responsive growth that the temptation elicits; and the response is stronger, more joyful, and more fully Eve's that it could have been without the difficulty to be overcome. Her designation of Adam as "thou for whom / And from whom I was formed flesh of thy flesh, / And without whom am to no end, my Guide / And Head" is (except for its central echo) her own idea. The voice that leads her to Adam calls him "hee / Whose image thou art," and Adam tells her that he lent his bone to give her being, but neither subjects her. The voice promises, "him thou shalt enjoy / Inseparablie thine," and Adam wants "to have thee by my side." Her response is not abject but magnanimous. It shows a quality Raphael recommends to Adam, "self-esteem, grounded in just and right / Well managed" (8.571–72); she emerges from her brush with narcissism "self-knowing, and from

thence / Magnanimous to correspond with Heav'n, / But grateful to
acknowledge whence [her] good / Descends" (7.510–13):

> For wee to [God] indeed all praises owe,
> And daily thanks, I chiefly who enjoy
> So farr the happier Lot, enjoying thee
> Praeeminent by so much odds, while thou
> Like consort to thy self canst no where find.
>   [4.444–48]

Fifth, Eve's second calling invokes attention to the differences between the "sweet and gladsome society" of Adam and Eve and the
humorless and truly narcissistic union of Satan and Sin. Unlike
Adam and Eve, Satan resents and denies having received the gift of
life from another, claiming that he is "self-begot, self-rais'd" (5.860).
At the other extreme, his incestuous union with Sin is so indistin-
guishable from the rest of his self-absorption that he promptly forgets
all about her, and her narration to her consort of her beginning
(2.787–814), the proleptic parody of Eve's, is necessary to remind
him who she is. She too has sprung from her consort's "left side op'n-
ing wide"; she is his "perfect image"; and, much as Eve will say to
Adam, "My Author and Disposer, what thou bidst / Unargued I
obey," Sin says to Satan, "Thou art my Father, thou my Author,
thou / My being gav'st me; whom should I obey / But thou, whom follow?" But the events within this parodic frame are monstrous opposites to those of the human marriage. Satan is surprised by Sin, who
springs from his head with "miserable pain"; he is at first "averse"
and in their infernal encounter he fails to recognize her. Adam pleads
for Eve in "celestial Colloquie" with God, painlessly watches God
create her °with his hands" from his own rib, receives her "overjoyd"
and recognizes her at once as "Flesh of my Flesh" and "dearer half"
(8.455–99). At the birth of Sin "amazement seis'd / All th' Host of
Heav'n; back they recoild affraid," while at the marriage of Adam
and Eve "all Heav'n, / And happie Constellatins on that houre / Shed
thir selectest influence; the Earth / Gave sign of Gratulation" (8.511–
14). The birth of Sin is surrounded by war, Eve's by the peaceable
kingdom. Satan with Sin becomes "enamour'd," and, she reminds
him, "such joy thou took'st / With me in secret, that my womb conceiv'd / A growing burden"; and she gives birth to Death, the devour-

ing shadow, who promptly rapes his mother "in embraces forcible and foul" and begets the hounds of Hell. Eve is brought "where no shadow staies / [Her] coming" to enjoy the "Perpetual Fountain of Domestic sweets" that is the "source of human offspring" and "all the Charities" (4.750–60).

Finally, the relation that is imitated by Eve's to Adam and parodied by Sin's to Satan is the source of all selfhood and all connection, the relation the Son expresses to the Father as "image of thee in all things . . . Whom to obey is happiness entire" (6.736, 741).[28] In both *De Doctrina Christiana* and *Paradise Regained,* as well as *Paradise Lost,* Milton stresses the distinct personality of the Son: Father and Son are one in substance, sharing Godhead, but different in essence, distinguishing wills, so that the Son's responsive acts of creation and redemption are acts of love. Similarly, Adam and Eve, who are God's images not only in their persons but in their relation, are one flesh, sharing and propagating humanity, but different persons, distinguishing wills, so that their union too may be one of voluntary love. If their love is to be a fountain of charity, and not a pool of Narcissus, they need to learn to recognize and promote each other's personal essence, and the sifting of true and false images at the lake is a part of this process.

At the Fall, both Adam and Eve will succumb to narcissism. But that is not what this scene prefigures. On the contrary, a timely remembrance of the experience by the lake might have saved them from embracing shadows at their falls. What the scene does prefigure is Eve's initiating step toward reconciliation after the Fall, which completes the poem's reversal of the tale of Narcissus. For Echo cries to Narcissus, "Forsake me not so cruelly that loueth thee so deere"; but Narcissus prefers to die of self-love and betakes himself "to the Well of *Styx,* and there both day and night / Standes tooting on his shadow still as fondely as before."[29] Eve, echoing Echo, pleads, "Forsake me not thus, *Adam,* witness Heav'n / What love sincere, and reverence in my heart / I beare thee" (10.914–16); and Adam, unlike Narcissus, "relent[s] / Towards her" and "with peaceful words uprais[es] her soon" (10.940, 946). And these first steps of regenerate life imitate steps for which the whole poem prepares the reader who turns from the poem's perpetual streams, and the mirror they form, to the life they nourish.[30]

"Proportion Due"

From the moment of recognition at the lake, Adam and Eve receive delight and instruction from each other's developing abilities, enjoying a "union of mind" enriched by diverse perspectives. Eve's reminiscences differ in notable ways from two parallel passages, Adam's accounts to Raphael of the same episode and of his own first moments; and each gains distinction from the other.

From Adam's point of view, God has created Eve in response to Adam's own plea (8.357–499). He knows that she was preveniently intended, but at the time of his seeking he has had to recognize his need and pluck up courage to ask, "presumptuous," for something more than the paradisal plenitude he has surveyed and named. The Creator, testing him, smilingly chides, "is not the Earth / With various living creatures, and the Aire / Replenisht?" and Adam persists:

> Among unequals what societie
> Can sort, what harmonie or true delight?
> Which must be mutual, in proportion due
> Giv'n and receiv'd. . . .
>   Of fellowship I speak
> Such as I seek, fit to participate
> All rational delight. . . .

Further trial elicits from Adam an eloquent speech on the purposes of marriage, and the Son replies that Adam's self-knowledge expresses

> well the spirit within thee free,
> My Image, not imparted to the Brute,
> Whose fellowship therefore unmeet for thee
> Good reason was thou freely shouldst dislike.

It is exactly her creation in God's image that makes Eve meet for Adam, "Thy likeness, thy fit help, thy other self, / Thy wish, exactly to thy heart's desire." In a trance, Adam watches as God creates from his own rib and fresh life-blood the sum of loveliness, "Manlike, but different Sex," whose looks Adam says

> infus'd
> Sweetness into my heart, unfelt before,
> And into all things from her Aire inspir'd
> The spirit of love and amorous delight.

Adam has in fact received more than he had asked for: not only "rational delight" but also "amorous delight," a bounty which Adam could not have imagined for himself, which the more ascetic of the Fathers would have found unsuitable, and by which Adam is well-nigh overwhelmed. By stirring the passion that is Adam's "good temptation" and the "ingredient of vertu" he most needs to temper, Eve provides the challenge to Adam's "manly grace / And wisdom" by which he chiefly grows.

What happens next is loss and seeking. The dream-Eve disappears and Adam wakes to behold the real one

> Led by her Heav'nly Maker, though unseen,
> And guided by his voice, nor uninformd
> Of nuptial Sanctitie and marriage Rites:
> Grace was in all her steps, Heav'n in her Eye,
> In every gesture dignitie and love.

At this point, the two accounts differ. In Adam's (8.491–520) it is after his ecstatic expansion of Genesis, "they shall be one Flesh, one Heart, one Soule," that Eve turns away. Adam, having heard Eve's self-mocking explanation, interprets her act more courteously.

> She heard me thus, and though divinely brought,
> Yet Innocence and Virgin Modestie,
> Her vertue and the conscience of her worth,
> That would be woo'd, and not unsought be won,
> Not obvious, not obtrusive, but retir'd,
> The more desirable, or to say all,
> Nature her self, though pure of sinful thought,
> Wrought in her so, that seeing me, she turn'd;
> I follow'd her, she what was Honour knew,
> And with obsequious Majestie approv'd
> My pleaded reason.

This winningly youthful, halting speech is a lover's idealization of the moment of weakness Eve has honestly confessed. Its broken phrases, its air of casting about, and its apt synoeceosis "obsequious [obedient] Majesty [sovereignty]" show that Adam is still struggling with the problem of having asked for an equal and been given instead someone who is engagingly different. He is still off balance in the re-cital (8.521–59) of "vehement desire" and "commotion strange" that follows his epithalamion. He polarizes woman as Milton's age too often did when he calls Eve "th'inferiour, in the mind / And inward Faculties" resembling less God's image particularly in the faculty of dominion, yet "so absolute" that "All higher knowledge in her presence falls / Degraded," while "Authority and Reason on her waite, / As one intended first, not after made / Occasionally." Eve is neither "absolute" nor made "occasionally," but part of an intended pair. The fact is, Adam has fallen into a dualistic opposition of the passion and the reason, and of the "outward" and "inward Faculties," that need to be integrated in each partner, in due proportion, and in the marriage. That need, recognized and coped with in the next lines, is part of the good temptation for Adam that corresponds to Eve's reflection in the lake. Raphael's rebuke, though pertinent, is incomplete, and elicits from Adam a better response. Adam is still free to "approve the best," and Eve's real nature is manifest in "those graceful acts, / Those thousand decencies that daily flow / From all her words and actions mixt with Love" (8.611, 600–602).

Both accounts of their meeting express in different ways a problem common to free and conscious beings. Self-knowledge and consciousness of worth, wooing and choosing, are only first steps to love. Further steps are called for, and although Eve has to be called by God and then, twice, by Adam, her second calling and her recalling of it provide opportunities for them both: for Adam to recognize that though he has given her substantial life she has also essential life of her own, free and responsive to "pleaded reason"; for Eve, to respond freely; for both, to grow in understanding of personhood and love.

The second passage to which Eve's account of her awakening should be compared is Adam's account of his own (8.250–355). Eve's perceptions are subordinate to Adam's, but necessary to them, illuminating them as fancy brightens reason and as poetry kindles virtuous deeds. Both find themselves reposed on flowers, Adam in sunlight and Eve in shade. Adam looks "strait toward Heav'n," Eve towards heaven's mirror. Adam, too, hears "liquid Lapse of murmuring streams" but notices more than Eve does. Both peruse themselves, but Adam consciously, "Limb by Limb," while Eve does not know that the charming face she peers at is her own. Adam at once tries speech, while Eve is content with looks. Adam deduces from his own existence that there must be "some great Maker," an instance of Milton's belief that every man is endowed with sufficient reason to infer the existence of God. Adam asks the other creatures how he may

know and adore his Maker, but "Answer none return'd": he falls
asleep and dreams of "One . . . of shape Divine" who bids him rise
and tells him "call'd by thee I come thy Guide"; waking to find "all
real" he sees approaching "Presence Divine" who raises him from his
knees and says "Whom thou soughtst I am." Eve has to be called, and
although she follows "strait," she wavers. The pattern "seek and ye
shall find" is established in Adam's first hours, soon to be reaffirmed
in his redoubled seeking and finding of Eve. The pattern for Eve is of
conversion from a blank innocence to a pure one and of growing response to her calling.

Adam comes off better, yet both patterns are needed. Eve does not
have Adam's sureness and alacrity of recognition or his capacity for
reasoning straight to first causes, but his instruction of her will exercise his intellect as well as hers. Her first perceptions test the bound-
aries of fact and illusion, while his explore those of natural and divine revelation. Adam's responses are more direct. He is "for God
only," she "for God in him." And this, I think, is the point of her story.
Both are images of God, but she is also an image of Adam. This is
the situation God has given them; it is in itself good, but like all good
things it has liabilities. God has given his images freedom, therefore
separateness, and seeds of growth. Hence he has not joined Eve to
Adam of necessity. Rather, having "edified" her from his very bone,
he sets her apart. She wakes, like Adam, alone. She and Adam, on
their own, have to discover themselves and each other, distinguish
themselves from each other, become two selves in order to become
"one Soule." For a start, Eve sees herself mirrored in a lake and
Adam sees himself mirrored in her. This phase is necessary but rapidly to be outgrown. As they grow, they break through the mirrors
of self, consciousness encountering consciousness for the enlargment
of both, and regard each other and the creation in their charge with
"looks Divine" in which "the image of thir glorious Maker shon." Thus,
mimetically, Milton calls us to break through our own reflections in
the poem to its essential life and then to "words and actions mixt with
Love."

"Forg'd Illusions": Eve's Dream

A second "good temptation" that exercises the abilities of Adam
and Eve to sort out truth from illusion and to use poetic imagination

aright is the dream that Satan induces in Eve (4.799–809)[31] and Eve
relates to Adam (5.28–93). The dream, far from being a proof of
Eve's weakness or a step in her corruption, shows that Eve is uncloistered, not only in the sense of being a free agent in a world where evil
too roams free, but even in the sense that neither God, nor Adam,
nor her own innocence protects her from the intrusion of evil into
her mind and imagination. In Milton's Paradise, blessedness consists not in being sheltered but in developing powers of goodness able
to cope with all occasions. Here Eve is responsible, with Adam's
help, for coping with evil even in her innermost thoughts.

Faculty psychology allows the possibility of such a process occur-
ring without sin, which enters, not when the lower faculties desire an
action, but when the will prefers it to obeying God. Richard Baxter,
wondering how sin can have infected rational creatures of God, speculates:

> At present it seemeth to me, that *sin* entred in this method. 1. *Sense*
> perceiveth the forbidden thing: 2. The appetite desireth it: 3. The
> imagination thinketh on its desirableness yet further.   4. The *intellect
> conceiveth* of it (truly) as *good,* by a *simple apprehension.*   5. The *Will* ac-
> cordingly *willeth* it by a *simple complacency* or *volition.* Thus far there was
> no sin: But 6. The *Will here adhered* to it too much, and took in it *an ex-
> cess of Complacency,* when it had power to do otherwise; And here *sin*
> begun.[32]

Baxter's reason for this cautious analysis is to deny that God could be
the author of sin by showing all human faculties to be originally good
and free. Milton, imagining innocent faculties functioning freely, is
particularly concerned, as a poet, with the faculty of imagination, or
fancy. In his representation of Eve's dream, he agrees with Baxter
and disagrees with Andrew Willett, who states that "whereas the
Devill internally tempteth only two wayes, either by alluring the
sense by some object, or else by moving and working the phantasie,
our parents before their fall could not be so tempted, having no inordinate motion."[33] If Adam and Eve were immune to temptation
through the senses and the imagination, those faculties would not be
free, and the exercise of reason and will would be reduced. For Milton, the keenness, the creativity, the liberty, and therefore the vulnerability of the subordinate faculties and the calling to keep them
free by the exercise of right reason and upright will are among the

risky opportunities for independent virtue that fill life in Paradise with challenge and delight.

In the dream episode, Eve's will takes no complacency in the forbidden thing when it has power to do otherwise. On the contrary, she is horrified that the forbidden tree—a thing not evil in itself but evil because forbidden—should have entered even as far as her imagination, and wholly without her volition, as a desirable object. "Assaying by his Devilish art to reach / The Organs of her Fancie, and with them forge / Illusions as he list," Satan has induced a dream in which, looking like an everyday angel, he claims that the forbidden fruit can "make Gods of Men" and thereby increase God's honor; she flies with him to the clouds and, in a proleptic parody of the revelation to Adam and an analogy of the temptation of Christ, beholds "The Earth outstretchd immense, a prospect wide / And various." But Ithuriel interrupts Satan's work and Eve awakes—not, as Satan had hoped, full of "inordinate desires / Blown up with high conceits engendring pride," but "O how glad . . . / To find this but a dream!" (4.801-11; 5.54-93).[34]

Surely this episode sweeps away any thought we may have that life in Paradise was tiresomely simple, or that the growth of moral understanding depended on the Fall, or that innocence meant ignorance of evil. Milton says in *Areopagitica* that perhaps the "doom which *Adam* fell into of knowing good and evill" was that "of knowing good by evill."[35] He does not say that this indirection was a blessing, but calls it a doom. Like the "essentiall joy" of Donne's *Second Anniversary,* the joy of Paradise does not depend on contrast. Adam and Eve know good in its essence. But evil exists, and God has judged that it is better for them to have the opportunity to resist it freely and sufficiently than to be protected from it. Milton therefore shows Adam and Eve learning a great deal about both good and evil without doing evil: the good by direct experience and the evil by instruction from Raphael and by Satan's perverse revelation to Eve.[36]

Raphael's account of the War in Heaven provides sufficient intellectual grasp of evil for conscious moral choice; Eve's dream, rightly responded to, provides opportunity for imaginative and emotional grasp as well. In particular, it makes Adam and Eve more aware of the potential uses and abuses of the faculty of fancy, whose office, as Edward Reynolds explains, is to assist "both the understanding and the will," and whose liberty is essential to "all Poeticall Fictions";[37] it is especially important to the poet as the faculty whose healthy operation as the wholly free servant, but not the master, of reason produces poetry able "to allay the perturbations of the mind, and set the affections in right tune." Eve's unfallen ability to narrate dreamed evil and to reject it justifies — and also embodies — Milton's ability as a poet of regeneration to imagine evil with such dramatic force; and the remembered dream might later have strengthened the tempted Eve, just as the remembered poem may strengthen the tempted reader.

By responding to Satan's manipulation of Eve's fancy as unfallen or regenerate men and women should respond — by rejecting the evil thought and determining on right action — Adam and Eve show themselves "sufficient to stand" in spite of the most unsettling perplexity. Because it allows Eve directly, and Adam in response to her, to experience evil without doing evil, the dream might have helped prevent the Fall if each had remembered and used it well. For the same reason, it permits us to apply the principles of *Areopagitica* concerning uncloistered virtue to the experience of Adam and Eve and, conversely, to compare their experience with our own.[38] Like all prelapsarian events in *Paradise Lost,* it prefigures and guides the process of regeneration.

The applicability of the dream episode to the lives of the regenerate is reinforced by the scriptural allusions that frame it, for Eve's account is introduced by a passage reminiscent of the Song of Solomon and followed by a passage reminiscent of an episode in the life of Christ.

Adam's joyous morning song to Eve resonates with echoes from the Song of Solomon, with the difference that here pleasure is fused with responsibility:

> Awake
> My fairest, my espous'd, my latest found,
> Heav'ns last best gift, my ever new delight,
> Awake, the morning shines, and the fresh field
> Calls us, we lose the prime, to mark how spring
> Our tended Plants, how blows the Citron Grove,
> What drops the Myrrhe, and what the balmie Reed,
> How Nature paints her colour, how the Bee
> Sits on the Bloom extracting liquid sweet.
> [5.17-25]

Unlike the *aubade* that laments the sunrise because it ends the secret pleasures of the night, Adam's song rejoices in the harmony of their love with the life around them and in their work of nurturing that life:[39] Adam and Eve are constantly aware that "Man hath his daily work of body or mind / Appointed, which declares his Dignitie, / And the regard of Heav'n on all his waies" (4.618–20); and after Eve tells her dream and he cheers her, Adam's song concludes with the wholesome suggestion that they resume their pleasant labors:

> let us to our fresh imployments rise
> Among the Groves, the Fountains, and the Flours
> That open now thir choicest bosom'd smells
> Reservd from night, and kept for thee in store.
> [5.125–28]

The dream is an invitation to transcend and spurn the pleasures and responsibilities delegated by God as means to grow "by degrees of merit" (7.157), and the song is a remedy for the dream.

The allusion to the Song of Solomon reminds us that Eve, like the Spouse in the Canticles, is traditionally interpreted as a type of the church,[40] and both patristic and Protestant expositors submerged the literal meaning in allegorical or "mystical" explication. Later, however, Milton calls the place where Satan finds Eve "more delicious" than either "those Gardens feign'd" of Adonis and Alcinous or "that, not Mystic, where the Sapient King / Held dalliance with his fair Egyptian Spouse" (9.439–43). When Milton writes about scriptural gardens, he is writing about real ones. They may have allegorical and anagogical implications, but these must be rooted in the literal meaning. His use of scripture is not allegorical but typological and mimetic, and this habit of mind applies even to his uses of King Solomon's "divine pastoral drama."[41] Nevertheless, the marriage of Adam and Eve in *Paradise Lost* has implications for the marriage of Christ and the church, as Milton interprets it, in the letters of St. Paul, and his allusion to the Song of Solomon provides connotations for his readers to choose from, as always, in the light of his drama.

In patristic exegesis, the Spouse is often the mystical church, or, in Origen's words, "the perfect soul";[42] for Reformers, she is primarily the visible church and the pilgrim soul, contending with frailties within as well as persecutions without.[43] For the Fathers, her separation from the Bridegroom means her sojourn in the corruptible world and flesh, whereas for the Reformers it signifies her error in following the traditions of men—that is, the unscriptural practices they wish to reform. But both patristic and Protestant commentaries contain a variety of attitudes toward the relations between the church or the soul and the world, and Milton's poem accords with some and departs from others in each.

One attitude that Milton rejects, although it persists in the commentaries of both traditions, is that which opposes the soul to the flesh and the church to the world. Most commentators have felt obliged to warn against outward and carnal interpretations of the Canticles to the extent of denying their literal meaning altogether. Origen believes that Genesis tells about the creation of inward and outward man, "the first *in the image and likeness of God,* and the second *formed of the slime of the earth,*" and advises that no one should read the Canticles until, having "ceased to feel the passions of his bodily nature," he has learned to "spurn and despise" corporeal things and "reach out for the things unseen and eternal which, with spiritual meaning verily but under certain secret metaphors of love, are taught in the Song of Songs."[44] Milton vehemently opposed the notion of a dual creation, showing discords of body and soul to be effects of the Fall that the regenerate must try to repair. In *Paradise Lost,* the love of unfallen Adam and Eve is both as chaste and as sensuous as that "not Mystic" of the Song of Solomon and is perfectly in accord with the divine love they are learning to imitate.

The desire for withdrawal from the world asserts itself most often in the commentaries of the earlier Fathers and the later Reformers. Jerome advises Eustochium not to follow the example of the Bride in the third Canticle: "Ever let the privacy of your chamber guard you. . . . Do not seek the Bridegroom in the streets."[45] However, Augustine rejects with some heat the notion that the elect can withdraw from the communion of mankind.

> Christ the Lord unto the Church saith, "As a lily in the midst of thorns, so is my best Beloved in the midst of the daughters." He said not, in the midst of them that are without, but "in the midst of the daughters." . . . and whilst the net which is cast into the sea, and gathers together all kinds of fishes, as saith the Holy Gospel, is being drawn to the shore, that is, unto the end of the world, let [the faithful person] separate himself from the evil fishes, in heart, not in body; by changing evil habits, not by breaking sacred nets."[46]

Although Milton could not support Augustine's point about the purity of the church, he showed in his portrayal of Eve that one must separate oneself from evil in the heart, not try to isolate oneself from it in the world. And the most famous medieval commentator on the Song of Songs, Bernard of Clairvaux, though more dualistic than Milton, describes the Bride's mission in the world:

> It is no small proof of virtue to live a good life among the depraved, to preserve the pureness of innocence, and gentleness of character, among the evil-disposed. It is a still greater one to be peaceful with those who are hostile to peace, and to show yourself a friend to your enemies themselves. That will evidently constitute a special degree of likeness to the lily, which does not cease to adorn and beautify with its own fairness the very thorns which pierce it.[47]

The Reformers reflected their own concerns by regarding the Spouse as the visible church in the fallen world and infusing a sense of moral and historical process often expressed in the pertinent metaphor of gardening. William Gouge says that the Bride going early to the vineyard "to see if the vine flourish" is promising "to enquire and learne . . . when she may come to be perfectly knit to Christ."[48] John Cotton exhorts us "to keep Christs garden clean from weeds and vermine."[49] Richard Sibbs explains that "the care of this blessed Husbandman is to prune us so, as to make us fruitful. . . . So when God prunes us by crosses and afflictions, and sowes good seed in us, it is a signe, he means to dwell with us, and delight in us."[50] On the whole, Protestants followed and even exceeded the Fathers in allegorizing the lovemaking, explaining, for example, that "by the bed is ment the Temple, which Salomon made,"[51] "breasts are the Ministers that suckle the children of the church,"[52] and "her *palate,* to weet, her speech and doctrine, should be like *good wine,* to comfort and revive bitter and heavy hearts."[53] Indeed, some so strained the limits of historical allegory as to suppose that the garden to which the Bridegroom descends after long absence is Wittenberg[54] or that the teeth of the Beloved are Luther, Melanchthon, Bucer, Zwingli, and Calvin.[55]

A few moderate Protestants, however, were able some of the time to escape the prevalent dualism, partly because they had a high opinion of marriage. John Robotham describes the Song as "a declaration of that mutuall intercourse and vicissitude of divine love, pass-

ing betweene Christ, and the Church his Spouse; set forth by a most
sweet and comfortable, by a most excellent and ravishing Allegorie,
of a Marriage-Song: Marriage being the most joyfull passage of all
our life, and a Song being the highest expression of joy."[56] Further,
although many commentators find in the imagery of the dove undefiled and the garden enclosed a warrant for withdrawal and exclusion, some found means to widen the Bridegroom's embrace. Gouge
says that "it is the property of true love to be desirous that others also
may haue a liking of the thing beloued";[57] and John Donne, dispos-
ing like Milton of the division between outward and inward life, expresses the full breadth of the Anglican *via media* with an unabashed
acceptance of sexual metaphor:

> Betray kind husband thy spouse to our sights,
> And let myne amourous soule court thy mild Dove,
> Who is most trew, and pleasing to thee, then,
> When she is embrac'd and open to most men.[58]

These writers began to mend the marriage of earthly and heavenly
love that both transcendental and historical allegorists annulled.

As the English Puritans increasingly separated themselves, or felt
themselves to be driven, from the established church, the sense of
disparity between outward appearance and inward truth and the
urge to separate the elect from the vessels of wrath reasserted itself.
John Cotton says that "a garden enclosed" means "a necessity of separation between the Church and the World," for "if a whole Nation
be received into the Church . . . It will make the Church as *Sardis,*
the body of Christ dead";[59] for Ainsworth the passage signifies that
the protected Bride must preserve her chastity by "keeping watch
lest the enemies should invade," and the final verses are "the prayer
of the Spouse unto Christ, desiring the end of his Kingdom in this
World, where his people are persecuted and afflicted, and the trans-
lating thereof into the highest heavens."[60] Thus, interpretation of the
Song of Solomon comes full circle, from the sense of separation and
persecution of the early church in Rome to that of the separatists in
Amsterdam and Boston, while between these extremes the more
moderate Fathers and Reformers taught that the church and the individual Christian must strive for integrity within the world and be,
if possible, a blessing to the world even when tempted and afflicted
by it.

In his characterization of Eve, Milton accepts those strands in both traditions which have to do with the chastity of the Spouse, but he rejects those which would enforce it by separation from the world. It is not God's way, he shows, to enclose his garden in a manner that isolates his people from trial and choice. Just as Satan lightly leaps the hedge of Paradise (4.181), "Wolves shall succeed for teachers" in the church (12.508); and it is these wolves, not God, who "force the Spirit of Grace it self, and binde / His consort Libertie" (12.525–26). Similarly, because his use of the Song of Solomon is mimetic rather than allegorical, Milton avoids the divorce of spirit and flesh that other interpreters make, using marriage not only as an analogue of divine love but as the very means and source of "all the Charities" (4.755). The Song of Songs is, after all, an impassioned love poem; and one finds in Milton's use of it none of the strain to disembody or reembody the divine lovers that one finds in the allegorical annotations. It is Satan, in the dream, who tempts Eve to want translation "to the highest heavens"; but Eve, whose dreams until now have been of Adam and their daily work, finds in this one nothing but "offence and trouble" (5.34), and in this she is obedient to her calling.

Milton's Eve, then, represents in the state of innocence, not the visionary church, but the visible church, and her trials typify its trials. Because, for Milton, regeneration and reformation resume the processes of generation and formation interrupted by the Fall, unfallen Eve represents by her actions the growth through trial that both the church in the process of reformation and the soul in the process of regeneration freely undertake. Like the historical church, she encounters difficulties and frustrations, and in her dream she is tempted, like it, to indulge in superstition on the one hand and excessive otherwordliness on the other. There is warning in the allusion, too. Eve, like the church, will fall into idolatry, and Adam, like Solomon, will be seduced from God by a fair idolatress. But these lapses are not inevitable. Like each prefiguration in the prelapsarian events, Eve's dream and the echoes from the Song of Solomon that surround it shadow forth, not only the Fall that in fact occurred, but also the obedience that could have continued and the regeneration that was to come. If Adam's song reminds us of the marriage of Christ and the Church, it also illuminates, by its context of both lurking evil and responsible activity, the distinction between the mystical church of allegory and the embattled church of warfaring Christians. It both compares and contrasts "the dalliance of the Sapient King" in a garden enclosed with the callings of Adam and Eve in a garden exposed — one that, although full of beckoning delights, is also in need of being providently dressed and watchfully kept.

Eve herself retells her dream (5.28–93), as she has retold her first awakening and her marriage, and she rejects it as she has rejected the pool of Narcissus in the previous trial. Although nothing in the dream is intrinsically unpleasant — except the false angel's eating of the fruit, at which she says "mee damp horror chil'd" — she is properly disturbed by her brush with evil. Her first words on waking affirm with joy and relief her love for Adam:

> O Sole in whom my thoughts find all repose,
> My Glory, my Perfection, glad I see
> Thy face, and Morn return'd.

She tells of a dream so unnatural that she wonders whether it was indeed a dream, in which a voice like Adam's parodies her own song of the previous evening.[61] Seeking Adam, she meets instead a figure in the familiar shape of an angel, who promptly eats of the forbidden fruit and offers her some, saying, "Happier thou mayst be, worthier thou canst not be": a reversal of their developing sense that they are replete with happiness and capable of infinite improvement. Promising that she will "Ascend to Heav'n," Eve continues, the angel

> drew nigh, and to me held,
> Even to my mouth of that same fruit held part
> Which he had pluckt; the pleasant savourie smell
> So quick'n appetite, that I, methought,
> Could not but taste. Forthwith up to the Clouds
> With him I flew.

At this point Milton offers one of those choices by which he reveals to us our own interpretive assumptions. Does Eve, in imagination, taste the fruit? Four possibilities present themselves. Either she does not taste, and remains free of even imagined disobedience; or she does not taste, but is inclined toward actual disobedience by the dreamed impulse; or she does taste, and is tainted by disobeying even in "forg[d] / Illusions"; or she does taste, by Satan's manipulation of the "organs of her Fancie," but her waking will and reason are still free to reject the imagined evil and better prepared to reject the real one because her unwilled dream rehearses deception and excites repugnance.[62] The last interpretation fits best with Milton's belief that the way to preserve virtue, far from circumscribing it, is to broaden its scope. Whether she tastes or not, there is no reason to think that the dream corrupts her. Her own response assures us that her waking will has not been infected by a desire to act out Satan's scenario, for, after describing her "flight" and "high exaltation," she exlaims, "O, how glad I wak'd / To find this but a dream," and Adam comforts her with hope that "what in sleep thou didst abhorr to dream, / Waking thou never wilt consent to do" (5.127–31).

Two influential critics who propose variants of the *felix culpa* tradition have commented on Eve's dream in ways that obscure its relevance to unfallen and regenerate growth. E. M. W. Tillyard thinks that is proves Eve already flawed and believes that perpetual innocence would have been dull. William Empson thinks that the dream justifies her disobedience and admires her pluck in defying a God he regards as wicked and unfair. In this, he out-Satans Satan, who only pretends to think that.

According to Tillyard, Eve would not have been so distressed if she had not already "passed from a state of innocence to one of sin."[63] This is to confuse innocence, or moral purity, with ignorance of evil — the error Milton wrote *Areopagitica* to correct. Paradise offers, not freedom from evil, or from proper emotional responses to it, but boundless opportunity for good. Since, by God's permissive will, an evil spirit is lurking in the garden, Adam and Eve must learn to resist evil, not to ignore it. By permitting Satan to be there, God allows Adam and Eve the dignity of choice and the means of moral growth. The dream Satan imposes on Eve is an important step in their education. Further, God sends Raphael to teach them about the nature of evil and the process of disobedience, as well as the nature of good and the process of obedience; and the forbidden tree itself affords continuous opportunity to "see and know and yet abstain" (4.311).

In his explanation of Eve's dream (5.95–121), Adam sums up another pertinent statement from *Areopagitica*. "Evil into the mind of God or Man / May come and go," he consoles her, "so unapprov'd, and leave / No spot or blame behind." "To the pure all things are pure," Milton reminds Parliament, "not only meats and drinks, but all kinds of knowledge whether of good or evil; the knowledge cannot defile . . . if the will and conscience be not defil'd." What he says of "bad books" may also be said of bad dreams: they "serve in many respects to discover, to confute, to forewarn, and to illustrate"; the dream shows that in prelapsarian as in regenerate life, with regard to "those actions which enter into a man, rather than issue out of him, and therefore defile not, God uses not to captivat under a perpetuall childhood of prescription, but trusts him with the gift of reason to be his own chooser" (4.308, 309, 310). Milton's God does not censor the dream Satan intrudes into Eve's mind; rather, he permits an experience that reveals and sets in motion the operations of reason and imagination, and the responses of Adam and Eve illustrate the distinction between a "blank virtue" and a "pure" one (4.311).

In his attempt to justify Milton's Eve at the expense of Milton's God, William Empson proposes that "Adam and Eve would not have fallen unless God had sent Raphael" to tell them, echoing Eve's dream, that "God expects them to manage to get to Heaven, and that what they eat has something to do with it."[64] Satan in angel form tells Eve in her dream, Empson points out, that if she eats forbidden fruit she may be "not to Earth confind / But somtimes in the Air, as wee, somtimes / Ascend to Heav'n," while Raphael says "from these corporal nutriments perhaps / Your bodies may at last turn all to Spirit, / . . . and wingd ascend / Ethereal, as wee" (5.496–99). However, Milton is again using here a technique he also used in describing the birth of Sin before the creation of Eve; that is, he presents to us the perverse parody of an episode before the episode itself, and thus challenges us to make careful distinctions.[65] The dream provides the parody of Raphael's better speculations; his metaphor of nurture is the true "poetical fancy" that cures the defect of fancy Satan tries to breed in the dream. Attention to the differences at the time of the waking temptation might have helped Eve resist.

In the dream, the forbidden fruit somehow contains knowledge and can confer it as from above: it is "able," Satan pretends, "to make Gods of Men." In Raphael's explanation of the cosmic process of nurture (5.404–33, 469–505), "The grosser feeds the purer" and is "by gradual scale sublim'd" to nourish the faculties of life, sense, fancy, and understanding, "whence the Soule / Reason receives, and reason is her being." The dream-voice asks, "And why not Gods of Men?" Raphael states that each created being is assigned to its own "active Sphear . . . / Till body up to spirit work, in bounds / Proportioned to each kind," and further that each kind converts its nourishment to its own "proper substance." In the dream, the fruit supposedly confers the ability to fly to heaven "forthwith"; Raphael says that even angels must "concoct, digest, assimilate, / And corporeal to incorporeal turn." The dream-voice tells Eve, "Happier thou mayst be, worthier canst not be"; Raphael says that they may be "Improv'd by tract of time . . . / If ye be found obedient" and that meanwhile they should enjoy their "happie state . . . incapable of more." Satan's imagery of ascent is foggily transcendental, Raphael's accommodatingly organic. Satan's emphasis is upon sudden flight, Raphael's, on gradual refinement; Satan's on the pretended efficacy of the fruit, Raphael's, on their responsibilities for the proper use and nurture of their faculties and nature's gifts. In his reply, Adam stresses the measured progression wherein "By steps we may ascend to God," and Raphael reaffirms the responsibility from which their freedom and dignity derive: "That thou art happie, owe to God; / That thou continu'st such, owe to thy self, / That is, to thy obedience; therein stand" (5.512, 520–22). The contrasts between Eve's dream and Raphael's teaching point up the fact that the Fall was in no way fortunate, but perverted a process of growth and fruition that might have continued through obedience and that regeneration would restore. As Virginia Mollenkott has said, "The grace is fortunate, the sin is not. . . ."[66]

Adam's explanation of Eve's dream shows another way of using it as an aid to virtue: it can help them to discriminate between "Fansie," or imagination, when it is working properly as the servant of reason, and "mimic Fansie," when it apes reason; it can help them (and us) to distinguish between substantial and illusory images, right and wrong uses of imagination, true and perverse poetry. Adam's faculty analysis places fancy next in importance to reason, since it composes the unlimited images that reason selects and joins together in making general propositions in its quest for truth. For the Christian poet, the regeneration of fancy is essential to his craft; and, in the dream and Adam's analysis, Milton shows distinctions between the abuses of poetry and its right uses so often debated in Renaissance poetics. In particular, the dream cautions against two opposed abuses: the wanton sensuality of libertinism and the contempt of this world for the sake of contemplative ecstasy of Counterreformation mysticism.

It is easy for modern readers steeped in Freud to see that the dream is an attempted seduction. But the attempt is twofold: Satan will be satisfied if he can either debase Eve's innocent sensuousness to irresponsible sensuality or inflate her innocent interest in heavenly things to an irresponsible kind of mysticism — the two tendencies in contemporary poetry Milton strove to rectify by his own. The temptation to transcendence — a natural and, from the point of view of the Reformation, an unregenerate reaction to the temptation to sensuality — was one of which Milton's contemporaries were well aware. In Cicero's *Somnium Scipionis,* for example, which with Macrobius's commentary went through numerous Renaissance editions, Scipio's guide cautions the dreamer (like Raphael and unlike Satan) that heaven is attained by virtuous action, not sudden transport: "Men were created with the understanding that they were to look after the Sphere called Earth. . . . Wherefore, Scipio, you and all other dutiful men must keep your souls in the custody of your bodies and must not leave this life of man except at the command of the One who gave it to you, that you may not appear to have deserted the office assigned to you."[67] Similarly, John Donne warns, "Man sometimes withdrawes the soule from the body, by neglecting the duties of this life for imaginary speculations."[68] And in *Adam in Ballingschap,* the version of the drama of Adam and Eve nearest in time to Milton's, Joost van den Vondel attributes to Eve a moment of ravishment comparable to her dream in *Paradise Lost,* with the very important difference that her waking thought is influenced by the bridal song of a poetical archangel rather than her sleeping fancy by Satan — a distinction that shows how careful Milton is not to suggest that God or his agents are sources of error or that Eve is inherently weak. In Vondel's version, Eve exclaims:

> Stand we in Eden, or among the stars?
> What heavenly yearning ravishes my soul?
> My feet can feel no earth: it sinks away.
> The godlike sound of holy bridal song
> Unties the bond that couples soul with body.
> The soul, intent upon its heavenly nature,
> Rejects the earthly and becomes a flame
> That seeks the high, first Source of its own being.

Adam protests, "Do not fly from me! . . . Here is thine element. Thy lover calls thee"; and Eve replies, "Now I am brought back to myself again."[69] In *Paradise Lost,* Eve's response to her dream expresses Milton's sense of the original integrity of body and soul and the original harmony of heaven and earth.

Eve's unwilled dream is an opportunity to confirm and strengthen her freely willed obedience by means of a fully informed imagination; and her response gives Adam hope "That what in sleep thou didst abhor to dream, / Waking thou never wilt consent to do." There is irony in his words, of course, for she will consent in spite of this hard lesson; but, until she does consent, her dream can be an instrument of moral growth. Adam and Eve are learning to choose between good and evil; they are learning it without disobeying God; they have been tested, have stood, and have grown in the process. Their experience shows that Milton's Paradise is not a place of languorous idleness but one that elicits deep feeling, hard thinking, and active accomplishment. For Milton, whether in heaven, in Paradise, or in the world we know, the peace of God is not the absence of labor or even of evil, but the power and grace to resist evil and achieve good.

The dream episode begins with echoes from the Song of Solomon that signal its applicability to the processes of regeneration and reformation, not in tranquil repose, but in difficult experience. It concludes with another scriptural echo, this time from the Gospel of Luke. For Eve, after Adam's comforting words,

> was cheard,
> But silently a gentle tear let fall
> From either eye, and wip'd them with her haire;
> Two other precious drops that ready stood,
> Each in their Chrystal sluce, hee ere they fell
> Kiss'd as the gracious signs of sweet remorse
> And pious awe, that feard to have offended.
> [5.129–35]

Eve's remorse is not proof that she has sinned, only that she "Feard to have offended." But to signify again the correpondences of unfallen responses with regenerate ones, the passage echoes the episode in the life of Christ in which a penitent woman bringing precious ointment "began to wash his feet with tears, and did wipe them with the hairs of her head." Jesus says, "Thy faith has saved thee, go in peace"; with prayer, Adam and Eve "Firm peace recovered soon and wonted calm." The dream is not inevitably a step toward the Fall, for "all was cleard"; it allows a growth in moral understanding and the proper use of fancy that might have proceeded in innocence; and their response to it prepares for the first steps in their regeneration and issues in the answerable deeds which are, for Milton, the right use of recovered peace: "On to thir mornings rural work they haste."

Notes

1. Empson, *Some Versions of Pastorale* (New York, 1968), p. 177; Collett, "Milton's Use of Classical Mythology in *Paradise Lost*," *PMLA* 85 (1970): 88–96; Harding, *The Club of Hercules: Studies in the Classical Background of "Paradise Lost"* (Urbana, 1962); quoted in A. B. Giamatti, *The Earthly Paradise and the Renaissance Epic,*, p. 81 n. According to Giamatti, "a classical allusion in the Christian tale will always do two things: it will invariably indicate the higher Truth and greater splendour of the garden and of Adam and Eve; but it will also, obliquely, by what it recalls and by the very fact that it is there, prepare for a context of falsity and disgrace. . . . We cannot escape what we know, and though the total effect of the perfect place is not diminished in any overt way, something lurks" (pp. 300 and 310). For Giamatti the something that lurks is a corrupting softness in nature and a corruptibility in Eve; but I suggest that it is, rather, the fallen archangel who has vowed "out of good still to find means of evil" (1.165).

Any interpretation of *Paradise Lost* that tries to take mythical or allegorical implications into account should adhere to two principles admirably expressed in recent articles. First, as Anthony Low reminds us, although "to a modern reader, *Paradise Lost* may seem a fiction," for Milton the Garden of Eden was "real, literally as well as figuratively and spiritually"; *MiltonQ* 13 (1979): 96–97. Second, as Philip J. Gallagher shows, "Milton . . . uses allusion in *Paradise Lost* not merely as a literary device, but as a way of reconstructing primordial truth from scattered fragments in various Greek myths" that have been perversely inspired by "the Father of Lies" as infernal muse: "*Paradise Lost* and the Greek Theogony," *ELR* 9 (1979): 144 and passim.

2. Anne B. Long has shown that Milton regularly pairs mythical and scriptural allusions to show "the continuity between natural and spiritual elements in the human condition," the continuity of God's ways in all dispensations, and the responsibility of all men to respond uprightly to the opportunities provided through nature and natural understanding rectified by faith. "The myths emphasize the human effort necessary in [the] process of regeneration, a human effort which Adam and Eve also exhibit in their growth," while the scriptural allusions "share characteristics of the mythological allusions but . . . add the supernatural assistance accepted by upright and regenerate men." By conjoining myth and Scripture, "Milton directs his reader's associations with the classical tradition towards the emphasis upon natural faculties, effort, and fertility as parts of God's plan": "The Relations Between Classical and Biblical Allusions in Milton's Later Poems" (Ph.D. dissertation, University of Illinois, 1967), pp. 364, 253, 309 and passim.

3. *The Whole Works of Homer,* trans. George Chapman (London, 1616)

4. Augustine equates Ceres with Isis (*Of the Citie of God,* pp. 280–81), who is identified as one of the fallen angels in 1.427. To clear Eve of the turpitude associated with Isis and with the Eleusinian mysteries, Milton compares her with "*Ceres* in her Prime, / Yet Virgin of *Proserpina* from *Jove*" (9.395–96). Pomona "when she fled / Vertumnus" (9.394–95) is fleeing seduction, and yields, as Eve has yielded to Adam, only after his true nature has been revealed to her (Ovid, *Metamorphoses,* 14). The one clearly degrading comparison is to Eurynome, which of course occurs after the

Fall and as a pagan version of sacred history (10.581–82). For a discussion of the pictorial analogues, see Frye, pp. 276 ff., especially the comparison of Titian's and Rembrandt's versions of Flora quoted from Julius S. Held, "Flora, Goddess and Courtesan," in *Essays in Honor of Erwin Panofsky,* ed. Millard Meiss (New York, 1961), 1:206.

5. Sir Thomas Elyot, *The Defence of Good Women* (1540), fac. ed. Edwin Johnston Howard (Oxford, Ohio, 1940), sig. D.v.

6. See especially the articles by Barker, Samuel, Lewalski, and Blackburn cited in notes 4–6 to ch. v.

7. Ralegh, *History,* p. 32.

8. Milton, letter dated London, 1657, trans. David Masson, 12:27.

9. Milton, *The Doctrine and Discipline of Divorce,* 3:440–41.

10. See for example Andrea Alciati, *Emblemata* (Frankfurt, 1597), p. 84, and Michael J. B. Allen, ed. and trans., *Marsilio Ficino: The "Philebus" Commentary* (Berkeley, 1975), p. 448.

11. Homer, *The Odyssey,* 10.138; Vergil, *The Aeneid,* 7:11; Boccaccio, *La Geneologia de gli Dei Gentili,* trans. Gioseppe Betusi da Basano (Venice, 1569), p. 63; *Omnia Andreae Alciati . . . Emblemata* (Antwerp, 1581), pp. 284–87. For other discussions of the allegorical and emblematic complexities of the Circe myth, see Leonora Leet Brodwin, "Milton and the Renaissance Circe," *Milton S* 6 (1975): 21–83, and Joan Larsen Klein, "From Error to Acrasia," *HLQ* 41 (1978): 173–99.

12. Alexander Neckham [?], *Albrici philosophi liber ymaginum deorum* (cod. Vat. 3413), paraphrased by Jean Seznec in *The Survival of the Pagan Gods,* trans. Barbara F. Sessions (New York, 1961), p. 172. According to Seznec, this treatise "exerted a profound and lasting influence on the iconography of the gods" (p. 170).

13. The tradition of multiple Venuses is discussed by Richard H. Green in "Alan of Lille's *De Planctu Naturae,*" *Speculum* 31 (1956): 649–74, and by Kathleen Williams in "Venus and Diana: Some Uses of Myth in *The Faerie Queene,*" *ELH* 28:101–20.

14. For example, Antonio Rizzi's statue of Eve clearly imitates the "Capitoline" *Venus;* Cranach's Eve assumes the position of *Aphrodite Combing Her Hair;* Albertinelli's *Virgin of the Annunciation* echoes the Venus Pudica motif; and paintings by Fra Angelico and Giovanni de Paolo the topos of *The Annunciation with the Expulsion.* That these visual comparisons were not accidental is substantiated by Durer's statement that "just as they [the pagan people] represented Venus as the most beautiful woman we shall chastely display the same features in the image of the Holy Virgin, Mother of God"; K. Lange and F. Fuhse, *"Durers schriftlicher Nachlass auf Grund der Originalhandschriften und theilweise neu entdecker alter Abschriften* (Halle a.S., 1893), p. 316; trans. in Erwin Panofsky, *Studies in Iconology* (New York, 1962), p. 70.

15. Allen, pp. 448 and 482.

16. See for example Jon S. Lawry, *The Shadow of Heaven* (Ithaca, N.Y., 1963), p. 175; A. B. Giamatti, *The Earthly Paradise and the Renaissance Epic,* pp. 9 ff.; Jonathan H. Collett, "Milton's Use of Classical Mythology in *Paradise Lost,*" *PMLA* 85 (1970): 88–96; Douglas A. Day, "Adam and Eve in *Paradise Lost* IV," *TSLL* 3 (1961).

17. These include Dennis Burden, *The Logical Epic* (Cambridge, Mass., 1967), pp. 83–85; Arnold Stein, *Answerable Style* (Minneapolis, 1953) p. 93; H. V. S. Ogden, "The Crisis of *Paradise Lost* Reconsidered," *PQ* 36 (1957): 1–19; J. M. Evans, *"Paradise Lost" and the Genesis Tradition* (Oxford, 1968), 253–54.

18. Lee A. Jacobus, "Self-Knowledge in *Paradise Lost.* Conscience and Contemplation, *MiltonS* 3 (1971): 103–18; Don Parry Norford, "The Separation of the World Parents in *Paradise Lost,*" *MiltonS* 12 (1978): 3–24.

19. Norford, "The Separation of the World Parents," pp. 14, 10, 21.

20. *The Tempest* II.i. Shakespeare puts these words into the mouth of a character whom the sea has "cast" in the vulgarest sense of the word, since he responds unregenerately and destructively; but most of the characters are recast in the senses of being re-formed and given new parts.

21. Sir Philip Sidney, *The Defence of Poesie* (London, 1594; repr. Cambridge, 1904), pp. 57, 34, 22, 16, 19.

22. Milton discusses this concept in *De Doctrina Christiana,* 15:199.

23. Ralegh calls this a "strange opinion" (*History,* p. 34).

24. Elegies, I.xv, trans. Christopher Marlowe, in *The Works and Life of Christopher Marlowe: Poems,* ed. L. C. Martin (New York, 1931, repr. 1966), p. 178.

25. Nature as a mirror for Eve's vanity in other versions of Genesis is discussed in ch. IV and V below. Examples of woman-headed serpents are given in ch. I.

The image of the watery mirror, on the other hand, can signify the temperate "love of self" that goes hand in hand with love of neighbor as a duty second only to love of God. Edward Reynolds, in *A Treatise of the Passions and Faculties of the Soul of Man* (London, 1658), quotes, perhaps as a proverb, *"as Face answereth to Face in Water, so the heart of Man to Man"* (p. 85). George Sandys comments that Teiresias's prophecy that Narcissus would not thrive unless "he know not himself" is "as strange as obscure; and seeming contradictory to that oracle of *Apollo:* To know a mans selfe is the chiefest knowledge": *Ovid's Metamorphosis Englished, Mythologiz'd, And Represented in Figures* . . . (Oxford, 1632), p. 103. See also Milton's primarily benign use of the Narcissus myth in *A Mask.*

26. Giovanni Pico della Mirandola, *A Platonick Discourse upon Love,* trans. Thomas Stanley [1615], ed. Edmund G. Gardner (Boston, 1914), pp. 74–76.

27. Sources and revisions of the rite are compared in F. E. Brightman, *The English Rite: Being a Synopsis of the Sources and Revisions of the Book of Common Prayer* (London, 1920).

28. Charles Williams compares the relation of Adam and Eve to that of Father and Son as "derivation-in-love" and contrasts them to Satan's refusal of derivation in his introduction to *The English Poems of John Milton* (Oxford, 1940). Mother Mary Christopher Pecheux discusses the analogies of the holy and the infernal trinities and the human family in "The Second Adam and the Church in *Paradise Lost," ELH* 34 (1967): 173. Stella P. Revard discusses the relation of Father and Son as a voluntary bond of love in "The Dramatic Function of the Son in *Paradise Lost:* A Commentary on Milton's 'Trinitarianism,'" *JEGP* 66 (1967): 45–58. Joseph H. Summers points out sound patterns in the speeches of Eve and the Son that distinguish redemptive love from its parodies in *The Muse's Method,* ch. VII.

29. *The XV Bookes of P. Ouidius Naso, entytuled Metamorphosis,* trans. Arthur Golding (London, 1567), pp. 38–38.

30. I am glad to find related views in two recent articles: Janet Adelman's comparison of the creation of Eve to Milton's creation of his poem, "Creation and the Place of the Poet in *Paradise Lost,*" in *The Author in His Work: Essays on a Problem in Criticism,* eds. Louis L. Martz and Aubrey Williams (New Haven, 1978); and Patricia Parker's comparison of Eve's situation to the reader's in "Eve, Evening, and the Labor of Reading in *Paradise Lost," ELR* 9 (1979): 319–42. On the poem as a "good temptation" of the reader see Stanley Fish, *Surprised by Sin,* pp. 38–56.

31. William B. Hunter, Jr., explains this process in the light of "contemporary dream and demon lore" in "Eve's Demonic Dream," *ELH* 8 (1946): 255–65; and John S. Diekhoff discusses Satan's agency in "Eve's Dream and the Paradox of Fal-

lible Perfection," *MiltonQ* 9 (1970): 5–7, affirming that the dream "reveals [Satan's] ethos, not Eve's" (p. 6).

32. Richard Baxter, *A Christian Directory* (London, 1678), 1:81. Cf. Ambrose, "For to have seen is no sin, but one must be careful that it be not the source of sin," in *Two Books of Saint Ambrose . . . Concerning Repentence,"* *SLNPNF,* Second Series, 10:340.

33. Andrew Willett, *Hexapla in Genesin,* p. 37.

34. Joan Larsen Klein's description of the dream-temptation of Red Cross in *The Faerie Queene* suggests crucial differences between it and Eve's, in "From Error to Acrasia," pp. 184–85: "Though Red Cross rejects the attempt to seduce his mind, Archimago has been able to infect it. Now a clear example of the weakness of unregenerate man, Red Cross is 'beguiled' by the art of the succubus . . . [and] returns to sleep, to be made once again to dream of the substance of lust. . . . This time, however, he does not waken at the coming of his hidden foe." Eve, in contrast, returns at once to wholesome labor.

35. Milton, *Areopagitica* 4:311. Ralegh makes similar distinctions between fallen and unfallen knowledge of evil in his *History,* p. 60.

36. Edward Reynolds, in *A Treatise of the Passions and Faculties of the Soul of Man* (London, 1656), includes among the causes of "the Errors which are in the Fancie" the "ministry of *evil Angels*" (p. 27).

37. Ibid., pp. 18 and 24.

38. Some critics feel that *Areopagitica* is inapplicable to the unfallen state; see, for example, John S. Diekhoff, "Eve, the Devil and *Areopagitica,"* *MLQ* 5 (1944): 429–34. Although the applications obviously need to be made with caution, Milton's principle that regeneration restores the faculties of original righteousness allows the same principles to apply to the growth of virtue in both states.

39. Howard Schultz points out that Satan's song to Eve in the dream (5.38–47) also alludes to the Song of Songs, but by contrast; it is a *serenade,* which like its morning counterpart, the *aubade,* is usually an adulterous seduction song: "Satan's Serenade," *PQ* 27 (1948): 17–21.

40. See Mother Mary Christopher Pecheux, "The Second Adam and the Church in *Paradise Lost,"* pp. 173–87. Thomas Peyton, in *The Glasse of Time* (1620), says that God in marrying Eve to Adam, "Made her the Tipe our senses all to rouse, / Of Christ himselfe, and of the Church his spouse"; in Watson Kirkconnell, *The Celestial Cycle,* p. 268.

41. "The Scripture also affords us a divine pastoral Drama in the Song of Solomon consisting of two persons and a double *Chorus,* as *Origen* rightly judges"; *Reason of Church-government,* 3: 237–38.

42. Origen, *The Song of Songs: Commentary and Homilies,* trans. R. P. Lawson, in *Ancient Christian Writers,* ed. Johannes Quasten and Joseph C. Plumpe (London, 1957), 26: 21.

43. The differences between Catholic and Protestant exegesis of the Song of Solomon and between allegorical and typological interpretations are discussed by Barbara Kiefer Lewalski in "Typology and Poetry: A Consideration of Herbert, Vaughan, and Marvell," in *Illustrious Evidence: Approaches to English Literature of the Early Seventeenth Century,* ed. Earl Miner (Berkeley, Los Angeles, and London, 1975), pp. 41–69. On the basic significance of typology see also Lewalski's *Protestant Poetics and the Seventeenth-Century Religious Lyric* (Princeton, 1979).

44. Origen, *Song of Songs,* pp. 25, 23, 44.

45. Jerome, Letter XXII, "to Eustochium," in *SLNPNF,* Second Series, 6:32.

46. Augustine, *Concerning Faith in Things Not Seen,* in *SLNPNF,* First Series, 3: 343.

47. *The Life and Works of Saint Bernard,* ed. John Mabillon, ed. and trans. Samuel J. Eales (London, 1896), 4:292–93.

48. William Gouge, *An Exposition of the Song of Solomon* (London, 1615), p. 57 [mispaginated as p. 65].

49. John Cotton, *A Brief Exposition with Practical Observations upon the whole Book of Canticles* (London, 1655), p. 105.

50. Richard Sibbs, *Bowels Opened, or, A Discovery of the Neere and deere Love, Vnion and Communion betwixt Christ and the Church, and consequently betwixt Him and every beleeving soule* (London, 1639), p. 16.

51. *The Bible and Holy Scriptures conteyned in the Olde and Newe Testament. Translated . . . with moste Profitable Annotations* (Geneva, 1560), intro. Lloyd E. Berry (facs. ed., Madison, 1969), p. 281.

52. Cotton, *Brief Exposition,* p. 164.

53. Ainsworth, *Solomons Song of Songs,* p. 52.

54. Cotton, *Brief Exposition,* p. 212.

55. Thomas Brightman, *A Commentary on the Canticles,* in *The Workes of that Famous, Reverend, and Learned Divine, Mr. Tho. Brightman* (London, 1644), p. 1046–47. Sibbs advises against too narrowly historical an interpretation and says that most passages also agree "to the Spirituall estate of the Church in every age" (p. 4).

56. John Robotham, *An Exposition on the whole booke of Solomons Song, Commonly Called the Canticles* (London, 1651), sig. A2.

57. Ibid., p. 9.

58. *The Complete Poetry of John Donne,* ed. Shawcross, p. 350.

59. Cotton, *Brief Exposition,* p. 105.

60. Ainsworth, *Solomons Song of Songs,* pp. 34, 59.

61. Mary S. Weinkauf discusses the imagery of Eve's dream in "Eve and the Sense of Beauty," *TSLL* 14 (1969): 102–9, showing that Satan's song is a perversion of Eve's love of nature. It does not follow, however, that Satan's echoes of Eve's response to nature are actually a step in her perversion, or that Eve must reject earthly beauty in order to ascend to heavenly beauty in her regeneration. The elements of the dream are the same ones Milton praises in "Il Penseroso."

62. The prevailing assumption has been that the dream manifests and increases a susceptibility in Eve to Satan's suggestions. Dan S. Collins refutes this view in "The Buoyant Mind in Milton's Eden," *MiltonS* 5 (1973): 234–37. Critics who take a position on the question of whether, in the dream, Eve tastes the fruit offer a wide range of interpretations. Mary Ann Nevins Radzinowicz feels that "in her dream she has eaten and awakes to 'a sweet remorse'" but "in her susceptibility has experienced alone the pattern of choice she repeats in the Fall" (*Reason and Imagination: Studies in the History of Ideas, 1600–1800,* ed. J. A. Mazzeo [New York, 1962], p. 170). Barbara Kiefer Lewalski, on the other hand, states that "Eve's virtual experience of evil . . . could more greatly enhance her ability and determination to shun the actual experience" ("Innocence and Experience," p. 103). Irene Samuel is convinced that Eve "does not taste the fruit. Rather, dream-fashion, the sequel skips over the supposedly requisite preliminary" and emphasizes Eve's conscious response: "The dream of Eve gives opportunity for . . . proof of merit" and "in advance of the later trial which they fail marks Eden as a place of growth" ("*Purgatorio* and the Dream of Eve," *JEGP* 63 [1964]: 444, 441). Stanley Fish agrees that Eve does not eat but thinks that she "remains untouched by the experience" (*Surprised by Sin: The Reader in "Paradise Lost"*

[Berkeley, 1967], pp. 222-25). Arthur E. Barker, in a comment on the present essay, believes that Eve does dream of eating and that the full imaginative experience of evil is what makes the dream a potentially powerful instrument of perceptively willing obedience: "Eve has to know as fully as possible, by *dream,* what evil *is;* and Adam has to be able to say it is a *willed,* not a dreamt, act." This view, in accordance with Milton's doctrine, exonerates Eve by increasing, rather than by circumscribing, her opportunity for a virtuous response.

63. Tillyard, *Studies in Milton* (London, 1951), p. 12.

64. Empson, *Milton's God* (London, 1961), p. 150.

65. Eve's dream parodies both Raphael's ensuing discourse and Adam's dream, experienced earlier but narrated later (8.291 ff.).

66. Mollenkott, "Milton's Rejection of the Fortunate Fall," *MiltonQ* 6 (1971): 2.

67. Cicero, *Scipio's Dream,* trans. William Harris Stahl (New York, 1952), p. 72. The passage is a warning against suicide.

68. Donne, *Sermons* 7:104.

69. Vondel, (1664), trans. Kirkconnell, in *The Celestial Cycle,* pp. 459-60.

IV

"The Hand of Eve":
Ingredients of Virtue

When Milton shows Adam and Eve engaged in the art of gardening, he departs radically from the iconographic and literary traditions he inherited and provides the world its first demonstration of what a productive and responsible active life before the Fall might be. Cultivating one's garden is an activity of such universal application that there is scarcely any art, science, emotion, virtue, or ethic for which it cannot stand; and Milton's mimesis of it is his pattern for a regenerate response to one's calling to do the work of this world, including his own work of poesie, in response to the divine voice. It is curious, therefore, that so many readers have seen the gardening of Adam and Eve as an inconsequential pastime, or a simple allegory of emotional order, and in particular have thought Eve's suggestion to Adam that they separate for a while to concentrate on their work a mere whim, a bit of feminine dabbling, or an excuse for willful roving. On the contrary, Milton's Eve is distinguished from all other Eves by the fact that she takes her work seriously.

A possible reason for the failure to take Eve's seriousness seriously is that modern psychology, and perhaps a pervasive subjectivity in moral life,[1] lead us in questions of motive to look for desires, appetites, "emotions" (as distinguished from the seventeenth-century "motions"), inward needs, and self-assertions. Nothing could be farther from the seventeenth-century conviction that one is called by God and empowered by his Spirit to do her or his work in the world, and that this delegation of creativity and providence is the fount of human dignity and right relation and a major source of joy. The pre-lapsarian conscience as Milton represents it is *called* (and so grows) by what is outside itself: by God, by other beings, by needs and beauties and glories one's talents fit and move one to serve. The Garden is not only, as it is so often seen, a mirror of Adam's and Eve's emotional states, though it is affected by them. It is an organic community of interconnected lives to which their healthy minds delightedly respond. Eve's suggestion that she work on her own for a bit is a part of her response to her callings. God has called her, and the Garden calls her. Her motives or "motions" are not merely the devices and desires of her own heart. They are objective tasks to which her heart responds, and above all the voice of God commending all "kinds" to the care of humankind who are images of his generous love. Before we look at the reasons why, on a particular morning, Eve feels moved to work alone and at the potential validity and risk of that method of working, we need to be aware of the objective importance of the interrelated tasks to which God calls her and Adam, both mutually and individually.

"Fresh Imployments"

In the first conversation between Adam and Eve we hear, Adam joins work, praise, and love:

> . . . let us ever praise [God], and extoll
> His bountie, following our delightful task,
> To prune these growing Plants, and tend these Flours,
> Which were it toilsom, yet with thee were sweet.
> [4.436–39]

Inviting Eve to evening repose, he adds:

> Man hath his daily work of body or mind
> Appointed, which declares his Dignitie,
> And the regard of Heav's on all his waies.
> [4.619–21]

The ensuing description of "wanton growth" alarms some readers as the mirror of an emotional life that is apt to get out of hand, yet for Milton choosing and ordering amid fertile efflorescence is just what temperance is, and Eve will echo the speech to that purpose later on. Since perfection is a process, it is fitting that Edenic profusion asks the discipline that produces finer fruits, and Adam's talk of "reform" and "riddance" links their work to the reformation of the church.

In their evening prayer, Adam and Eve thank God for the day

> Which we in our appointed work imployd
> Have finisht happie in our mutual help
> And mutual love, the Crown of all our bliss
> Ordaind by thee, and this delicious place
> For us too large, where thy abundance wants
> Partakers, and uncropt falls to the ground.
> But thou hast promis'd from us two a Race
> To fill the Earth. . . .
>
> [4.726-33]

Both Adam and Eve often mention their hope of progeny to share the work and the bounty, linking the commandments to dress and keep the Garden and to increase and multiply. After her dream, Adam bids Eve "Awake, the morning shines, and the fresh field / Calls us, we lose the prime, to mark how spring / Our tended Plants," and as they recover from their first distress he resumes, "let us to our fresh imployments rise" (5.20–22, 125). In their morning prayer they praise the Parent of good who is "dimly seen / In these thy lowest works, yet these declare / Thy goodness beyond thought," and invite all nature to join their song; then

> On to thir mornings rural work they haste
> Among sweet dewes and flours; where any row
> Of Fruit-trees overwoodie reachd too farr
> Thir pamperd boughes, and needed hands to check
> Fruitless imbraces: or they led the Vine
> To wed her Elm; she spous'd about him twines
> Her mariagable arms, and with her brings
> Her dowr th'adopted Clusters, to adorn
> His barren leaves.
>
> [5.157-59, 211-19]

Clearly, this is a natural garden that responds to care in familiar ways, and their labor in it is a high delight. At the same time, it teaches Adam and Eve much about its Maker, about themselves, and about their "mutual help / And mutual love."

Insofar as their work in the Garden is a metaphor for marriage, it highlights the dower, not the dependence, of the Vine. Throughout their life in the Garden, Eve innocently exercises special talents and responsibilities without breach in mutual help and love. The first of her contributions, we learn in retrospect, has been the naming of the flowers, which she has often tended by herself; when Michael announces their expulsion she mourns her flowers,

> My early visitation, and my last
> At Eev'n, which I bred up with tender hand
> From the first op'ning bud, and gave ye Names,
> Who now shall reare ye to the Sun, or ranke
> Your Tribes, and water from th'ambrosial Fount?
> [11.275–79]

Adam's naming of the creatures is commonly cited as proof of his intelligence, since Hebrew names denote the nature of their bearers, and right naming signifies right knowing: "I nam'd them," Adam tells Raphael, "and understood / Thir Nature, with such knowledge God endu'd / My sudden apprehension" (8.352–54). But Eve was not thought to have had a part in this act of naming, and two famous preachers deny her the capacity for it. William Perkins, explaining that Eve's failure before her fall to recognize fraud in the Serpent was an innocent and not a sinful kind of ignorance, states that "the naming of the creatures, which argues knowledge of them, was not giuen to Eue, but to Adam";[2] and John Donne, in a marriage sermon on Genesis 2:18, exhorts the bride,

> Since she was taken out of man's side, let her not depart from his side, but show herself so much as she was made for, *Adjutorium,* a Helper. But she must be no more: If she think herself more than a Helper, she is not so much. He is a miserable creature, whose Creator is his Wife. God did not stay to join her in commission with Adam, so far as to give names to the creatures; much lesse to give essence . . . to her husband.[3]

But in *Paradise Lost,* as Adam names the beasts and understands their natures, Eve names the flowers and understands theirs; and, while subordinate on the scale of nature to Adam's charge, the "bright consummate floure" which "spirits odorous breathes" is Raphael's epitome of the process by which all forms of life become "more refin'd, more spiritous, and pure" and is the precursor of "fruit / Mans nourishment" (5.474–83). In both classical and scriptural imagery, flowers are metaphors of regeneration.[4]

On two occasions before the separation for which she is so often blamed, Eve goes forth alone on gracious errands. When Raphael comes to dinner, she "Bestirs her then, and from each tender stalk / Whatever Earth all-bearing Mother yields . . . She gathers, Tribute large, and on the board / Heaps with unsparing hand" (5.337–38, 343–44). During the lecture on astronomy, she

> Rose, and went forth among her Fruits and Flours,
> To visit how they prosper'd, bud and bloom,
> Her Nurserie; they at her coming sprung
> And toucht by her fair tendance gladlier grew.
>
> [8.44–47]

Milton is careful to add that she goes "not, as not with such discourse / Delighted, or not capable her eare / Of what was high;" she prefers to ask her husband, who will "intermix / Grateful digressions, and solve high dispute / With conjugal Caresses." Meanwhile, her "fair tendance" of "her Nurserie" is no trifle. Nature responds to her as she and Adam respond to each other, and as the children they prepare for might have responded, with glad growth. Adam shows no lack of confidence at these departures, though the first was preceded by a disturbing dream and the second by Raphael's warning of a lurking foe.[5]

These passages prepare for the scene in which Eve decides that the Garden and the marriage will be better served if she and Adam work separately for a spell; and all of these separations differ from the work of Milton's predecessors, who never dramatized the prelapsarian callings of Adam and Eve nor supposed Eve capable of any good purposes of her own, much less "what was high." Her going forth among her fruits and flowers prepares also for the nurturing employment in which Satan finds her "oft stooping to support / Each Flour"; and we know that this personal task is a long-practiced art, for the Serpent approaches "Among thick-wov'n Arborets and Flours / Imborderd on each Bank, the hand of Eve" (9.437–38).

These passages suggest that the relation of Adam and Eve to God, to each other, and to the rest of the creation has been developing, through their participation in the work of the "sovran Planter" (4.691), long enough to teach them much about themselves, God's ways, and nature's ways. By encouraging and shaping the responsive growth of nature's various forms, they dress and keep not only the Garden but also the harmonious responses to the whole creation and the good uses of their own talents that keep their love free and fruitful. In these creative, procreative, and recreative tasks, Eve is both meet help and inspired artist whose work is a figure of the poet's own.

"Immortal Fruits"

In representing the art of gardening, Milton chose to "lop overgrown, or prune, or prop, or bind" three interwoven traditions: the patristic and medieval, which accepted the mystical implications of cultivation and marriage but as we have seen sometimes denied their literal applications, advocating contemplation in preference to action and celibacy in preference to the practical consequences of marriage; the Protestant, which, especially in its puritan branches, advocated marriage and a sense of calling, but distrusted the sensuous and imaginative powers of love, art, and Eve; and the Renaissance revival of classical pastoral poetry by humanist writers who, comparing Eden to Arcadia, extolled Eve's beauty but gave her nothing to do. Milton selected and refined the parts of these traditions that could be used to display active goodness, and integrated them into his vision of original righteousness.

Although interpreters of Genesis agreed with the gravedigger in *Hamlet* that "the Scripture says Adam digged," tradition reserves this activity for his fallen and laborious tilling of the earth from whence he came; in neither art nor literature do Adam and Eve do anything useful between his naming of the animals and their penitential toil. Ideas about original righteousness are abundant but abstract. According to a representative medieval poem,

> Adam oure fadur hade to byn hys
> The joy and myrth of Paradys,
> It to wonen and to welde to syche ende,
> Til that he shulde ther to hevyn wende;
> But . . . sone he hit alle for-les. . . . [6]

Most interpreters assume that Adam and Eve fell the day they were made, with no effort to wend to heaven by righteous rule, and the few who imagine them living sinlessly do not imagine them living productively, but roaming the enamelled gardens of allegorical time-

and placelessness. There was much discussion of what God's image in man consists of, as "reason, vnderstanding, knowledge, wisedome, and memorie, with Iustice, equitie, courage, temperance, Chastity, love, pitty, and all manner of holinesse, with a beautiful proportion of the body, and excellent gifts of the mind, yea with Lordship and Dominion ouer all these earthly Creatures,"[7] along with perfect health, vigor, and immortality sustained by the Tree of Life. But there was little thought about how Adam and Eve might have put all these powers to use. In *Paradise Lost* their virtues are challenged and exercised by the complexities of experience, by the richness of their own natures, and by their "daily work of body or mind / Appointed, which declares [their] dignity, / And the regard of Heav'n on all [their] ways" (4.618–20).

Milton's gardeners have no precedents, but many unused resources, in the exegetical environment. In general, rabbinical and patristic commentators interpret the commandment to dress and keep the Garden allegorically, the rabbis as the keeping of the Law and the Fathers as the contemplation of God's goodness and the cultivation of virtue, while the Reformers prefer its practical applications to the stewardship of nature, the duty of useful employment for the common good, and the mutual help of marriage. All three regard the Garden as a type of the church, Christian expositors adding to the mystical exegesis of the rabbis the typology of Christ, the second Adam, at work in his vineyard. The writer who provides the link between allegorical Fathers and literal-minded Protestants is Augustine, who accepts figurative meanings as long as they are rooted in literal ones. Some people, he says, "understand all its trees and fruit-bearing plants as virtues and habits of life, as if they had no existence in the external world, but were only so spoken of or related for the sake of spiritual meanings. As if there could not be a real terrestrial Paradise!" However, once one accepts "the truth of holy Scripture" in fact, one need not deny that

> Paradise may signify the life of the blessed; its four rivers, the four virtues, prudence, fortitude, temperance, and justice; its trees, all useful knowledge; its fruits, the customs of the godly; its tree of life, wisdom herself, the mother of all good; and the tree of the knowledge of good and evil, the experience of a broken commandment.

Proceeding from allegory to typology, Augustine continues:

These things can also and more profitably be understood of the
Church, so that they become prophetic foreshadowings of things to
come. Thus Paradise is the Church, as it is called in the Canticles; the
four rivers of Paradise are the four gospels; the fruit-trees the saints,
and the fruit their works; the tree of life is the holy of holies, Christ;
the tree of knowledge of good and evil, the will's free choice. For if
man despise the will of God, he can only destroy himself; and so he
learns the difference between consecrating himself to the common
good and reveling in his own.[8]

Although in these passages Augustine omits the sense of process that
Milton infuses into the work of Adam and Eve, in *De Genesi ad Litteram* he considers the commandment to dress and keep the Garden
literally and recognizes the concinnity of rational and natural processes and, to a degree, the correspondence of human and divine
providence that makes the gardening of Adam and Eve at once an
active and a contemplative art.

For what greater or more marvelous sight is there, or where can human reason speak, in a way, with nature better than this: when the
seeds are sown, the sprouts set down, the shrubs moved, the mallet-
shoots grafted, and it is as if every force in root and seed is asked what
it can do and what it cannot; whence it can grow and whence not; what
effect on its increase comes from its unseen strength within, and what
from tending provided from without. Even in this consideration, one
should note that neither he who plants nor he who waters is anything,
but only God who gives increase (I Cor. 3.7); and that even that labor
which comes from without comes through him whom God no less created and, all unseen, governs and ordains.[9]

Subsequently, Augustine points out correspondences between agri-
culture, government, and all good arts.

Milton places more emphasis on the efforts of those who plant and
water, not to diminish God's providence but to increase the freedom
and responsibility with which God encourages them to use the
"strength within" he has provided: "For God towards thee hath done
his part, do thine." This reciprocity of providential grace and responsive effort is central to English Protestantism. Its rhythm appears in
the post-communion prayer Thomas Cranmer added to the liturgy
in 1549: "We therefore most humbly beseech thee, O heauenly Father, so to assist us with thy grace, that we may continue in that holy
fellowship, and doe all such good workes as thou hast prepared for us

to walk in." John Donne also urges doing one's part. Although God gives grace of "his own meer, and unmeasurable goodnesse," yet "there is nothing in grace, that was not first in nature, so farre, as that grace always finds nature, and naturall faculties to work upon"; so that, when we cleanse and dispose our faculties to receive it, "that which thy soule began but in *good nature,* shall be perfected in grace."[10] The rhythm of grace and response is at the heart of the experience of Adam and Eve and is recreated in their work. In Cranmer's words, God prepares, they beseech, God assists, they continue in holy fellowship and do good works.

The aptness of the trope of gardening for this process is picked up by Ralegh. Having argued against pure allegorists that "there was a true and locall Paradise Eastward, in the Countrie of Eden," he agrees with Augustine that Paradise may be taken in both "corporall" and "spirituall" senses, "of which *Suidas* giueth this allowable iudgment: . . . *As man was created at one time both sensible and intelligible: so was this holy groue or garden to be taken both waies, and endued with a double forme.*" But he also combines Augustine's sense of the kinship of natural and moral processes with a Protestant humanist sense of responsibility in his discussion of man as microcosm and his assertions about free will. "As the sappe and iuyce, wherein the life of Plants is preserued, doth euermore ascend or descend," he remarks, "so is it with the life of man, which is alwaies either increasing towards ripenesse and perfection, or declining and decreasing towards rottennesse and dissolution." Proceeding to an exposition "of the free power, which man had in his first creation, to dispose of himselfe," Ralegh continues,

> God set before [man], a mortall and immortall life, a nature celestiall and terrene, and (indeed) God gaue man to himselfe, to be his own guide, his owne workeman, and his owne painter, that he might frame or describe vnto himselfe what hee pleased, and make election of his owne forme. . . . Such was the liberalitie of God, and mans felicitie: . . . God gaue vnto man all kinde of seedes and grafts of life, (to wit) the vegetatiue life of Plants, the sensuall of beastes, the rationall of man, and the intellectuall of Angels, whereof which soeuer he tooke pleasure to plant and cultiue, the same should futurely grow in him, and bring forth fruit, agreable to his owne choyce and plantation.[11]

The gardening of Adam and Eve, then, is susceptible to all the levels of interpretation worked out through centuries of scriptural and literary exegesis: it is literally the care and cultivation of nature; morally, the cultivation of virtue in response to God's laws, both natural and revealed; ethically, the nurture of marriage and children, which Milton stresses in his similitudes, and the formation of a godly community; and anagogically the regeneration of "all the faculties" and the union of Christ and the church, both celestial and terrene. Moreover, Milton so cultivates the sense of organic process, of mimesis, and of the interinanimation of nature and grace emergent in the liveliest Renaissance and Reformation thought, that his fit audience might see in the handiwork of Adam and Eve the cultivation of "all kinde of seedes and grafts of life," as they integrate the contemplation of God's ways and the imitation of them and thus nurture the divine image in themselves and each other through providential and creative acts.

"The Regard of Heaven"

By cultivating the Garden and by that means advancing the growth and refinement of their own natures as images of God, Adam and Eve integrate what puritans thought of as a twofold calling: the general calling to salvation (in the case of Adam and Eve to proceed to heaven by degrees of merit) and the particular calling by which each member of the household of faith serves God and men. According to William Perkins,

> Mans particular calling was to come into the garden of Eden, to keepe it, and to dresse the trees & fruits thereof. This shewes vnto vs a good lesson, that euery man must haue a particular calling wherein hee ought to walke. . . . Adam's general calling was to worship his Creator, to which he was bound by the right of creation, considering the morall law was written in his heart by natvre. . . . Man was made a goodly creature in the blessed image of God: but by *Adams* fall men lost the same, and are now become the deformed children of wrath: our dutie therefore is, to labour to get againe our first image, and indeauor our selues to become new creatures.[12]

Like Milton, Perkins sees the callings of Adam as a pattern for regeneration, but unlike Milton he tends to segregate its parts, as

many puritans did much more strenuously. The reason for this segregation may be seen at its extreme in William Prynne's reduction
of Calvinist predestinarianism. In reaction to what he supposes to be
a belief in salvation through works, Prynne asserts

> 1. That God from all eternity hath, by his immutable purpose and
> decree, predestined unto life, . . . only a certain select number of par-
> ticular men . . . ; others hath he eternally and perpetually reprobated
> unto death.
> 2. That the only moving or efficient cause of election, or predestina-
> tion unto life, is the mere good pleasure, love, free grace and mercy of
> God; not the preconsideration of any foreseen faith, perseverance,
> good works, good will, good endeavors, or any other prerequired
> quality or condition whatsoever, in the persons elected.[13]

In contrast, Milton states in *De Doctrina Christiana* that "God invites
the whole of mankind, in various ways, but all of them sufficient to
the purpose to the knowledge of the true Deity"; the only reason for
reprobation is that God does not compel men to be saved: "our own
co-operation is uniformly required," both for regeneration and for
"spiritual increase," which "unlike physical growth, appears to be to
a certain degree in the power of the regenerate themselves" (15:347–
48). He does not diminish the "free grace and mercy of God" but
shows that "good works, good will, good endeavors" are means of
apprehending and responding to grace, so that "the true worship of
God consists chiefly in the exercise of good works," which are "those
we perform by the Spirit of God working in us through true faith."
Thus "the primary efficient cause of good works . . . is God," while
"the *proximate causes of good works* are . . . good habits, or, as they are
called, *virtues;* in which is comprised the whole of our duty towards
God and man. . . . *Obedience* is that virtue whereby we propose to ourselves the will of God as the paramount rule of our conduct, and
serve him alone" (17:3, 5, 27, 69). The obedience of either the unfallen or the regenerate depends on free will. When one "is regenerated
by God after his own image . . . for no one generates, except the Father," he is renewed "in all the faculties of his mind; that is to say, in
understanding and will. . . . This renewal of the will can mean nothing, but a restoration to its former liberty." But, again, one has to
make use of liberty: "we could ask nothing more of God, than that,
being delivered from the slavery of sin, and restored to the divine
image, we might have it in our power to obtain salvation if willing.

Willing we shall undoubtedly be, if truly free, and he who is not willing, has no one to accuse by himself. But if the will of the regenerate
be not made free, then we are not renewed, but compelled to embrace salvation in an unregenerate state" (15:371–73).[14] Since the
same image is generated and regenerated, Eve's argument that freedom is necessary for obedience in the separation colloquy is perfectly
sound; and that obedience is figured forth in the work of Adam and
Eve, which integrates the twofold calling to worship their Creator "in
the exercise of good works" and to preserve and improve the creation
for the common good.

In general, Protestant expositors interpreted Genesis 2:15 and
2:18, the calling to dress and keep the Garden and the creation of
woman as meet help, as proof that everyone should engage in a "particular calling," with marriage a help to that end. John Cotton gives
three tests by which to know a warrantable calling, all of which apply
to Milton's gardeners. It is one "wherein we may not onely aime at
our own, but at the publike good," and it is known "when God gives
a man *gifts* for it, that he is acquainted with the mystery of it, and
hath gifts of body and minde sutable to it" and "when a man enter-
prises not a calling, but in the use of such meanes as he may see Gods
providence leading him to it." These requirements met, he advises,
"If thou wouldst live a lively life, and have thy soule and body pros-
per in thy calling . . . , serve God in thy calling, and doe it with cheer-
fulnesse, and faithfulnesse, and an heavenly mind."[15]

Protestant commentary on Adam's calling tends to be as literal as
the Fathers' was mystical, partly because of the segregation of nature
and grace already noted, partly because of a distaste for "Popish"
allegory that, by supposing the scriptures enigmatic, makes them the
property of ecclesiastical authority, and partly because of a desire,
which Milton shared, to assert their historical truth and apply their
lessons to immediate ethical concerns. By taking the commandment
to dress and keep the Garden seriously, Protestants gave Milton the
opportunity to heal the breach they themselves created between literal and figurative meanings by his mimetic integration of them; his
"fit audience," though never before confronted with a dramatization
of original righteousness that answered to their sense of calling, were
prepared by the commentators to receive one and apply its implications to themselves. Calvin's commentary, Englished in 1578, provides a model:

> Seeing God would haue man to be exercised in tilling of the earth, he
> condemned in his person, all idlenesse. . . . Moses addeth that Adam
> was made ouerseer of the garden, thereby to declare, that upon this
> condition we possesse those thinges which the Lorde giueth vnto us,
> that we being content with the moderate and temperate vse of them,
> may lay vp in stoare the remainder. He which possesseth land, must
> so receive the yearly fruit thereof, that he suffer not the ground through
> carelessenesse to decay, but ought to endeauour him selfe to leaue the
> same to his posteritie as good, or rather better then he found it. . . . let
> euery man consider that he is the Lordes steward, in all those thinges,
> which he hath vnder his hand.[16]

Other commentators often stressed the dangers of idleness more than
the responsibilities of stewardship. Salkeld suggests that the work of
cultivating Paradise was "a pleasure and a voluntary effect of [Adam's]
well-disposed mind" provided specifically to help him keep himself
from sin;[17] and Gervase Babington adds, *"God sette man in this Garden,
to dress and keepe it,* not allowing Man in his most innocencie to bee
idle: no, hee would not his Angels to wante what to doe, but made
them ministring Spyrits."[18] Alexander Ross and Andrew Willet,
both moderate Anglicans, sum up generally accepted literal, moral,
and cautiously mystical interpretations. To the question "Should
man have wrought in Paradise?" Ross replies, "Yes: but not for need,
and with trouble, as now: but with pleasure, to keepe himselfe from
idlenes. Secondly, thereby to stirre him vp the more to contemplate
heauenly things. And thirdly, to try the diuers natures of grounds,
and of those things that grow on the ground."[19] And Willet comments
that Adam's delightful labour was enjoined both "that beeing thus
occupied in continuall beholding of the goodly plants in Paradise, he
might thereby bee stirred vp to acknowledge the goodnesse and
bounty of the Creator" and to instruct us against idleness.[20] Both Sir
Thomas Browne and John Donne defend the nonallegorical, but
nonetheless moral, nature of Adam's calling. Browne rejects the
common notion that man was made erect to fix his eyes on heaven,
appealing to Galen's opinion that "Man is Erect, because he was
made with hands, and was therewith to exercise all Arts, which in
any other Figure, he could not have performed."[21] Donne argues
that "Adam was not put into Paradise, onely in that Paradise to contemplate the future Paradise, but to dresse and keep the present";
and like Calvin he makes stewardship a continuing obligation: "We

are bound amongst other duties, to keep the world in reparation, and leave it as well as we found it." Summing up the two callings which Milton will mimetically unite both to each other and to their "Spirituall" meanings, Donne adds, "We have here two employments, one to conserve this world, another to increase God's kingdom."[22]

All of these explicators agree that idleness, the proverbial nurse of vice, had no place in Paradise, and implicitly support Eve's concern for the Garden as a part of the process of obedience. But they do not mention Eve. Milton is the first to dignify her calling as meet help by giving her meet work to do, "gifts of body and minde sutable to it," and an understanding of "the mystery of it" that not only equals but sometimes surpasses Adam's.

"Unceasing Care"

Of the three traditions under consideration, the one most tending to deny Eve a responsible role is the pastoral, adopted with the intention of Christianizing Arcadia, but often with the effect of paganizing Eden. Critics who have noticed Milton's affinity with classical pastoral but overlooked his emphasis on active response to calling have produced two lines of interpretation: the nostalgic reading, which makes prelapsarian life charming but irrelevant,[23] and the rebel reading, in which the Fall is an escape from a tiresome bucolic repose.[24]

One of the recurrent motifs of the pastoral tradition is natural abundance and freedom from labor, and this theme gained topical interest from disastrously optimistic reports from the New World. Classical and neoclassical examples of "earth's innocence of cultivation" have been gathered by J. M. Evans, who cites Vergil's fourth *Eclogue:* "the fields become golden with soft corn and the ripening grape will hang from the unpruned thorn . . . the soil will not suffer the plowshare or the vine the pruning knife"; and Hilary's adaptation to Genesis: "And the cornfield was already bringing forth fruit from the tender ears of grain, while no yokes existed nor any plowshare for the plow, and no bull lowed in the furrowed fields. Lo, even the vine already laden with juicy clusters of grapes, not having felt the pruning fork and still without knowledge of the hard iron, was weaving shades of vine-leaves on the high hills." Meanwhile, according to Dracontius, Adam and Eve "would walk through the flowers and the rose-gardens everywhere, through the scented crops and the green groves, innocently, like the tame herds or the wild animals," while according to Proba, "Gardens fragrant with yellow flowers beckon them amid the perfumed grove of laurel, and the earthe bore everything of itself . . . quite spontaneously."[25] Milton's Adam, of course, distinguishes man's daily work, which declares his dignity and heaven's regard, from the rovings of "other Animals" that "unactive range, / And of their doings God takes no account"; and Milton arms Eve with "such Gardning Tools as Art yet rude, / Guiltless of fire had formd, of Angels brought" (9.391–92).

Reversing the rabbis' association of the cultivation of the Garden with the keeping of God's law, much pastoral poetry associated freedom from cultivation with freedom from external law and government. Ovid's description of the Golden Age, popularized by Golding's and Sandys's translations, was often echoed in Renaissance poetry and applied to the New World where many hoped to see the Golden Age revived:

> Then sprang vp first the golden age, which of it selfe maintainde,
> The truth and right of euery thing vnforst and vnconstrainde.
> There was no feare of punishment, there was no threatning lawe
> In brazen tables nayled vp, to keep the fold in awe. . . .
> The fertile earth as yet was free, vntoucht of spade or plough,
> And yet it yielded of it selfe of euery thing inough.[26]

The coincidence of the revival of classical literature and the discovery of a New World full of economic and evangelical opportunities naturally brought forth an association of scriptural Eden, classical Arcadia, and the "Fruitfullest Virginia" Spenser urged his queen to claim.[27] According to the more idealistic — and also to the more avaricious — advocates of colonization, the Americas were an earthly paradise offering liberty, abundance, and the chance of a commonwealth in which the inconveniences of man's estate caused by Adam's fall could be relieved by scientific, economic, and political means. Milton alludes to this undoctrinal optimism when he comments in *Areopagitica*, "To sequester out of the world into *Atlantick* and *Eutopian* polities, which can never be drawn into use, will not mend our condition" (4:318). But while the polities of Bacon and More recommended piety and industry, others looked for ease, inspired by reports such as those of Captain John Smith and of Captain Barlowe, who wrote to Ralegh in 1584, "Wee found the people most gentle, louing, and faithfull, void of all guile, and treason, and such as liued after the manner of the golden age. The earth bringeth forth all things in aboundance, as in the first creation, without toile or labour."[28] Drayton's ode to Virginia reflects this vision of effortless living and virtuous heathen as it extolls

> Earth's onely paradise,
> Where nature hath in store
> Fowl, venison, and fishe,
> And the fruiteful'st soyle
> Without your toyle,
> Three haruests more,
> All greater than your wish.

Her natives are happy folk "To whome the golden age / still natures lawes doth giue."[29]

Gonzalo mimics these fantasies in *The Tempest* while trying to divert the king from his untimely grief: were this his colony, his says, he would admit "no name of magistrate" and "no occupation—all men idle, all; And women too, but innocent and pure"; he would have "no sovereignty"—a liberty which, owing to the shipwreck that inspired the play, the colonists at Jamestown had experienced to their sorrow—but

> All things in common nature should produce
> Without sweat or endeavor. . . . Nature should bring forth,
> Of its own kind, all foison, all abundance,
> To feed my innocent people. . . .
> I would with such perfection govern, sir,
> To excel the Golden Age.
>
> [2.1.145–68]

Shakespeare, like Milton, prefers a more realistic and responsible attitude toward both tilth and virtue, for in Prospero's wedding masque for the future rulers, Ceres and Juno link earth's fertility with the joys of chaste and fruitful marriage, and Ceres' domains are explicitly cultivated ones, unlike Gonzalo's "tilth, vineyard none," for she comes from fields of tended grains, "meads thatched with stover," "banks with pioned and twilled brims," and a "pole-clipped vineyard" to promise "barns and garners never empty" (4.1.60–117), all products of providential husbandry.

The moral and practical deficiencies of New World Utopianism brought criticism from both the stage and the pulpit. The villains in *The Tempest* provide a running gloss on Gonzalo's dream—"all idle, whores and knaves"—and in *Eastward Hoe* Seagull assures Scapethrift in that "there we shall haue no more Law then Conscience, and not too much of either."[30] The strenuous puritan William Crashaw told the Virginia Company in 1609 that "those who want present profit and scoff at the purpose of planting a Church proclaim themselves *Sowes that stille wallow in the mire* of their profit and pleasure."[31] But rumors of three harvests a year tempted the Ferrars to send colonists to Jamestown so ill-provisioned that thousands died. In 1622 John Donne sought with greater tact and sympathy to rectify the Company's expectations, already brought closer to reality by hardship, frustration, and a massacre, reminding them of their evangelical responsibilities in a sermon on Acts 1:8. "*Libertie* and *Abundance*," he says picking up the twin golden-age themes, "are Characters of kingdomes, and a kingdome is excluded in the *Text;* the *Apostles* were not to looke for it in their employment, nor you in this your Plantation."[32]

Milton's impatience with the flaccidity of otiose views of either man's first estate or his present condition, his contrasting sense of process in nature and in men's relations to it, and his lifelong insistence on the responsible use of creative energy are already apparent in his own poems in the pastoral tradition, *Arcades*[33] and *Lycidas,* and in his *Mask.* In *Arcades,* the Genius of the northern Wood says that it is his job to "nurse the Saplings," save plants "from nightly ill," "heal the harms" of thunder, unpropitious planets, and "hurtfull Worm," and, like Eve, hasten forth early to "Number my ranks, and visit every sprout / With puissant words, and murmurs made to bless" (44–60). In the *Mask . . . at Ludlow-Castle,* to Comus's doctrine that nature's bounty is to be enjoyed, the Lady replies with asperity that it is to be justly used (705–78). And in *Lycidas,* comparing the pastoral calling to that of both poet and priest, Milton contrasts the "unceasing care" of the true shepherd both to the levity of those who "sport with Amaryllis in the shade" and to the greed of "blind mouths" who "scarce themselves know how to hold / A Sheep-hook, or have learn'd ought els the least / That to the faithfull Herdmans art belongs!"

In *Paradise Lost,* the cultivation of God's gifts by human effort and imagination demonstrates Milton's belief in active response to grace.

By showing Adam and Eve caring for the Garden, he differs sharply from many contemporaries. For example, in Serafino della Salandra's *Adamo Caduto* (1647), Adam, surveying nature's bounty, exclaims,

> The gift is all the greater, in that we
> Ourselves supply no merit, while the Giver,
> No past or future servitude imposing,
> Has lavished treasure of such amplitude.

With a frivolity, even a rapacity, utterly opposed to the concern of Milton's Eve for "her Nurserie," della Salandra's Eve replies,

> Each hour that fills my bosom with such flowers
> Equals the rapture of a thousand years.
> It seems each calls you to adorn with it
> Your hand and breast, and says: "O gather me!
> 'Tis for your sake I stand upon my stem!"[34]

The opposition of grace and merit, though intended for the glory of God, seems inevitably to lead to a life of self-indulgence for the less contemplative Eve. In Andreini's *L'Adamo,* Eve wanders through the Garden, before she has met the Serpent, beckoned by flowers she sees vainly, as does della Salandra's Eve, as adorning and adoring her. Nature, as Eve's mirror, is idolatrous, desirous, and entrapping. "Yonder leafy tree," she muses,"Weaving its foliaged arms to rival Heaven, / Desires above my tresses to spread out / A rich sky of green leaves." Distant flowers

> Turn their glad eyes on me and seem to say,
> "Let neighboring flowers rejoice to be a carpet
> Beneath your feet, but we, like eagles proud,
> Gaze from afar but to behold your face,
> A humble image of the Face divine."

Other flowers, "desiring / That I should sit among them," form themselves into hedges and "in a thousand gentle knots / Weave with such skill a secret snare of herbs / That the unwary scarcely shall escape — / The hand that frees the foot itself is caught."[35] In *L'Adamo,* nature is opposed to grace and allied with Eve. In *Paradise Lost,* Eve by her art is a participant in grace.

Taken literally, the commandment to subdue the earth and exercise dominion over its creatures is unpalatable to modern readers who see it abused as an excuse for exploitation. Its allegorical mean-

ing, the government of passions and appetites, should serve as a cor-
rective to such abuse. In dealing with its literal implications, Milton
refines their application to experience. "Dominion," from *dominus,*
means lordship. As images of a providential God, Adam and Eve are
"Lords of all" whose calling is to foster life. One of the pleasantest
features of most hexamera is the eager obedience of the beasts as
they pay homage to Adam. In *Paradise Lost* both the beasts, who are
"duteous at her call" (9.521), and the flowers that spring at her coming are responsive to Eve. The Garden responds in its vegetable
way, the beasts in their animal way, and men in their rational way to
beneficent lordship, and this response, as we have seen, is the way
each being grows toward its singular perfection. By this process of
calling and response rendered visible in their gardening, Adam and
Eve go hand in hand with nature.

The relations between the operations of nature and the operations
of art, dominion, and grace in Milton's Garden are rooted in the definition of nature Milton provides in *De Doctrina Christiana,* in which
he distinguishes between the laws of nature, which God's providence
upholds, and nature itself, which is the "power and efficacy" of his
own voice.

> His ordinary providence [as distinguished from special providence]
> is that whereby he upholds and preserves the immutable order of
> causes appointed by him in the beginning. This is commonly, and in-
> deed too frequently described by the name of nature; for nature cannot
> possibly mean anything but the mysterious power and efficacy of that
> divine voice which went forth in the beginning, and to which as to a
> perpetual command, all things have since paid obedience. [15:93]

"Nature," then, is the calling and enabling by the divine voice, and
the operations of nature are responses to that voice, a concept that is
powerfully dramatized in Raphael's account of the creation. As creatures of God, Adam and Eve are responsible to that voice within
themselves, which is their own nature as rational beings: "Our
Reason is our Law" (9.654). As creative and providential images of
God, Adam and Eve obey the divine voice within themselves and
exercise its power by bringing the inward powers of other creatures
to full fruition.

We have seen, then, that Milton accepts and develops some
strands of the patristic, the classical pastoral, and the Protestant tra-

ditions concerning man's first estate and rejects or amends others. From the Fathers he keeps and develops implications about the divine image, the virtues of original righteousness, the figurative meanings of the Garden, and the first commandments, but he rejects ideas of an immediate, inevitable, or fortunate Fall, the preference for contemplation and celibacy, and the notion that woman represented the bodily and corruptible part of man. From the pastoral tradition he preserves a love of beauty and a delight in sensuous and amorous pleasure, but rejects the trend toward love of idleness and irresponsibility. From Protestant commentary on Genesis, he cultivates and applauds commendation of marriage and the idea of calling, but avoids the puritan tendency to be suspicious of art and pleasure and to separate man's natural from his spiritual good. With regard to calling, this distrust of the things of this world separates worldly work from heavenly grace. With regard to marriage, it suggests that sexuality is intrinsically corrupt, a superstition roundly exorcised in Milton's celebration of "the Rites / Mysterious of connubial Love" (4.742 ff.). Binding together the joint callings of Adam and Eve to work and marriage and the joint endeavors of body and soul for the perfecting of both, Milton shows Adam and Eve engaged in the "mutual help," and preeminently the "mutual help to piety" (4.88) through all other helps, that for Milton is the essence of marriage. Of all the Reformation writers on marriage, except perhaps Donne, Milton makes all its pleasures and responsibilities most mutual. Of all writers on calling, only Milton gives Eve equal work, equal talent, and equal opportunity for growth and accomplishment.

"An Art that Nature Makes"

The dualism that opposes grace to merit and nature to art produced numerous attacks on poetry and the theater and, in reaction, numerous defenses of them, often embedded in literary texts, crowned by Sidney's *Apologie*. As Edward Tayler has shown,[36] pastoral poetry in the Renaissance often opposed art and nature, a bit suicidally it would seem, and it became the business of poets to show in their craft how art and nature, in Sidney's words, go hand in hand. Milton did not write a tract defending poetry, but he wove one through his prose, and he embodied one in the gardening of Adam and Eve, and especially in Eve.

Attitudes toward art in descriptions of God's Garden are varied, but they have in common the absence of a responsible human gardener. The *Mundorum Explicatio* (1661), attributed to Samuel Pordage, agrees with other Golden Age poems in making cultivation—and, by implication, all human arts—a postlapsarian phenomenon: "No dainty Flower, which art makes now to flourish, / But then the earth did naturally nourish."[37] In contrast, in a creation poem often compared to Milton's, Du Bartas manages to combine *otium* with the opposite artistic excess of "curiosity" as Adam "vnderneath a fragrant Hedge reposes, / Full of all kindes of sweet all-coloured Roses, Which (one would think) the Angels daily dress / In true-loue knots, tri-angles, lozenges."[38] Eve's attitude toward roses repudiates both Pordage's and Du Bartas's. She goes hand in hand with nature as "them she upstaies / Gently with Mirtle band" and waters "from th' ambrosial Fount."

Du Bartas's "true-loue knots, tri-angles, lozenges" alludes to a vogue among courtly gardeners analogous to a vogue among courtly poets for intricate versifying, both more conducive to admiration of the artist than to the health of their fruits. Tudor and Stuart gardens were highly architectural and ornamental, laid out in careful geometric patterns containing walks and terraces, pyramids, mounts, arbors, turrets, statuary, fountains, mazes, complicated herbal "knots," open "knots" or flower-beds, and elaborate topiary pruning.[39] The horticultural sun-dial in Marvell's "The Garden" represents a common artifice, as does Shakespeare's "curious-knotted garden."[40] A taste for such niceties is often attributed to women, or recommended as a pastime to keep them out of mischief. Barnabe Googe suggests that rosemary is appropriate to be "sette by women for their pleasure, to grow in sundry proportions, as in the fashion of a cart, a peacock, or such by things as they fancy."[41] So it is not surprising that George Puttenham in his *Arte of English Poesie,* which develops a theory of art on the familiar metaphor of the garden, devotes a chapter to what might be called topiary poetry, shaped in "triangles, lozenges," and other fanciful forms, which like Googe he relegates to the ladies, as it is "fittest for the pretie amourets in Court to entertain their seruants and the time withall, their delicate wits requiring some commendable exercise to keepe them from idleness."[42]

In contrast to these curiosities, Adam and Eve assist the natural fruitfulness of the Garden by lopping wanton growth that makes embraces fruitless, by "scant manuring," watering, propping and upstaying, and by clearing green alleys enough "to tread with ease."

Milton repudiates the fashionable trivializing of both art and nature when he chooses blank verse over rhyme and when he describes the flowers of Paradise "which not nice Art / In Beds and curious Knots, but Nature boon / Powrd forth profuse on Hill and Dale and Plaine" (4.241–43). At first glance Milton seems to oppose art to nature in these lines as simpler poets had done. But the distinction is not between art and nature but between degenerate art, which is "nice" and "curious," and the art Adam and Eve practice in their Garden and he in his poem as likenesses of the "Sovran Planter." Art increases fruitfulness when it goes hand in hand with nature, which is the art of God, whose images the artists are.

The relation between the art of poetry and the art of gardening, or the perfecting of nature, is declared in Renaissance manifestos about the nature of art.[43] Sidney presents the view that the poet is the vicar of God's voice, himself a product of the art of God, the Maker of makers or the Poet who composes poets; these in turn go "hand in hand with nature" not only by imitating her forms but by participating in her productive ways.

> Neither let it be deemed too sawcy a comparison, to ballance the highest point of man's wit with the efficacie of nature: but rather give right honor to the heavenly maker of that maker, who, having made man to his owne likenes, set him beyond and over all the works of that second nature, which in nothing he showeth so much as in Poetry: when with the force of a divine breath, he bringeth things foorth surpassing her doings: with no small arguments to the incredulous of that first accursed fall of Adam, since our erected wit maketh us know what perfection is, and yet our infected will keepeth us from reaching unto it.[44]

If Adam had not fallen, presumably poets and gardeners would not only surpass but perfect that second nature, since there would have been no cleavage between wit and will or between art and life to be bridged and no infections to be remedied.

The distinction between the art that perfects nature's forms and the art that creates forms nature herself would not have made concerns George Puttenham, who discusses the related arts of gardening, poesie, and physic.

> In some cases we say arte is an ayde and coadiutor to nature, and a
> furtherer of her actions to good effect, or peraduenture a meane to
> supply her wants, by renforcing the causes wherein shee is impotent
> and defectiue, as doth the arte of physicke. . . . Or as the good gardin-
> er seasons his soyle by sundrie sorts of compost . . . and waters his
> plants, and weedes his herbes or floures, and prunes his branches, and
> vnleaues his boughes to let in the sunne: and twentie other waies cher-
> iseth them, and cureth their infirmities, and so makes that neuer, or
> very seldome any of them miscarry, but bring foorth their flours and
> fruites in season.

Other practices of poets and physicians, however, make "arte not
only an aide and coadjutor to nature in all her actions, but an alterer
of them . . . as to make a single gilliflour . . . double: and the white
rose, redde." The arts of language, Puttenham continues, are not
counterfeit arts, but natural ones perfected by exercise. But the poet
most admired, because most natural, not only does "as the cunning
gardiner that vsing nature as coadiutor, furders her conclusions,"
but works "even as nature her selfe working by her own peculiar vertue and proper instinct."[45]

Shakespeare makes similar distinctions in *The Winter's Tale* when
Perdita rejects "streaked gillyvors" because "there is an art which in
their piedness shares / With great creating Nature." Polixenes replies,

> Say there be,
> Yet Nature is made better by no mean
> But Nature makes that mean. So, over that art
> Which you say adds to Nature, is an art
> That Nature makes.
>
> [4.4.82–86]

His example is grafting, which he links to breeding; and Perdita replies by rejecting hybrids, also in sexual terms. The passage distinguishes, like *Paradise Lost,* between "art" (which Polixenes defends)
and "nice" or "curious" art (which Perdita denounces). Adam and
Eve do not graft or hybridize, and their tools are "guiltless of fire," so
that their practice agrees with Perdita's ideal. But they do exercise
"an art that nature makes" in shaping and adorning as well as ordering and nurturing, in such integrated ways that, as Polixenes argues,
"art itself is Nature."

Nature, like art, can mirror one's inward states. Readers often see
reflections of distempered passions in the Garden's "wanton growth,"

of self-discipline in the work of clearing and pruning, of sexual pleasure and fertility in its abundance of delights, and of the "Paradise
within" in its tranquil beauty.[46] Inferences about self-cultivation, self-
awareness, and self-fulfillment should be drawn with caution, as we
know from the scene at the lake. If the Garden is only a mirror, or a
simulacrum of inward states, Eve in turning to her work is turning
from one well of Narcissus to another. If it is a "true and locall Paradise" but dualistically separate from "spiritual increase," then Eve as
she upstays her roses, "mindless the while, / Her self, though fairest
unsupported Flour," is not just mindless of the approaching Serpent,
as the passage literally means, but also mindless of her responsibilities toward Adam and toward God. But if Adam and Eve cultivate
all the faculties of the mind *by means of* cultivating a real garden with
real claims, and for its sake as well as their own — "For the performance of good works" — then there is no rivalry between the Paradise
without and the Paradise within, or faith and works, or nature and
art. In their experience, "inward" growth results from attention to
"outward" responsibilities, toward God, toward each other, toward
future children, and toward the Garden; the "Paradise within" is the
result of "answerable deeds." Eve's work in the Garden is a means of
perfecting her faculties, including memory, and if she is self-forgetful
among her roses she need not on that account forget God's commands, one of which she is engaged in obeying. It is not her poignant
mindlessness, either of herself or of what she supposes to be a perfectly harmless beast, that brings about her fall, but her forgetfulness of
her real responsibilities in order to give full attention, as Satan pretends, to "inward Powers" (9.600). Until then, she is still God's image,
fostering that image unselfconsciously by fostering life, and mindful
of "each Flour."

The particular gardens that Milton compares with Eve's handiwork suggest that art is more fully united to nature and human merit
to divine grace in Milton's Paradise than in its analogues. When
Satan finds her, Eve is at work in a "Spot more delicious then those
Gardens feign'd / Or of reviv'd *Adonis,* or renownd / Alcinoüs, host of
old Laertes' Son" (9.439–41). Homer's description is of a carefully
planned and fully humanized garden in which "the King did aime, /
To the precisest order he could claim."[47] It suggests a prudential manipulation of nature quite different from Edenic profusion, and does
not direct attention to the voice of God either in the gardener or in

his material. On the other hand, Spenser's allegorical garden of Adonis is a place of spontaneous generation, artless nature, and uncultivated grace, wholly sustained by "that divine voice which went forth in the beginning."

> No needs there Gardiner to set, or sow,
>   To plant or prune: for of thir owne accord
>   All things, as they created were, doe grow,
>   And yet remember well the mightie word,
>   Which first was spoken by th'Almightie lord,
>   That bad them to increase and multiply:
>   No doe they need the water of the ford,
>   Or of the clouds to moysten their roots dry;
> For in themselves eternall moisture they imply.
>
> .   .   .   .
>
> And in the thickest covert of that shade,
>   There was a pleasant arbor, not by art,
>   But of the trees owne inclination made,
>   Which knitting their rancke braunces part to part,
>   With wanton yvie twyne entrayld athwart,
>   And Eglantine, and Captifole emong,
>   Fashioned above within their inmost part,
>   That neither Phoebus beams could through them throng,
>   Nor Aeolus sharp blast could worke them any wrong.
>   [3.6.34, 44]

In a series of unmistakably allusive contrasts, in Milton's Garden "whatever was created, needs / To be sustained and fed" (5.414–15); trees need to be planted and pruned, flowers to be "water[ed] from the'ambrosial Fount" (11.279), and the vine "led . . . to wed her elm" (5.215–16). The "blissful Bower" whose roof "of thickest covert was inwoven shade / Laurel and Mirtle" (4.690–94) combines divine and human arts, for it was designed by God, and adorned by Eve.

At the opposite extreme from the artlessness of the Garden of Adonis in *The Faerie Queene* stands the depraved artifice of the Bower of Bliss. Here, the obvious sexual connotations of gardens which in the Garden of Adonis, *The Winter's Tale,* and *Paradise Lost* pertain (among other things) to human generation are no longer procreative. Like the trees and flowers of the earthly paradise in the *Roman de la Rose,* whose portress is Idleness, those of the Bower of Bliss are symbols of refined but inorganic delectation. Its wanton and illusory abundance, reached by the Idle Lake, exemplifies the art that conceals art: "And that which all fair works doth most aggrace, / The art which all that wrought, appeareth in no place" (2.12.58). Neither of Spenser's allegorical gardens of human sexuality is cultivated by a visible gardener. One spontaneously obeys the inward voice of God, while the other is contrived by a parodic and hidden artificer. In Milton's garden, the voice of God, issuing the linked commandments to dress and keep the Garden and to increase and multiply, elicits responsible human action. And so, as Satan approaches Eve employed among her roses, we know exactly whose hand has been at work: "the hand of Eve."

Notes

1. For an excellent account of the habit of objective intellectual analysis of moral choices in Milton's age see Camille Wells Slights, *The Casuistical Tradition in Shakespeare, Donne, Herbert, and Milton* (Princeton, 1981).

2. Perkins, *The Whole Treatise of the Cases of Conscience,* in *Workes,* 2:57.

3. Donne, *Sermons,* 2:346.

4. In, for example, Ovid's *Metamorphoses* and both patristic and Protestant explications of the Song of Songs. The *Exposition of the Song of Songs* published by William Gouge (London, 1615) explains that the Spouse gathers "flowers for the solemnization of marriage. That is, to furnish her selfe with spirituall graces . . ." (p. 57, mispaginated 65). The verse "I am the rose of Sharon, and the lily of the valleys" (2.1) provides figures of Christ. The Fathers often allegorized flowers as the prayers of the saints. An anthology of "spiritual helps" published in 1610 is titled *A Garden of spirituall Flowers* (and cf. the etymology of *anthology*).

5. As Stella Revard points out, "If Eve were truly unable to bear the responsibility of 'separateness,' surely Raphael would have cautioned Adam here at this very moment of the danger of allowing Eve to fare forth alone" ("Eve and the Doctrine of Responsibility," p. 72).

6. Robert Grosseteste [d. 1253], *The Castle of Love* (a fourteenth-century translation from the Anglo-Norman), ed. James Orchard Halliwell (Brixton Hill, 1849), p. 3.

7. Thomas Morton, *A Treatise of the Threefold State of Man. Or, An Anatomie of the Soule* (London, 1629), pp. 310–11.

8. *The City of God, SLNPNF,* First Series, 2:256. For additional examples of allegorical readings see Evans, *"Paradise Lost" and the Genesis Tradition,* pp. 69–77.

9. *De Genesi ad Litteram,* in J.-P. Migne, *Patrologiae Cursus Completus,* Seria Prima [Latina] (Paris, 1844–), 34:379; hereafter cited as *PL*. This translation is by David F. Bright.

10. Donne, *Sermons,* 5:176–77. The point of Donne's distinctions may be clarified by comparison with Prynne's *Anti-Arminianism,* cited below. For a full discussion of Donne's doctrine of nature and grace and its applications to marriage, see Lindsay Alfred Mann, "John Donne's Doctrine of Marriage in Its Historical Context" (Ph.D. dissertation, University of Illinois, 1965).

11. Ralegh, *History,* pp. 35, 39, and 32.

12. Perkins, *An Exposition of the Creede, Workes,* 2:152–53. Conventionally both kinds of calling apply to each man. Milton uses the terms differently in *De Doctrina Christiana,* to emphasize his belief that all men are called to salvation, though many do not respond, when he speaks of the "general calling" of all mankind to salvation and the "special calling" of "particular individuals in preference to others" for special purposes (15: 347–51).

13. Prynne, *Anti-Arminianism* (1630), p. 72; quoted in Woodhouse, *Puritanism and Liberty* (London, 1938), p. 232. Milton firmly rejects the deterministic idea of pre-destination to reprobation: "It has been the practice of the schools to use the word predestination, not only in the sense of election, but also of reprobation. This is not consistent with the caution necessary on so momentous a subject, since wherever it is mentioned in Scripture, election alone is uniformly intended" (*De Doctrina Christiana,* 14: 91).

14. Milton's terminology of renewal makes distinctions which sustain and clarify his sense of process and of the relation of the natural and the supernatural. The key terms are *restitutio, redemptio, renovatio,* and *regeneratio,* translated by Bishop Sumner as *restoration, redemption, renovation,* and *regeneration* (Book I, chapters XIV–XVIII). *Restoration* is the most general term, encompassing *redemption* and *renovation;* renova-tion in turn covers *natural renovation,* or *calling,* and *supernatural renovation,* or *regenera-tion:* "The *restoration of Man* is that act whereby man, being delivered from sin and death by God the Father through Jesus Christ, is raised to a far more excellent state of grace and glory than that from which he had fallen. In this restoration are com-prised the *redemption* and *renovation of man.*" Milton does *not* say "a more excellent state . . . than if he had not fallen," and since Adam and Eve are in the process of being raised by grace and merit before the Fall, we need not think that their disobedience was fortunate or that the Son's participation need have been less triumphant without it. Milton continues, "*Redemption* is that act whereby *Christ, being sent in the fulness of time, redeemed all believers at the price of his own blood, by his own voluntary act, conformably to the eternal counsel and grace of God the Father.*" Prevenient grace, or "gratuitous redemp-tion," he continues, is seen in the Judgment, which promised a saviour before man's repentance. *Renovation* is "that change whereby *he who was before under the curse, and ob-noxious to the divine wrath, is brought into a state of grace.*" It proceeds in two "modes," the "natural" and the "supernatural": "By the natural mode, I mean that which influ-ences the natural affections alone. This includes the calling of the natural man, and the consequent change in his character. [¶] *The calling of man* is that natural mode of renovation whereby *God the Father, according to his purpose in Christ, invites fallen man to a knowledge of the way in which he is to be propitiated and worshipped; insomuch that believers, through his gratuitous kindness, are called to salvation, and such as refuse to believe are left with-out excuse.*" This calling is universal, is sufficient for each man, and enables his re-sponse by freeing his will, which since the Fall is entrapped in sin; and it induces the co-operation of the hearer: "The change which takes place in man by reason of his calling, is that whereby the natural mind and will of man being partially renewed by a divine impulse, are led to seek the knowledge of God, and for the time, at least, undergo an alteration for the better." This part of renovation is natural and may be temporary, since each man may refuse the calling or fail to persevere in repentance and faith; the restoration of the whole man depends on his regeneration: "The intent of *supernatural renovation* is not only to restore man more completely than before to the use of his natural faculties as regards his power to form right judgment, and to exer-cise free will; but to create afresh, as it were, the inward man, and infuse from above

new and supernatural faculties into the minds of the renovated. This is called *regeneration*, and the regenerate are said to be *planted in Christ.*" Regeneration, though the last division of Milton's analysis of the process of renovation, is also the summary and completion of all its parts, and its definition reproduces that interaction of grace and responsive service, each growing in response to the other, and of reciprocally increasing liberty and obedience found in all parts of the process—an interaction divided here for the sake of clarity into "natural" and "supernatural" stages but reintegrated in those "planted in Christ" and originally unified in Adam and Eve in the process of planting and being planted in God's Garden. See Barker, *Milton and the Puritan Dilemma,* especially ch. XVII, and "Structural and Doctrinal Pattern," p. 171-72, and passim, especially the statement, "What supernatural renovation restores, in men who exercise their responsibility, their naturally renovated and their new powers thus to obtain salvation, is the divine image. Milton was never moved to revise his belief that the unwritten Law of God is that 'law of nature' given to the first man, of which remnants and a kind of reflection remain in all men's hearts, and which in the regenerate is day by day being renovated in the direction of its primitive (or prelapsarian) perfection" (p. 172).

15. John Cotton, *The Way of Life* (London, 1641), pp. 439-40.

16. Calvin, *A Commentarie vpon Genesis,* pp. 68-69.

17. Salkeld, *A Treatise of Paradise,* p. 144.

18. Gervase Babington, *Certaine Plaine, brief, and comfortable Notes, vpon euery Chapter of Genesis* (London, 1596), p. 21.

19. Ross, *The First Book of Questions and Answers upon Genesis,* p. 45.

20. Willet, *Hexapla in Genesin,* p. 26.

21. Browne, *Pseudodoxia Epidemica,* pp. 212-13.

22. Donne, *Sermons,* 7:104, and *Essays in Divinity* (London, 1652), pp. 154-55.

23. See for example John R. Knott, Jr., "Symbolic Landscape in Paradise Lost," *MiltonS* 2 (1970).

24. Basil Willey states that Milton did not really like the Edenic myth because it contained a yearning for "the blank innocence and effortlessness of a golden age" which he could not share (*The Seventeenth-Century Background* [London, 1934], p. 229); and Tillyard argues that "reduced to the ridiculous task of working in a garden which produces of its own accord more than they will ever need, Adam and Eve are in the hopeless position of Old Age pensioners enjoying perpetual youth" (*Milton,* p. 282). J. M. Evans counters that "if Adam and Eve stopped working the wilderness outside would soon engulf them," and that furthermore their gardening represents the control of passion and the preservation of virtue (*"Paradise Lost" and the Genesis Tradition,* pp. 249-50). But the work of Adam and Eve not only keeps order and preserves fertility, which if allowed to wanton would destroy itself, but also improves the beauty, strength, and quality of the fruit, of their own virtues, and of their relationship.

25. Evans, pp. 114, 118-19, 131. Translations, from Evans's notes, are his unless otherwise cited. Quotations are from Virgil, *Eclogae,* trans. E. V. Rieu (1961 reprint), 4:28-41; Hilarius Arelantensis, *Metrum in Genesim,* lines 101-7, in *Corpus Scriptorum Ecclesiasticorum Latinorum* 23; Dracontius, *Carmen de Deo* 1.437-45, in Migne, *PL* 60; Proba, *Cento,* 163-69, in *CSEL* 16.

26. *The XV Bookes of P. Ouidius Naso, entytuled Metamorphosis,* trans. Arthur Golding (London, 1567), pp. 2-2ᵛ.

27. In *The Faerie Queene,* proem to Book II, and 4.11.22. Spenser makes the discovery of the New World analogous to the liberation of the poetic imagination.

28. Master Arthur Barlowe (to Sir Walter Ralegh, 1584), in Richard Hakluyt, *The Principall Navigations, Voiages, and Discoveries of the English Nation* (London, 1589), p. 731.

29. Michael Drayton, *Poemes Lyrick and pastorall* (London, 1616?), sig. C4.

30. Geo. Chapman, Ben. Jonson, Joh. Marston, *Eastward Hoe* (London, 1605), sig. E.

31. Crashaw, "A New-Yeeres Gift to Virginea" (preached to the council of the Virginia Company and Lord De La Warr, at the Temple, 1605), sig. C2ᵛ.

32. Donne, *A Sermon Preached to the Honourable Company of the Virginian Plantation* (London, 1622), in *Sermons* 4:269. Here and in a verse letter to the Countess of Huntingdon ("That unripe side of earth," in Shawcross, p. 214), Donne, like Milton in 9.1115–18, indicates that the American Indians, like everyone else, are fallen and in need of regeneration.

33. The anti-Arcadian theme of *Arcades* is discussed by John M. Wallace as "a pilgrimage from the profane to the religious, from the classical south to the Christian north," in "Milton's *Arcades*," *JEGP* 58 (1959): 627–36; revised and reprinted in Barker, *Modern Essays,* pp. 77–87.

34. Della Salandra, trans. Kirkconnell, *The Celestial Cycle,* p. 298.

35. Andreini, *L'Adamo* (Milan, 1613 and 1617), trans. Kirkconnell, *The Celestial Cycle,* p. 242.

36. Edward Tayler, *Nature and Art in Renaissance Literature* (New York, 1964). Tayler documents a wide range of viewpoints regarding the relations of art and nature in Renaissance thought.

37. In Kirkconnell, p. 425.

38. Du Bartas, *Deuine Weekes and Workes,* trans. Joshua Sylvester (London, 1613), p. 228. Grant McColley discusses the possible relations of Du Bartas and Milton at length in *"Paradise Lost: An Account of Its Growth and Major Origins, with a Discussion of Milton's Use of Sources and Literary Patterns* (Chicago, 1940).

39. Such gardens are described, with excellent illustrations, by Alicia Amherst in *A History of Gardening in England* (London, 1896), ch. VI and VIII. She points out that Tudor books on the art of gardening regularly included patterns for mazes, knots, and topiary pruning; John Parkinson recommends the privet as "apt . . . to be cut, lead, and drawn into what forme one will, either of beasts, birds, or men armed or otherwise," and William Lawson tells how "your Gardiner can frame your lesser wood to shape of men armed in the field, ready to give battell: or swift-running Grey Hounds to chase the Deere, or hunt the Hare." George W. Johnson reports that one of Lord Burleigh's gardens at Theobalds reputedly contained "nine knots artificially and 'exquisitely' made, one of which was set forth in likeness of the King's arms" (*A History of English Gardening* [London, 1829], p. 60). See also Niels Bugge Hansen, *That Pleasant Place: The Representation of Ideal Landscape in English Literature from the Fourteenth to the Seventeenth Century* (Copenhagen, 1973), p. 56 and passim. As Hansen points out, "With a better sense of decorum than Du Bartas, [Milton] did not compose his Paradise as a perfect type of 17th century garden with parterres, canals, and rigid symmetry. The French style in garden design prevailed in England in Milton's time, and both in European poetry and painting this fashion had been followed in representations of Paradise" (p. 154).

40. Shakespeare, *Love's Labours Lost,* I.i.249.

41. Quoted in Amherst, pp. 125–6.

42. George [or Richard] Puttenham, *The Arte of English Poesie* (London, 1589), p. 104; facsimile edition, intro. Baxter Hathaway (Kent State University Press, 1970).

43. On Renaissance poetics, see Arthur E. Barker, "An Apology for the Study of Renaissance Poetry," in *Literary Views,* ed. Charles Carroll Camden (Chicago, 1964), pp. 15–43.

44. Sir Philip Sidney, *The Defence of Poesie* (London, 1594), pp. 11, 12–13.

45. Puttenham, *The Arte of English Poesie,* pp. 308–13. The analogy of gardening and physic is particularly appropriate to poetry as a regenerative art. Gardening and medicine were closely related in the Renaissance, and recipes for herbal cures were regularly included in handbooks on gardening.

46. Joseph H. Summers comments that "Those readers who have complained that Milton's Paradise is dull, that it lacks scope for action, must either have failed to respond to Milton's evocation of sensuous and sexual fulfillment or else have considered it unrespectable" (*The Muse's Method* [London, 1962], p. 94).

John G. Halkett finds that "marriage reflects the sensuousness and order of the Garden itself," and "the Garden becomes a consistent and subtle mirror image of their married happiness" (*Milton and the Idea of Matrimony,* pp. 109 and 141). Barbara K. Lewalski points out that Adam and Eve are themselves "'planted' by God" and are "gardeners also of their own paradise within, that is, responsible for perfecting their own natures," and argues that when Eve "goes forth to work in the external garden" she is "'mindless' of her prior responsibility toward the Paradise within" ("Innocence and Experience in Milton's Eden," pp. 91, 93–94). Although I agree with the gist of these comments, I believe that the language of mirrors and reflections can be misleading, for reasons that will appear in the text, and that no dichotomy between "inward" and "outward" Paradises exists in Milton's Eden or in Eve's going forth.

47. *The Whole Works of Homer,* trans. Geo. Chapman, p. 102.

"Summon All":
The Separation Colloquy

The Book of Genesis does not record what Adam was doing while the Serpent was beguiling Eve. It leaves the reader free to imagine whether Adam and Eve were together or apart and, if apart, why. What one imagines reveals one's assumptions about their natures, about their relations, and about God's ways.

Since it seems unlikely that Adam would stand idly by and watch Eve fall,[1] writers have devised various accounts of his conduct or explanations of his absence. Renaissance painters usually conflated the two temptations and assigned to Adam various degrees of remonstrance or collusion.[2] Titian's Adam, though seated, puts out a restraining hand, while Raimondi's and van Scorel's seem to give the fruit to Eve. Most, however, show Eve receiving fruit from the Serpent and giving it to Adam in one fluid motion. Dramatic and poetic versions, proceeding in time and requiring dialogue, could not epitomize the Fall in this way. They nearly always show Satan seeking out Eve separately on the clairvoyant assumption that she will be easy prey. The simpler ones merely present the scene: Eve [alone]; enter Serpent.

As dramatic poets of the Renaissance paid increasing attention to motivation, their craft required them to explain why she was alone. Milton's predecessors found an abundance of ready-made reasons based on the stereotype of female vanity. If Milton was to "assert Eternal Providence" he had now to do something that was indeed "unattempted yet in Prose or Rhime": he had to explain the separation in a way that manifests Eve's sufficiency to stand. His radical solution was to represent Eve's departure as the result of a responsible and considered choice whose outcome might have been, though it was not, the greater good of an unfallen race.

By contrasting Milton's explanation with those of others, we may see that he corrects the entrenched imaginings of Eve's intrinsic vanity by applying to the relations of Adam and Eve the convictions of his arguments for Christian liberty and responsibility. At the same time, he invites richer imaginings of the immediacies and intimacies of unfallen life. In a piquant and portentous dialogue, resonant with tensions and responses that might become either fruitful or fateful in that or any life, Milton invites us to see the manifold possibilities not only of a potential fall but also of potential ascent by degrees of merit through light well used, by two gentle and vibrant beings whose finely-etched and sensitively interactive personalities call forth love and hope as well as prescient pity and grief, showing both capable of weakness but also preserving their freedom and sufficiency to choose well until the very moment of engorging sin. The separation scene shows Adam and Eve in that process of mental and emotional pruning and propping that is the unfallen version of what the reader is called to do in interpreting it: that Psyche-like sorting of the seeds of truth and error that, Milton tells us in *Areopagitica*, grow up together. But to do this circumspectly we need to identify the tares that Milton saw in the field of contemporary opinion. Comparison of Milton's treatment of the separation with those he may have known or inferred from ancient and still-current attitudes toward Eve will show that again and again Milton explicitly dissociates Eve from exactly the weaknesses that his predecessors and contemporaries assigned to her and carefully preserves her unfallen liberty and her delicate yet sufficient adherence to active goodness. If we read with informed and open minds, we may feel, within the perfect tension of painful and hopeful possibility that the scene sustains, that the Fall need not have happened, yet did happen, yet can be repaired, and that the beauty and goodness lost are worth the most exacting labors to regain.

Awareness of the assumptions Milton was resisting, and the more vigilant response to tone it allows, is the more important because the separation colloquy is habitually brought forward, even by subtle and learned interpreters, as proof of Eve's insufficiency, Adam's uxorious weakness, and the inevitability of a fall by creatures already "human"—as if human meant not "Godlike erect" but merely incompetent. A. J. A. Waldock blames the Fall on Eve's "obstinacy on the fateful day, her setting forth alone" and "Adam's weakness here." Balachandra Rajan states that by comparing Adam's response to Eve with contemporary opinion on the subjection of women we see "that he is doomed from the outset. We know that even before he has considered eating the fruit his uxoriousness has sown the seeds of his disaster." E. M. W. Tillyard agrees that "both are virtually fallen before the official temptation has begun," and Millicent Bell that the Fall is "not the onset of sin" but "the beginning of self-discovery by creatures essentially human, which is to say imperfect in a hundred ways." For Douglas A. Day the separation scene proves that Eve's "innate vanity and resistance to teaching which she had revealed in the pond-passage now have begun to be approved by her." Fredson Bowers finds that Adam upset the hierarchical order of creation by granting liberty to a woman, and that "in his role as protector Adam had no right to relieve himself from his responsibility to Eve by making her a free agent"; and Lawrence Babb that "Adam knows that Eve is not completely dependable. . . . Yet he lets her go. In both an internal and an external sense, he has violated the God-ordained scheme of subordinations: he has allowed a lower faculty (affection or passion) to rule the higher, and he has allowed the inferior creature (woman) to govern her superior. . . . She is, after all, a second class human being." Edward LeComte thinks that "the marital difference" is "a rift that becomes as wide as the mouth of hell."[3]

Several questions should be asked. Does human mean weak? Do weaknesses mean doom? Are Eve's motives vain? Did God make her a free agent? Does subordination mean insufficiency? Are Eve's arguments or Adam's permission products of passion? Does Eve govern Adam? Is she a citizen of God's commonwealth?

A second group of critics defend Adam and Eve as developing virtuously in previous scenes, but think the separation scene the beginning of the Fall. Dennis Burden defends Eve in the scene by the lake, seeing that it establishes the consent necessary to true marriage, but says that the liberty Eve claims in the separation scene "is not that liberty which her female nature was created to have" and that "Adam's crucial misjudgment was to approve (despite some gainsaying) her departure from him"; in this one place he finds Milton's epic less than logical, calling the apparent strength of Eve's case a "sleight of hand" Milton has to resort to "in order not to make Adam's intellectual failure too blatant." A. H. Gilbert, who otherwise defends Milton against the charge of misogyny, uneasily clears Adam of fault but not Eve: "Overtrusting Eve, he had allowed her to control the fate of both. Eve, on the other hand, by persisting in her course against the persuasions of Adam, had broken the harmony of ideal marriage. It would equally have been broken, however, if Adam had by force kept Eve at his side against her will." Both Arnold Stein and H. V. S. Ogden stress the importance of distinguishing between potential (but avoidable) and actual sin, seeing other prelapsarian scenes as part of a testing process that need not have led to the Fall; but Stein sees the separation as "the causal decision which already sponsors the act" and Ogden as proof that "Satan's attack on Eve's fancy has come to infect her will; we realize that the Fall itself is imminent"; and both Stein and William Riley Parker in his admirable biography reduce Eve's motive to a "whim." Even Barbara Kiefer Lewalski, who vigorously defends the prelapsarian life of Adam and Eve as one "not of declining innocence but of steady growth toward perfection and knowledge" finds that this process comes to a halt at "the fateful marital dispute"; and even J. M. Evans, who explains with care and clarity both the theological dilemma of supposing Eve fallen before the Fall and Milton's concept of innocence as virtue in the process of development, finds that "Eve's moral defection took place when she decided to leave Adam."[4]

A few critics have seen the separation not as a fatal breach but as an unfortunate but reparable error, a choice of the lesser of two goods, or a thing indifferent, arguing that Adam was right to respect Eve's freedom and that Eve, though perhaps mistaken in her use of it, was not thereby doomed to eat the forbidden fruit. Joseph H. Summers, a sensitive and lyrical celebrant of the innocence and love of Adam and Eve, finds that until each makes the decision to eat the fruit "Adam and Eve still possess their possibilities of freedom and are still perfect — not because problems do not exist, but because they can be solved; not because they do not make mistakes but because they are not fatal." Yet he feels that Eve's argument for parting is "full of obvious errors" and that Adam "abdicates his responsibility" because he "prefers the risk of her destruction to the risk of her momentary resentment." J. Max Patrick, on the other hand, sees the debate as a quarrel but includes it in the growth of Eve's

ability to reason independently and finds her intellectually superior
to Adam, demonstrating "a capacity for reasoning that was anything
but innocent and naive," while Adam's "rational superiority was only
potential, and he failed to achieve it. Instead he tended to yield to
another of his potentialities—his susceptibility to Eve's beauty,
charm, and sensuality." Eve is "a highly sophisticated woman" who
chose to fall "responsibly and freely . . . because she did not bother to
make good use of her faculties." Wayne Shumaker argues that the
prelapsarian scenes to not "dramatize bad states of conscience in
Eve" but rather "suggest the kinds of dangerous impulses which she
might some day cease to control," while "it was proper for Adam,
after expostulation, to allow his hierarchical inferior a measure of
self-determination, as God permitted it to him and to the angels."
Irene Samuel, who demonstrates that "nothing that can be the stuff
of growth is alien to Eden," suggests that Milton "invents the morning dispute between Eve and Adam to distinguish trifling from fatal
errors, as well as to provide a narrative sequence that makes the fatal
error plausible." Thomas H. Blackburn cogently states the theological and literary problems Milton was dealing with in showing Adam
and Eve knowledgeably innocent and truly free, and shows the process of temperate moral choice before the Fall to be compatible with
Areopagitica; of Eve's departure he says, "If, when she remains ada-
mant in her decision to labor away from Adam for a morning, she
does choose a lesser good over a greater, it is to be known as such
only by the outcome (which was not necessitated by her choice to
leave), and she departs forewarned by Adam's last 'reasoning words,'"
adding that "belief in the responsible use of freedom to choose their
own fate underlies Adam's arguments to dissuade Eve from separate
work in the garden, and is finally the reason why he lets her go."
Stella P. Revard makes a strong case for Eve's sufficiency and responsibility for faithful obedience to God and states that although in
this scene it "would have been better had Adam overcome his own
feelings of rejection and voiced the loving plea which might have
won his wife's consent," this "omission . . . is a tactical and not a
moral failure," for "if we would affirm Eden the true mirror-image of
Heaven, [Adam] must leave Eve free to choose and trust, like God,
that he has sent his creature forth sufficient to stand." Stanley Fish
affirms Eve's sufficiency of will, finding her argument in the scene

fallacious but denying that it has any relation to the Fall: her speech is "a negative test of the reader" in which "the reader's ability to perceive the fallacies in her argument measure the extent to which he *now* understands God's logic"; but "since the misconceptions Eve entertains cannot affect her performance at the moment of temptation ('the seat of temptation is in the will, not the understanding'), her speech is more important for the reader's state of mind than for her own; in relationship to the Fall, her state of mind does not matter."[5] Is there, in the decorum of Milton's drama, anything that, in relation to anything else, does not matter?

Finally, one scholar, Arthur E. Barker, has argued that "every prelapsarian action in *Paradise Lost* is so far from foreboding the Fall that it stands in sharpest contrast with it," and that "it may in due course even prove possible to prove that Eve's desire to work alone . . . is a perfectly legitimate, if hazardous (but all such situations are hazardous in the fallen or the unfallen state) expression of justifiably growing and developing (if feminine) individuality";[6] the challenge that initiated the work in hand. What remains is to demonstrate that the separation colloquy not only shows Eve "yet sinless," but also, while displaying the "liability to fall" that is their growing-edge, engages Eve and Adam in just the informed and active liberty, responsibility, truth-seeking, magnanimity, and love that form the gist of any paradise.

"What to Redress"

A week after Raphael's visit, after their morning prayer, Adam and Eve, as the narrator approvingly explains, "commune how that day they best may ply / Thir growing work: for much thir work outgrew / The hands dispatch of two Gardning so wide" (9.201-4). "Growing work" is both wordplay and Miltonic theme; work worth doing increases and multiplies. Eve, taking seriously God's commands, begins,

> *Adam,* well may we labour still to dress
> This Garden, still to tend Plant, Herb, and Flour,
> Our pleasant task enjoyn'd, but till more hands
> Aid us, the work under our labour grows,
> Luxurious by restraint; what we by day

> Lop overgrown, or prune, or prop, or bind,
> One night or two with wanton growth derides
> Tending to wilde.

> [9.205–12]

So far, Eve's speech attests how well attuned she is to the opportunities of their condition. Their task is to "dress" and "tend"; it is both
"pleasant" and "enjoyn'd"; they await "more hands"; discipline promotes abundance that requires further discipline, as the Garden
challenges their efforts by outgrowing their labor and becoming "lux-
urious," "wanton," and "wild." The garden in fact appropriates the
luxuria painters assigned to Eve, so that it becomes the object of her
sober thought as she ponders the challenges of disciplined growth.
"To dress," from *dirigere,* is a rich word, meaning to direct, rule, ar-
range, array, embellish, and remedy as well as till and prune. Responding to these attentions, as gardens do, with bursts of growth,
this Garden elicits progressive "degrees of merit" from its gardeners.

In addition to being a real garden really needing care, the Garden
is a metaphor for well-tempered passions and pleasures; and Eve, as
she tactfully mentions a few lines later, has overheard "the parting
Angel . . . As in a shadie nook I stood behind, / Just then returnd at
shut of Evening Flours" (9.276–78). What she has heard the Angel
say to Adam — who has just been wrestling aloud with his passion for
Eve — is "take heed lest Passion sway / Thy Judgement" (8.635–36).
The imagery of her speech is of the tempering of passions in response
to what Raphael's warnings and, no doubt, her own observations
have told her is Adam's greatest need.

She continues the metaphor by naming flowers that are traditional
emblems of marriage and by gently making explicit the problem of
tempering passion.

> Thou therefore now advise
> Or hear what to my minde first thoughts present,
> Let us divide our labours, thou where choice
> Leads thee, or where most needs, whether to wind
> The Woodbine round this Arbour, or direct
> The clasping Ivie where to climb, while I
> In yonder Spring of Roses intermixt
> With Myrtle, find what to redress till Noon:
> For while so near each other thus all day
> Our taske we choose, what wonder if so near

Looks intervene and smiles, or object new
Casual discourse draw on, which intermits
Our dayes work brought to little, though begun
Early, and th' hour of Supper comes unearn'd.
[9.212-25]

Roses, myrtle, ivy, and woodbine are symbols of conjugal love, but they are also cautionary emblems. Roses, soon to fall withering from Adam's slack hand, signify transient beauty and passion in *carpe diem* and courtly love poetry, and as both Venus's flower and Mary's they represent the choice between divisive *luxuria* and fruitful obedience. Ivy and woodbine, unless directed where to climb, provide similes for opportunistic or tyrannously dependent attachments that kill "as the Ivy climbeth up the Oak, and through time destroys the Tree it was supported by."[7] The ease with which these symbols of *caritas* become those of *cupiditas* urges the perpetual choice between love that obsesses and love that nurtures, the cistern of Narcissus and the fountain of charity. Eve's attention to the Garden, expressed in metaphors of marriage, shows to Adam her awareness that their flowering love for each other will remain harmonious in proportion to their participation in the harmony of all creation, and her question about looks that intermit and intervene is part of her "meet help" in the tempering of passions that could make them vulnerable to concupiscence and jeopardize their freedom.

Among a plenitude of Eves, Milton's is the only one whose motives spring naturally from God's word. Predecessors had provided, roughly speaking, three ways of explaining the separation for Milton to refute. The first attributes it to God's ordinance. The second attributes it to either simplicity, inadvertence, or mere bad luck, in effect equating innocence with incompetence. The third and by far the most frequent attributes it to female vanity and presumption. Obviously, none of these speak well for God's handiwork. If the separation is predestined or haphazard, or if it results from original human weakness or progressive prelapsarian depravity, God has not been provident. If Eve is not sufficient, with Adam's counsel, to stand without Adam's physical presence, her union with "God in him" is defective, her faculties are flawed, and her will is not free. If she is flawed, and Adam is to cleave unto her, God has created a predisposition to sin. One of the primary cruxes of Milton's justification of God's ways is his characterization of Eve; and the crux of his charac-

terization of Eve is her separation from Adam's physical presence on
the morning of the Fall.

The first kind of explanation, which attributes the separation to
God's ordinance, appears in Jewish apocryphal versions. Although
the separation is ordained, Eve proves insufficient to stand without
her guardian angel, whose departure is also predetermined. In the
Vita Adae et Evae, widely circulated in Latin up through the sixteenth
century, Adam on his deathbed tells his sons,

> But God gave a part of paradise to me and a part to your mother: . . . .
> (Moreover) God the Lord gave us two angels to guard us. The hour
> came when the angels had ascended to worship in the sight of God;
> forthwith the adversary found an opportunity while the angels were
> absent and . . . led your mother astray to eat of the unlawful and for-
> bidden tree. And she did eat and gave to me.[8]

In the version known as the *Apocalypsis Mosis,* Eve explains that all
the animals were divided between them, the males given to Adam
and the females to Eve. Further, "when the angels ascended to worship God, then Satan appeared in the form of an angel and sang
hymns like angels. And I bent over the wall and saw him, like an
angel." Then Satan's mouthpiece the serpent, draped over the wall,
persuades Eve to eat the forbidden fruit.[9]

Milton's contemporary John Lightfoot echoes such accounts when,
having attributed the apostacy of the fallen angels to their despising
their charge to minister to man, he explains that they then set out to
bring man into condemnation "by tempting him in his wife the weaker
vessel: shee not yet knowing that there were any Devils at all, but
well knowing that God had allotted her and her husband the custody
of angels, mistooke the Devill that spake in a serpent, for a good An-
gell, and so was deceived by him. . . . "[10] In the Old English "Genesis
B" Satan appears in angel form and announces that God has revoked
the prohibition.[11]

Vestiges of these legends remain in *Paradise Lost,* but significantly
altered and rearranged. The guardian angels are at the gates, not
hovering about *in loco parentis;* they intervene only when Satan is
dropping his ineffectual poison into the ear of sleeping Eve. It is in
this dream, dismissed as "mimic Fansie," that he appears in the form
of an angel. And the purpose of Raphael's visit "till Evening rise"
(5.376), when he ascends for angelic vespers, is not to guard but to

encourage inward readiness, as stressed in his valediction, "Perfet within, no outward help require" (8.642).

These differences all emphasize the responsibility of Adam and Eve for their own faithfulness or disobedience. In the legends, the separation is ordained by God; it is the absence of Eve's angel, not of Adam, that provides Satan's occasion; Eve falls as soon as the angel departs for daily worship; the segregation of the sexes suggests that the forbidden knowledge was sexual knowledge. In the poem, the separation is a carefully deliberated choice; Adam and Eve are entirely on their own and thoroughly prepared; Raphael aids them as teacher, not warrior; Eve is not "uninformed / Of nuptial Sanctitie and marriage Rites" (8.486–87); and she is neither ignorant of devils nor, thanks to her dream and Adam's fervent advice, of their ability to resemble angels or any other "faire appeering Good" (9.354).

The second kind of explanation of a separate fall, that of inadvertence or inattention, depends on the notion that Adam and Eve were either ignorant or simple-minded, a supposition that Milton's separation scene thoroughly forefends. Among early Christian poets, Avitus recounts that while "by chance / The happy young folk from a leafy branch / Were plucking rosy apples," the Serpent coiled himself up a tree and whispered in Eve's ear, apparently in Adam's sight but not his hearing;[12] and Prudentius remarks that "the treacherous serpent beguiled the simple heart of the maid to seduce her male partner and make him eat of the forbidden fruit," again implying that the Fall was sexual: "Each other's body (unlawful knowledge), after eating, they saw uncovered. . . ."[13]

In medieval plays the separation is often casual, again suggesting primitive simplicity. In many, as in most cyclical paintings, Eve has been present at the admonition to abstain from the forbidden fruit, but Satan's enmity has not been revealed to them. In the Norwich play, Adam takes leave of Eve in his first speech to her—curious behavior for a bridegroom—and does not stay for an answer. Naively, he assures her,

> I leve the here alone, I shall not tary longe,
> For I wyll walk a whyle for my recreacion
>   And se ouer Paradyce, that ys so stronge.
>   No thyng may hurt us nor do us wronge;
> God ys ower protectour & soverayn guyde;
> In thys place non yll thing may abyde.[14]

In the Towneley play also Adam departs to survey his lands without thought of inviting Eve:

> Eue, felow, abide me thore,
> ffor I will go to viset more,
> To se what trees that here been;
> Gresys, and othere small floures
> That smell full swete, of seyr coloures.

And Eve replies with cheerful docility, "Gladly, *sir,* I will full fayne; / When ye haue sene theym, com agane."[15] In the Coventry play it is Eve who goes off, after praising God's providence and vowing obedience:

> We may be both blyth and glad
> oure lordys comaundment to fulfyll . . .
> our witte were rakyl and ovyr don bad
> to fforfete Ageyns oure lordys wyll
>   in ony wyse
> in this gardeyn I wyl go se
> all the fflourys of fayr bewte
> and tastyn the frutys of gret plente
>   that be in paradyse.[16]

Renaissance versions in this group sometimes patch up the medieval Adam's want of gallantry by ascribing the separation to his ardent love. In Thomas Peyton's *The Glasse of Time,* Satan waits for Adam to leave his bride "To pluck perhaps a nut among the trees, / Or get a combe amongst the honey bees: / Or some such thing to give his welcome spouse";[17] and in Joost van den Vondel's *Adam in Ballingschap,* Adam asks Eve's permission "to turn aside, / To speak with God and in my solitude / Give thanks to him for thy companionship."[18]

In *Paradise Lost,* Adam views his domain before the creation of Eve and then asks God for a fit companion with whom to enjoy and care for it. Eve goes off alone to gather fruits and nuts for Raphael at Adam's bidding and without mishap. Prayers are always "said unanimous"; "both stood / Both turnd, and under op'n Skie ador'd / The God that made both Skie, Air, Earth and Heav'n" (4.736, 720–22). The reiteration of "both" stresses that Eve had equal part in worship, and the third "both" aurally links their unanimity to the integrity of creation.

Comparison with these versions illuminates the care Milton takes not to make divine decree, mere chance, or original fecklessness the occasion of sin.[19] By the discourses of Raphael and of Adam and Eve in the dream episode and the separation colloquy, he removes all question of ignorance or accident and gives Eve as well as Adam the dignity of inward virtue activated by informed and reasoned choice.

The third kind of reason for a separate fall that Milton refutes, regeneratively, by his separation scene is by far the commonest: the intrinsic vanity of women. The varieties of vanity given prominence in different versions include both worthlessness and vainglory: idleness, pleasure-seeking, light-mindedness, inconstancy, secretiveness, curiosity, concupiscence, self-love, presumption, and an innate desire to do whatever has been forbidden.

Idleness is endemic in the poetry of temptation. Personified, it tends the gates of the gardens of delectation in the *Roman de la Rose* and Chaucer's Knight's tale; topographically it provides passage to the Bower of Bliss. It is linked to the vice of effeminacy, or excessive yielding to women, in classical and Renaissance epics in which the disarmed warrior betrays his manhood in the arms of Circe or Armida. Poems and plays that link Eden with Arcadia exalt a blissful indolence uncomfortably akin to the bowers of effeminacy, and pictorial cycles represent labor only after Adam's "curse" of tilling a recalcitrant earth by the sweat of his brow. Until Eve makes her much-maligned suggestion in *Paradise Lost,* it seems not to have occurred to artists and poets that a keen involvement in interesting work might be one of the joys of Paradise.

Protestant commentators, as we have seen, found in the commandment to dress and keep the Garden a discipline, in Salkeld's words, "to keep [Adam] from idlenes, from sinne, for as it is true . . . that labour blunteth the arrowes of Cupid, so doth it no lesse other darts of the devill."[20] Some expositors blame the Fall directly on a failure to keep this commandment. Henoch Clapham states that since God "could not create anything bad," both the apostate angels and the woman fell "by not kepinge their first estate . . . *not kepinge,* implying Negligence or Idlenes."[21] David Pareus makes idleness the principle condition of the Fall:

> Si enim parentes in colendo horto juxta hoc Dei mandatum fuissent occupati, pro eo quod cùm serpente per otium confabulati, utique non fuissent seducti.[22]

[For if our parents had been employed in cultivating the garden according to the commandment of God, since they chatted with the serpent through idleness, they would not at any rate have been seduced.]

The motive Milton gives Eve for the separation explicitly removes the imputation of disobedience before the Fall that Pareus implies.

It is doubly remarkable that Milton assigns this motive to Eve. The expositors do not mention her; the Fathers were inclined to think that "Mulier typus est vitae mollis";[23] the temptresses in illusory paradises of myth and epic tempt first to idleness. One might expect from precedent that Adam would suggest getting to work and Eve, in voluptuous lassitude, decline. Instead, as she goes forth to tend her garden and to temper the intervening looks and smiles that might otherwise lead to the enervating dalliance of other gardens, it is industry, not covert idleness, that moves her, as we can be sure because work is what she is actually doing when Satan finds her.

A corollary vice incessantly assigned to Eve and to womankind is irrational changeableness, light-mindedness, variability, inconstancy, rashness, love of novelty, lack of perseverance, frivolity, and caprice. On this, too, classical poets, Fathers, medieval playwrights and Puritan moralists agreed: La donna è mobile. Aeneas, distracted by Dido from his manly pursuits, learns from (appositely) Mercury that "ever a various and changeful thing is woman."[24] "Of woman," Ambrose wrote to his sister, "change follows change, their hatreds alternate, their falsehoods vary."[25] Chrysostom explains that God set woman under subjection because she "is in some sort a weaker being and easily carried away and light minded."[26] In *Le Mistére du Viel Testament,* "Satan dressed in a serpent costume and the face of a girl" plots,

> Tout droit m'en vois, pour abreger,
> Tempter la femme en ce party,
> Qui a le couraige legier
> Troplus que n'a pas son mary. . . .[27]
> [To make it short, I'll go straight to tempt
> the woman of this lot, who has a lighter
> mind than her husband's.]

In the *Speculum Humanae Salvationis* the fiend, also in "serpents kynd" with "a womans face,"

> Halding Adam more warre / more wyse, more avysee
> Whils scho was fro the man / come he to hire in hye
> ffor rather man fallis soellel / than in gude companye.[28]
> [for man falls sooner alone than in good company.]

Du Bartas joins this chorus when Satan seeks out "poor woman, wavering, weak, and unwise, / Light, credulous, news-lover, giv'n to lies."[29] The indefatigable puritan compiler of proverbial opinion, Samuel Purchas, though pointing out woman's creation in paradise and her role in redemption, effuses,

> Feminine affections goe not, they runne, rush on, flie with impetuous force, and whatsoeuer they will, *valdè volunt,* they will with a witnesse, their passions generally are more eager, vehement, violent, vnbridled.[30]

Joseph Beaumont explicitly attributes the separation to a sort of mindless unreliability; the Serpent

> towards Eve did gently glide,
> Whom straying from her husband he espied.
> Unhappy Error that, which could invite
> The jealous Tempter to be bold, since she
> Has robbed herself of all her Spouse's Might
> By starting from his holy company.[31]

The absence of all Adam's might suggests that either the Fall was coerced by the "outward force" Milton's Adam denies (9.348 ff.) or that Eve is unteachable.

Perhaps the most thoroughgoing accuser of this kind of waywardness is Hugo Grotius. In *Adamus Exul,* Satan chooses Eve as his fit instrument and lists her useful frailties before he has encountered her, and indeed in the soliloquy with which the play begins, so that he has no warrant for his opinions except the assumptions of his audience. This a priori assertion of woman's inherent inclination to sin appears in Satan's plans in many medieval dramas and is implied by, for example, Eve-faced serpents, Ralegh's "vnquiet vanity," and Lancetta's "concupiscenza." Grotius's Satan muses,

> If Adam can be moved,
> Let him be tempted! But if naught can sway his faith,
> Let us assay his wife! Let this advantage nue,
> That he is not alone. The female mind is light;
> Prone to neglect commands, fickle in undertakings,

> She varies willingly; wanton in self-indulgence,
> She reaches ever in proud hope for greater gain;
> Loves only what she lacks, and finds familiar things
> Tarnish'd, and strange things fair. What is not new displeases,
> Her blest lot's tedium, her frail inconstancy,
> Vain hopes, the color of the sweet-appearing fruit,
> Her lust to taste—All these assure me my desire.
> Woman, apt source of ill, is sure without the rest.[32]

This list of faults is thoroughly commonplace; and in the course of the poem, particularly in the separation scene, Milton refutes them all. "The female mind is light"; Milton's Eve argues with high seriousness that they should not let Satan's envy impede their lives and labors. "Prone to neglect commands": she is specifically proposing to obey one. "Fickle in undertakings," "wanton in self-indulgence": that is just what she tells Adam they must not be. "Loves only what she lacks, and finds familiar things / Tarnish'd and strange things fair": she disclaims "object new" in favor of her "daily visitation." "Her blest lot's tedium, her frail inconstancy . . . assure me my desire"; Milton's Eve finds so little tedium in her lot that she finds it necessary to temper the multitude of interests that draw their discourse on, and then becomes so absorbed in her work that the Serpent himself has a hard job drawing her eye.

In opposition to assumptions of vascillation and rashness, Eve's going forth alone in *Paradise Lost* is a considered, deliberated, informed choice. It results from a decision not to let the Enemy win the victory of hampering their responses to their callings, constricting their God-given freedoms and responsibilities, or substituting physical restraint for constancy of heart.

Two other kinds of "feminine" weakness used to explain the separation are curiosity and love of secrecy. John Trapp in his commentary of 1662, perhaps drawing from literary versions, records the opinion that "the tempter set upon the woman alone and apart from her husband, as she was curiously prying into the pleasures of the garden."[33] This is the view of Troilo Lancetta in whose *Scena Tragica d'Adamo e d'Eua* Eve displays an insatiable desire to view the flocks and herds, glossed as "Curiosita d'Eua." After Adam has shown them to her she goes back to look again on her own and encounters the Serpent. When he asks why she has left her husband and set out alone, she replies,

Io sono vscita della mia stanza solita per riuedere alquanto lo stato di tutte le cose à noi soggette, & mi sono partita con buona licenza di mio marito; me commise perô che adempita questa mia curiositâ, me ne ritorni a casâ, & di già m'incresce tanta dimora.[34]

[I have left my customary room to see again something of the condition of all the things subject to us, and I left with the good permission of my husband; but he charged me, this curiosity of mine satisfied, to return home, and I already regreat so much delay.]

In a nearly identical sequence, in Hans Sachs's earlier *Tragedia von Schöpfung, fal und ausztreiben Ade ausz dem paradeyz,* the Serpent asks, "Weib, wo wilt du hin gehn allein? / Sag! wo ist der gemahel dein?" and Eve replies,

> Ich geh da spacieren hinumb,
> Beschaw desz garten schmuck und zir.
> Mein man hat das erlaubet mir.
> Ietz geh ich heim, er thut mein warten.[35]

[I am walking about, looking at this adorned and dainty garden. My husband has allowed me to. Now I'm going home, he's waiting for me.]

In both plays, the Serpent questions the separation and Eve stresses that she has Adam's permission. In neither does her one pang of conscience prevent her engaging in conversation with the Serpent, and in neither does her interest in the Garden extend beyond idle curiosity. That particular weakness, of course, is connected with lust for "forbidden knowledge," a rehearsal for a fall caused, Ralegh says, by "a desire to know what was most vnfitting for her knowledge, an affection which hathe euer since remayned in all the posteritie of her sexe."[36]

The temptation to secrecy occurs in the Anglo-Norman *Jeu d'Adam,* in which Satan comes undisguised to Adam and Eve separately before reappearing as a mechanical snake whose supposed whisperings the audience can only imagine. In the initial temptation, Diabolus tries to infect Adam with pride by belittling his calling.

> Ne munteras ja mes plus halt?
> Molt te porras tenir por chier,
> Quant Deus t'a fet sun jardenier?
> . . . .
> Forma il toi por ventre faire?
> Altre honor ne te voldra atraire?[37]

[Won't you ever rise higher? Can you congratulate yourself because
God has made you his gardener? Did he make you to take care of your
stomach? Don't you want to gain another honor?]

The clever implication that Adam's work is servile and merely fills
his belly is dealt with in Milton's multileveled vision of cosmic nurture and Adam's understanding that obedience to their calling declares their dignity. In the *Jeu d'Adam,* Adam virtuously repels Diabolus, who then attempts Eve, first swearing her to secrecy and particularly to secrecy from Adam. Eve's promise not to tell Adam the
content of their conversation is of course a step in the Fall. She and
Satan have become, in the words of the *Cursor Mundi,* "on o party /
To ouercome man with trichery" (ll. 727–28). Milton's Eve does not
fall into this sin until she swallows Satan's lies and decides to eat the
fruit without consulting Adam, then speculates that it might be profitable to "keep the odds of Knowledge in my power / Without Co-
partner" (9.820–21). In the separation scene, on the contrary, she
calls for candor, not collusion, and her initial credulousness derives
from a sinless, if misplaced, openness of heart.

A final and especially pertinent assumption about Eve's weakness
appears in a comment attributed to Martin Luther about Satan's
choice of Eve as his target: "Satan, therefore, directs his attack on
Eve as the weaker part and puts her valor to the test, for he sees that
she is so dependent on her husband that she thinks she cannot sin."[38]
This is exactly the trap that Milton's Eve refuses to fall into.

The most damaging explanations for the separation hold that Eve
before the Fall was not only weak but wicked. The sins they accuse
her of are inordinate self-love, evil concupiscence, and overweening
obstinacy.

A *locus classicus* of the belief that Eve was vainglorious and willful
before the Fall is Augustine's question in *De Genesi ad Litteram.*

Quando his verbis crederet mulier a bona atque utili re divinitus se
fuisse prohibitos, nisi jam inesset menti amor ille propriae potestatis,
et quaedam de se superba praesumptio, quae per illam tentationem
fuerat convincenda et humilianda?
[Under what circumstances would the woman believe these words,
namely that they had been prohibited from a good and useful thing by
Divine influence, unless there were already in her mind a certain love
of her own power and a certain proud self-presumption which should
have been defeated and humiliated through the temptation?][39]

The notion that Eve was infected with proud presumption and love of her own power before the Fall, as Evans has remarked, casts "the gravest doubts on her original integrity, and, by implication, on the benevolence and justice of her Creator."[40] However, even if these potentialities were latent in Eve (and Milton does not suggest either that they were actual or that she did not recognize and cope with their possibility), if they *had* been demonstrated and humbled by the temptation itself, without the disobedience, Eve's trial by the Serpent could have been one of those "good temptations" by which Milton says even the righteous may be tried "for the purpose of exercising or manifesting their faith or patience . . . or of lessening their self-confidence and reproving their weakness" (15:87).

Thomas Aquinas, careful like Milton not to let it appear that God has created a defective Eve, explicates Augustine's comment: "This does not mean that pride preceded the promptings of the serpent, but that immediately afterwards a pretentiousness invaded her mind with the result that she credited what the demon told her."[41] This is by no means an inconsequential quibble. That unfallen Eve can be perverted is a concomitant of free will. What matters is whether she can be good. If she is already vain and proud when she meets the Serpent, her nature or her situation has doomed her, and God has not played fair. In *De Doctrina Christiana,* Milton distinguished between the "liability to fall" with which man was created, and the "evil concupiscence" which is an effect, not a cause, of the Fall. "Liability" in the seventeenth century did not mean tendency but a state of being exposed to something and answerable for it. "Evil concupiscence" is the innate propensity to sin with which mankind was burdened by the Fall. Doctrinally, there could be no evil concupiscence before the Fall, but the idea of a "good temptation" raises the difficult question of exactly where temptation ends and sin begins. Milton dramatizes the difference in the Fall itself; until then both Adam and Eve resist temptation and thereby grow in strength and wisdom.

Milton's insistence in *De Doctrina Christiana* that neither Eve nor Adam could have been guilty of evil concupiscence before the Fall is clear in his discussion of original sin, or sin present in one from one's origin onwards. "Evil concupiscence," he says, "that law of sin, was not only naturally bred in us [that is, was not only "original sin"] but dwelt also in Adam after the fall, in whom it could not properly be called original." It is not, then, the same thing as original sin, for "our first parents, in whom . . . there could have been no original sin, were involved in guiltiness immediately upon their fall. . . ." To banish all doubt of the original righteousness of Adam and Eve, he adds, *'Spiritual death,* by which is meant the loss of divine grace, and that of innate righteousness, wherein man in the beginning lived unto God . . . , took place . . . at the very moment of the fall" (15:195, 197, 205). This distinction is also clarified in the ninth Article of Religion appendixed to the Book of Common Prayer:

> Original sin standeth not in the following of Adam [that is, in works of disobedience] . . . but it is the fault and corruption of the Nature of every man, that naturally is engendered of the offspring of Adam; whereby man is very far gone from original righteousness, and is of his own nature inclined to evil, so that the flesh lusteth always contrary to the spirit.

Salkeld makes the same distinction, with the same assumption that before the fall flesh and spirit were at one; sinful concupiscence is "a sickly, corrupt, or infected affection, or inclination" that "doth prevent, or ouerride reason" and "is deprived of original iustice, which in our first Parents, was a power above nature, yet connaturalized . . . vnto their nature . . . ; our originall iniustice consisteth in concupiscence the which though it doth remaine in the regenerate, yet it is not imputed vnto them."[42] This latter point, also made by Milton (15:197) and the ninth Article, constitutes the difference between the unfallen and the regenerate: unlike the former, the latter are afflicted by the inclination to sin; but the guilt of the inclination is removed by Christ's sacrifice, while (as long as the process of regeneration is going forward) they are preserved by grace and effort from its actual commission.

"Our original parents," then — and all three passages specifically include both parents — were, until the Fall, free of the concupiscence, or godless inclination, that afterwards infected them and their posterity. Yet to make doubly sure of their freedom and sufficiency, and of the reader's ability to apply their unfallen state to his own regenerate one insofar as possible, Milton provides Eve with two "good temptations" by which those natural desires which could become inordinate might be "convincenda et humilianda" without sin before the final trial: the lake and her dream; and Adam with one: Eve.

Other interpreters of the Genesis story were not so scrupulous as

Milton, Aquinas, Salkeld, and the Articles of Religion, but attributed pride, presumption, and concupiscence to unfallen Eve as a matter of course. In the most censorious of the analogues, they are the cause or condition of her separation from Adam, and in the most degrading of all, it is the desire for that which is forbidden, because it is forbidden, that draws her from him.

We have already seen that in Andreini's *L'Adamo* Eve sees nature as a mirror of her own beauty. In addition, Andreini imputes to Eve before her encounter with the Serpent the defects to which Augustine attributes her credulity. The Tempter, "disguised as a serpent with a female head, bosom, and arms," is accompanied at the outset by an ally called Vain Glory, suggesting "quaedam de se superba praesumptio." Before she meets him, Eve indulges in a long soliloquy[43] revealing "amor ille propriae potestatis" in which she moves from casting herself as God's servitor to casting God as hers. She begins,

> Handmaiden of a lofty Lord, a low
> And humble servitor, I ought to kneel
> With reverent knee upon the ground to praise
> The love divine and measureless of Him
> Who made me queen of all the Sun surveys.
> But if I raise my eyes and heart to heaven
> Is it not clear to Eve that she was made
> For everlasting and celestial marvels?
> So that in soul or veil'd in mortal flesh,
> Enjoyment should be hers in highest Heaven
> Or on this earth.

The description of nature that follows, with its idolatrous flowers, "thousand gentle knots" and "secret snare" is emblematic of the concupiscence of that anachronistic "mortal flesh." Andreini's Eve continues with an anthem to herself, parodically reminiscent of the prayers of gratitude for which she "ought to kneel" but actually expressive of insatiable ambition, in which she complacently sets nature, Adam, angels, and God himself at her own behest.

> If I should wish for food and drink, behold
> Ready for me are fruits, milk, honey, manna,
> And from a thousand springs, a thousand rills
> Water pours clear as crystal, cool and sweet.
> If I wish music, lo the tuneful birds

And banded angels sing their matchless songs.
If it is lovely day or night I wish,
Behold the Sun, behold the moon and stars.
If for a friend I ask, Adam responds.
If God I would invoke, behold in Heaven
The eternal Maker hearkens to my prayer.
If I crave subject creatures for my rule,
Behold a thousand creatures at my side.
What can I wish for more? What more obtain?
Nothing more, Lord. Eve's cup of honour's full.

On the surface, what she says contains all the traditional elements of Edenic bliss and pertinent praise, but her point of view perverts them to her own self-aggrandizement.

Milton uses the elements of this speech, but in contexts so wholly different as to constitute a deliberate acquittal of Eve.

First, the prayers of gratitude that Andreini's Eve thinks she ought to say alone, kneeling, and with exaggerated subservience, but does not say at all, Milton's Adam and Eve do say, together, standing, with dignity and unfeigned thankfulness. Not until after her fall does Milton's Eve think of herself as "low" and react to the thought with presumption.

Second, in her beautiful love song to Adam beginning "With thee conversing I forget all time" (4.639), Milton's Eve gathers the beauty of nature that in *L'Adamo* she takes as a compliment to herself and bestows it upon Adam: it is his presence, not hers, that gives nature its sweetness for her.

Third, the presumption, not only geocentric but egocentric, that the stars run at her pleasure that Eve reveals in *L'Adamo* has been elicited (in less vainglorious form), acknowledged, and dealt with early in Milton's poem. When Eve wonders why the stars shine when no one is awake to admire them, Adam reminds her both that the stars have other observers, for "Millions of spiritual Creatures walk the Earth / Unseen, both when we wake, and when we sleep," and that stars not only delight and "enlighten" but "Temper or nourish, or in part shed down / Thir stellar vertue on all kinds that grow / On Earth, made hereby apter to receive / Perfection from the Suns more potent Ray" (4.670–78). It is as a participant in this process of "influence," not in vain charm, that Eve is like the stars; later Adam will say, "I from the influence of thy looks receave / Access in every Vertue" (9.309–10).

Fourth, in *Paradise Lost* it is Satan, not Eve, whom nature reflects as a snaring maze: "Hee leading swiftly rowld / In tangles, and made intricate seem strait . . . as when a wandring Fire . . . Misleads th' amaz'd Night wanderer from his way / To Boggs and Mires" (9.631–41). Eve's roses, in contrast to the flattering and deceiving flowers that adore her in *L'Adamo,* not only share her beauty, innocence and vulnerability but thrive in response to her nurturing hand. She does not wander off seeking their admiration but goes forth purposefully to serve them.

Fifth, many passages in Milton's temptation scene are so similar to this one that they may indeed be influenced by it, but it is Satan, not Eve, who utters them.

> Fairest resemblance of thy Maker faire,
> Thee all living things gaze on, all things thine
> By gift, and thy Celestial Beautie adore
> With ravishment beheld, there best beheld
> Where universally admir'd;

all that is good in heaven and earth, he glozes,

> in thy Divine
> Semblance, and in thy Beauties heav'nly Ray
> United I beheld; no Fair to thine
> Equivalent or second, which compel'd
> Mee thus, though importune perhaps, to come
> And gaze, and worship thee of right declar'd
> Sovran of Creatures, universal Dame.
> [9.538–42, 606–12]

Moreover, Milton's Eve promptly reproves this outrageous flattery with good-humored asperity by commenting wryly on the quality of the "Reason" the Serpent claims he acquired by eating: "Serpent thy overpraising leaves in doubt / The vertue of that Fruit" (9.615–16).

When Eve repudiates her reflection in the lake, Milton implicitly rejects the tradition that makes either nature or Satan a mirror of her own corruption, and this theme is reinforced wherever Eve recognizes the dangers of self-love and presumption, while in the analogues they simply inhere in her. In other words, Milton shows that whatever self-willfulness attaches itself to the human condition as lords of creation can be "convicted and brought low," or rather manifested and transformed into gratitude and magnanimity, without sin. In

Paradise Lost Eve copes with her liabilities and thereby learns. In *L'Adamo* they are what she is.

Serafino della Salandra's *Adamo Caduto*[44] presents similar elements in subtler ways. To begin with, he frames the action with the medieval device of a debate between Omnipotence and Mercy, in which an emaciated Mercy complains that unless man sins she will have nothing to do. Therefore, prefigurations of the Fall found in the character of Eve are also preludes to the triumph of Mercy. Milton avoided the implication that one of the attributes of God could not act without sin by showing in Adam and Eve degrees of impercipience, immoderation, and mutability which are "yet sinless" and remediable by means of truthfulness and compassion.

Hints of Eve's perversity in *Adamo Caduto* are slight at first. She has perhaps an excessive interest in snakes, for Lucifer decides to "use that serpent as an interpreter, since I have seen him jesting with Eve, and nestling in her bosom," a motif emblematic of envy. Also, she admits after the prohibition that she finds the forbidden fruit "very pretty." But on the whole she is more intelligent and better informed than previous Eves, has discussed the admonition with Adam at length, and initially puts up a good resistance to the Serpent. Perhaps for that reason, della Salandra does not devise a pretext for her separation from Adam arising out of their dialogue. That is, he could absolve her of a perverse motive but could not, as Milton did, supply her with a responsible one. Instead, he has Adam lured away by Echo, who distracts him by warning them both that the Serpent will cause Eve to tell lies "with her mind and her mouth." Adam, wanting to know more, follows Echo, asking, maladroitly enough, "Dost thou wish my wife to come, or dost thou wish her to stay?" Echo, of course, echoes "Stay."[45]

As we have already observed, the relation of Adam and Eve to nature in this play is that of consumers without productivity. It is Arcadian and anti-Arminian in that human accomplishment is wholly discounted even as a provision of God. The gift of nature's uncultivated bounty is "all the greater," Adam exclaims, "in that we / Ourselves supply no merit." Milton's Adam epitomizes a more energetic response of obedient hearts to grace:

> Let us ever praise him, and extoll
> His bountie, following our delightful task

> To prune these growing Plants, and tend these Flours,
> Which were it toilsom, yet with thee were sweet.
>
> [4.436–39]

Della Salandra's Eve, like Andreini's, thinks that the flowers were created for her own pleasure and adornment and hears each call "O gather me! 'Tis for your sake I stand upon my stem!" Milton's Eve "upstaies" them.

In *Adamo Caduto,* when Adam leaves, with Eve's urging, to follow Echo, Eve roaming and admiring, like Andreini's and Lancetta's, sees the animals "coming to me in legions and legions, for whom the King of heaven created them. They make humble and reverent bows." Milton's Eve is not eager for such homage. As the Serpent approaches "fawning," Eve "busied heard the sound" but "minded not, as us'd / To such disport," and it is his "gentle dumb expression" that finally draws her eye (9.518–27). Della Salandra's Eve is allured at once by the creature she sees coiled in a tree, "Its face . . . that of a woman, its body like a serpent's." It is Eve who does the approaching, exclaiming "Oh, thou art beautiful, charming, agreeable, so variegated, that thou seemst another starry sky or enameled earth. . . . Thou art perfect; thou art all beautiful; speech alone is lacking." The Serpent, of course, proceeds to speak, and in the ensuing dialogue an eager and ambitious Eve elicits the temptation from a mock-reluctant Fiend.[46]

The full implications of the supposition that Eve was naturally attracted to the Serpent because of her inward concupiscence appear in Joseph Fletcher's *History of the Perfect-Cursed-Blessed Man* (that is, unfallen, fallen, and redeemed). Here, Satan "catcht the simple Woman by the snare / Of Serpents subtiltie." But although Eve is "simple," and although sin is defined in the poem as willful disobedience, Eve's part is set forth in a figure in which the blatancy of the grotesque sexuality is mitigated only by the banality of the verse.

> Though *Satan Father,* she was Mother first
> Of Sin, and so for Sin was next accurst.
> She had indeed both formerly conceiv'd;
> And brought forth Sin to Man.[47]

In *Paradise Lost,* Satan begets and conceives Sin autogenically.

In these versions Eve exhibits fully developed self-love and concupiscence before the Fall. In the most extreme antifeminine portrayals, her presumption is so complete that the admonition itself arouses desire for the fruit and she falls "self-tempted" on the grounds that the Wif of Bath claims for her sex, "Forbede us thyng, and that desiren we."[48] In the Chester play, Satan assumes, "That woman is forbyd to doe, / for any thinge therto will shooe," and in Grotius's version he counts on "her lust to taste."[49] In Gasparo Murtola's poem "Della creatione del mondo" (1608), the Serpent is scarcely mentioned. "The woman saw that apple. . . . Nearer she walked with recklessness alarming. . . . What will, o fool, makes you so resolute?"[50]

An extreme example of the notion that Eve fell by sheer "willful disobedience" appears in the work of "an Eminent Divine in Amsterdam" who denies that any Serpent or Apostate Angel tempted Eve at all. Instead, he explains, Eve sees an ordinary snake eating from the forbidden tree and thinks to herself the questions in Genesis. Observing that the beast is still healthy, she begins to resent the commandment, because, as she says at the Judgment, "It was very irksome to me to see the *Serpent* solace himself with the Fruit and that I (being more noble than that Brute) should be forc'd to look on contentedly without setting my Teeth in it also." "Whence we learn," the expositor advises "that man is the cause of his own misfortune, we don't lay the Fault on the Devil, but own it to be ours. . . . We assert that mankind is wholly corrupt, that he is naturally inclin'd to ill." This abject disavowal that God might have empowered Adam and Eve to achieve any "degrees of merit" whatsoever paradoxically begs the question it claims to answer; for the author gives as a reason for his heterodox reading, "if he hath given the Devil a Power and a Capacity to make that Brute speak, we should make no Scruple to Assert that God himself is the Author of Sin, and the cause of the Fall of our first Parents Adam and Eve."[51]

The *Adamo* of Milton's near contemporary Giovanni Francesco Loredano falls into this final and most damaging group of explanations of the separation by alleging a natural disposition in women to do whatever is prohibited. After Adam explains the admonition,

> The Woman became at those prohibitions the more curious. To forbid a woman, is to increase her appetite. He that denies anything, adds a spurre to that desire, which is ardent in all things; but, in things prohibited, insatiable.
>
> The Woman, therefore, transported by those impatiencies, that interposed between them and their felicity, left *Adam;* desiring to injoy

without testimonys, and without check, the sight of that fruit, which
being forbidden, was to be supposed the more exquisite.

The Woman, the more distant she is from her Husband, the more
adjacent she is to.Sin; and, whilst left alone, is in perill of destroying
herselfe, because she gives incouragement & opportunity to any one
to tempt her.

Needless, almost, to say, Loredano's Serpent has "the face of a dam-
sell," and his Eve is so ready to disobey that tempter and tempted are
reversed: "Having found the tree, she beheld the fruits with so much
curiosity, that it induced the Devill to tempt her."[52]

In *Paradise Lost,* it is not until the Serpent has entirely had his say
that Eve, worshipping the Tree, utters the blasphemy: "[God's] forbidding / Commends thee more" (9.753–54).

The reason for imputing evil concupiscence and pride to Eve before the Fall is not only a masculine attempt to blame women for sin.
It derives, I think, from a legitimate but ill-conceived desire to give
the experience of Adam and Eve a cautionary semblance to our own.
Its text is James 1:14, which Tyndale translates "But euery man is
tempted, drawne awaye, and entyced of his own concupiscence."
John Trapp, commenting on Eve's sin, derives the moral, "Satan
hath only a perswasive sleight, not an enforcing might. It is our own
concupiscence that carries the greatest stroke."[53] The point is that
Satan has power only by means of man's own collusion, and on this
Milton certainly agrees, since there would be no free will otherwise.
But to imply that either Eve or Adam through her was predisposed
to sin is to deprive them of free will from the beginning. If for Milton
regeneration means the restoration of God's image "in understanding
and in will" so that "the whole man is sanctified both in body and
soul, for the service of God, and the performance of good works,"
and if "this renewal of the will can mean nothing, but a restoration to
its former liberty," Milton must demonstrate the operations of the
original righteousness and the freedom to stand that regeneration renews. To do this, he must invent for Eve motives for her separation
from Adam at the Fall which will serve for the free obedience of regenerate men and women. If he can show that Adam and Eve are
truly not "self-tempted" but are developing in virtuous ways until the
Serpent perverts those ways, then he can show that not only has God
been provident, not only are their wills truly free, but their natures
(and their children's children's) can be restored by regeneration;

mankind is not hopelessly sinful, but, redeemed and regenerate, can with grace and effort walk again in God's ways.

"Reasoning Words"

When Eve suggests that they (like the poet) might sometimes do their best work in solitude, the discourse of Adam and Eve turns to the most serious matter they have yet encountered. Informed as they are by their own past trials and by Raphael's news of Satan's designs, they have to decide what effect they are going to allow the presence of evil to have on their lives.

Historically, the question of what an individual, a community, or a congregation must do to preserve both the integrity of faith and goodness and the liberty to exercise and develop them in the face of impurity and inticement has been called "the puritan dilemma." For the individual, the problem is whether it is possible to consort with "publicans and sinners" and keep one's constancy to God; for the church, it is whether strict and immutable forms of government and observance are necessary to avoid error and corruption, or whether discipline may be accommodated to the conditions of men with the general guidance of scripture and the Holy Spirit. The horns of the dilemma on which the puritan revolution was tossed were truth and liberty; translated into the choices of daily life, they are purity and charity. In the years that Milton devoted to trying to resolve the puritan dilemma, his steadfast position was, as Arthur E. Barker states it, that "reformation according to the word of God and true liberty are inseparable." Since Adam and Eve are in the process not of the reformation but of the formation of a holy community, Milton's answer must be, necessary changes made, applied to them also. If, as Barker continues, Milton believed that "human reason, rightly guided, is the image of God in us remaining," it will also be the image of God in Adam and Eve as yet untarnished. The right guiding is provided by the revealed word of God, which is not yet written but comes to Adam and Eve as the direct voice of God, as accommodated to their condition through the poet Raphael, and by the Spirit whom the poet Milton invokes as guide, who "from the first / [Was] present," and whose temple is "the' upright heart and pure" (1.17–20).[54]

In order to savor the tone of the dialogue that precedes the separation (9.226–384), we need to read it not only from our own point of view as readers who know that the Fall is going to happen and who bring with us our own experience of postlapsarian domesticity, but also from the points of view of the characters themselves, who know only that a fall is possible and that they have the responsibility not only to stand but also to preserve the freedom for the sake of which the possibility of falling exists. Since the scene has so predominantly been interpreted from the former point of view, with stress on fore-shadowings of sin, I shall adopt the latter, exploring Eve's freedom to stand as a good creature of God who need not and should not fall, with stress on foreshadowings of the freedom and responsibility that regeneration will restore.

The narrative voice moves from approval as Adam and Eve "commune how that day they best may ply / Thir growing work" to uneasiness within the tension of the dialogue to compassionate lament as Eve withdraws her hand. It provides a sympathetic frame, but between speeches intervenes to probe our sense of tone with comments that elicit our own habits of mind. We can hear in the narrator's comments the irritations of our experience of fallen discourse or not, as we choose; no word requires them, yet if we select their fallen connotations the sum of words permits them. Thus:

> To whom the Virgin Majestie of *Eve,*
> As one who loves, and some unkindness meets,
> With sweet austere composure thus reply'd.

Virgin Majesty: pristine and uncorrupted dignity. *As:* a comparison, not a direct description. *One who loves* (the loving is preeminent) *and some unkindness meets:* among much kindness. *With sweet austere composure:* with sweetness, simple gravity, and poise. Would such composure ring as disguised asperity in Adam's ears, or only ours?

> To whom with healing words *Adam* replyd.

Healing words; can there be wounds in innocence? These free beings, yet unfallen, express a full range of feeling; the peace of Paradise is neither nocent nor innocuous, but includes vulnerability, compassion, and remedy, and love's sensitivities want solace even there.

> So spake domestick *Adam* in his care
> And Matrimonial Love; but *Eve,* who thought
> Less attributed to her Faith sincere,
> Thus her reply with accent sweet renewd.

The narrator is more approving of Adam, admitting ambiguities, and testing our responses, towards Eve. "Less," Richardson explains, is "an Elegant Latinism" meaning "too little."[55] Yet Eve replies "with accent sweet." The phrase may unsettle and annoy us; we may suppose that only the accent is sweet. But since her faith is "sincere" there can be no duality between her outward expression and her inward thoughts. The divorce between the tongue and the heart occurs at the Fall.

> So spake the Patriarch of Mandkinde, but *Eve*
> Persisted, yet submiss, though last, repli'd.

Again, the nonparallelism of "the Patriarch of Mankinde" with simple *"Eve"* gives weight to Adam's speech, yet the wavering locution about Eve ends in balance. Eve, having kept her stand, is still submissive, though she has the last word. The economical "yet" means both "still" and "nevertheless." She submits to Adam's instruction and persists— is steadfast—in her intention. Like "sweet austere composure" and "accent sweet," "persisted" (from *stare,* to stand) catches our annoyance without having any etymological warrant to do so. I think that Milton purposely elicits these irritable responses from us by the narrator's collusion with them, yet the words that elicit them do so only by the connotations that we ourselves provide.

After the dialogue, however, the narrator's tone changes to yearning poignancy at the moment of Eve's departure, when "from her Husbands hand her hand / Soft she withdrew." The knowledge that the dialogue has been spoken handfast, or that before its conclusion Adam's hand has again seized hers, spreads an afterglow over its tone that should dispel any suspicion we might have had that it is a domestic squabble and confirm its gravity and tenderness. This tone and Eve's continued innocence are reaffirmed by the conclusion of the narrative frame. The nymphs and goddesses it compares to her are among the most blameless in the classical pantheon, personifying Eve's beauty, chastity, and nurturing care. She and Adam part as lovers:

> Her long with ardent look his Eye pursu'd
> Delighted, but desiring more her stay.
> Oft he to her his charge of quick returne
> Repeated, shee to him as oft engag'd
> To be returned by Noon. . . .

Then, in a rare instance of direct address comparable to Homer's to the beloved Eumaios, the narrator is moved to exclamation by his compassion for Eve; and again the lines test our response to Eve, this time in the form of surprise by syntax: "O much deceav'd, much failing, hapless *Eve*, / Of thy presum'd return! event perverse!" Again, we are tempted to think what the analogues have so insistently insinuated: that Eve herself is "deceiv'd" and "failing" before the Serpent tempts her. But after the enjambment we see that "much deceav'd, much failing" does not modify "hapless Eve," which is direct address, but her state of mind about her return. Of that she is deceived; of that she will fail; but so far, she herself is only "hapless," ill-chanced. It is the "event" — the still undetermined outcome — that is perverse, not Eve; and when she fails it is not because she is sinful beforehand but because, as Bunyan's pilgrim also finds and as Adam's pleas for vigilance might have prepared her to perceive, there is "a way to hell even from the gates of heaven."[56]

The language of the dialogue itself, as Beverley Sherry has demonstrated, remains within the decorum of unfallen discourse, as established by the contexts of infernal and celestial utterance and revealed in its honesty, its reasonableness, and its mutual responsiveness.[57] Its imagery, rhetoric, prosody, complexities of tone, and narrative frame all support the view that Adam and Eve are "yet sinless." Its perverse parodies are the soliloquies in which Satan tries to justify his separation from God, exhibiting the pride that forsakes God rather than the dignity that relies on God's having done his part, while its true models are the heavenly colloquys for whose "thousand vagancies" of joy and felicity it terrestrially strives.

The decorum of unfallen utterance does not flow with the naive simplicity of happy rural swains without a care. The difficulties Adam and Eve are coping with are both personal and cosmic, and the resolution of the "dilemma" will affect those multitudes Eve has been promised she will bear. The speakers are complexly and deeply human. There are hesitations, false moves, even moments of injury and defensiveness, though not of the bitter postlapsarian sort; and after each, poise is recovered, accommodation is made, so that the discourse is not discord but harmony with accidentals, those passing dissonances that enrich the song. These are not bashful lovers but "Lords of all" committed forever, and they work out their deepening relation through the intimacies of tension and distinction as well as attraction and agreement. The play of stress and courtesy in their tone springs from the freedom within conjunction of their marriage. That tone is knit to the theme of their dialogue, the nature of obedience for free and growing beings, and the theme to its form, a debate. Human reason is discursive, as Raphael observes (5.488–89), and truth proceeds afoot, by contraries, even before the Fall.

The *débat* begins with the reciprocal courtesies with which unfallen Adam and Eve habitually acknowledge one another. Adam addresses Eve as "Associate sole, to me beyond / Compare above all other Creatures deare." She begins her reply, "Ofspring of Heav'n and Earth, and all Earths Lord," and he antiphonally responds, "Daughter of God and Man, immortal *Eve*." As the dialogue proceeds the formality of these addresses, but not the dignity, gives way to fervor.

Adam's mild reply to Eve's proposal to divide their labors approves her desire to "fulfill the work which here / God hath assign'd us" and "good workes in her Husband to promote." He then considers its implications in the pro-and-con rhythm of discursive understanding, fitly dressed in metaphors of nurture and imagery of sweetness and satiety. The actual controversy begins when he says, "But other doubt possesses me, least harm / Befall thee sever'd from me." From this point on Milton compresses the questions of Christian liberty and responsibility that he labored over in his prose into intimate and urgent colloquy.

Adam's speech reveals an accurate apprehension of the nature of the Foe and his workings, known to both, "for thou knowst / What hath bin warn'd us." He speaks in the terms of equality at first — "each / To other speedie aide might lend at need" — and rightly speculates that Satan may attack either their fealty to God or the envied bliss of conjugal love.

Eve replies by acknowledging her awareness of the Enemy, "both by thee informd" and "from the parting Angel overheard."[58] But in fact Eve has "heard attentive" (7.51) the entire account of the war in heaven and the warning that

> hee who envies now thy state . . . is plotting how he may seduce
> Thee also from obedience, that with him
> Bereavd of happiness thou maist partake
> His punishment, Eternal miserie.

> [6.900–904]

Her allusion to Raphael here is a tactful reminder to Adam, who wishes to "shade" and "protect," of what the "parting angel" actually said; his valediction contains the premise of the rest of Eve's argument: "Perfet within, no outward aid require; / And all temptation to transgress repel" (8.640–41).

The increasing alliteration of the ensuing lines, flowing out of "firmness" and pitting "firm faith" against "fraud" and "fear," may ring in the reader's ear as either stubborness or perseverence. In his discourse on obedience, Raphael has addressed Adam in the singular, as the progenitor on whom the race depends: "thy state . . . Thee also . . . thou maist partake." Now Eve insists that she too is individually responsible for "firm Faith and Love." If that is presumption, it is a far cry from the presumption of other Eves, who presume to disobey God; she presumes a full share in the process of obeying.

Adam's healing reply contains one of his less effective arguments. He wants to avoid "Th' attempt it self," he says (contradictorily to his analysis of Eve's dream) because "hee who tempts, though in vain, at least asperses / The tempted with dishonour foul, suppos'd / Not incorruptible of Faith, not prooff /Against temptation." Eve replies to this part of his argument in a thoroughly Miltonic way that "foul esteeme / Sticks no dishonour on our Front, but turns / Foul on himself" and is, in fact, an opportunity for merit. The second point of Adam's speech, turning on the pivotal and habitual "nor" (306) of his careful reasoning, is better: Eve should not underestimate the malice and the guile of one "who could seduce / Angels" nor "think superfluous others aid." He then turns the graceful astronomical compliment, "I from the influence of thy looks receave / Access in every Vertue," which he rather spoils by wondering why Eve does not feel the same about him. At this point, then, each has made a small display of hurt feelings. But even if the play of sensibilities includes umbrage, whether sportive or earnest, is the reasoning wrong? Is Eve moved primarily by doubt of Adam's trust or by a genuine desire to be trustworthy? Is Adam spurred by wounded pride at Eve's supposing herself able to do without him for a while or by a real desire for mutual support? In cases of mixed motives the modern habit of mind is to take the baser motive as the "real" one; but paradisal discourse always gives opportunity for candor, which Milton defines as the virtue "whereby we cheerfully acknowledge the gifts of God in our neighbor, and interpret all [her] words and actions in a favorable sense" (17: 311).

So far the debate has preserved an emotional as well as a rational balance. In the first exchange, both have spoken reasonably and responsibly, though neither has fully acknowledged the kind of responsibility the other has in mind. In the second exchange, each has labored to express important principles, and each learns by the effort, but each also gives a hint of unsettled self-esteem. Compared with the previous speeches, these are groping ones, though still within the decorum of "Virgin Majesty" and "Matrimonial Love." Eve's next speech (9.322–41) recaptures moral clarity and turns the tide in her favor with a succinct compendium of *Aeopagitica.*

Eve's question is packed with Milton's libertarian fervor.

> If this be our condition, thus to dwell
> In narrow circuit strait'nd by a Foe,
> Suttle or violent, we not endu'd
> Single with like defence, wherever met,
> How are we happie, still in fear of harm?

Our condition: that is, the human condition, a long-term consideration. Eve addresses the condition of the human family they are to found, of the church for which the Garden is type and metaphor, and of each person laboring to increase in wisdom and goodness wherever wickedness and folly are at large. *Thus to dwell / In narrow circuit strait'n'd by a Foe:* Even, Milton says in *Areopagitica,* if it were possible to expell sin by shutting people up in hermitages (but "ye cannot make them chaste, that came not thither so"), even then

> look how much we thus expell of sin, so much we expell of vertue: for the matter of them both is the same; remove that, and ye remove them both alike. This justifies the high providence of God, who though he command us temperance, justice, continence, yet powrs out before us ev'n to a profusenes all desirable things, and gives us minds that can wander beyond all limit and satiety. Why should we then affect a rigor contrary to the manner of God and of nature, by abridging or scanting those means . . . both to the triall of vertue, and the exercise of truth. It would be better to learn that the law must needs be frivolous which goes to restrain things, uncertainly and yet equally working to good, and to evil. And were I the chooser, a dram of well-doing should be prefer'd before many times as much the forcible hindrance of evill-doing. For God sure esteems the growth and compleating of one vertuous person, more then the restraint of ten vitious. [4:320]

The only phrase that needs changing for this passage to apply to the condition of Adam and Eve is the last, to "the restraint of ten for fear they might become vitious"; for Adam and Eve are constantly aware of "younger hands" whose growth and completing will be encouraged or hindered by the policy they choose now.

The most questionable word in this part of Eve's speech is "single." On the whole, singular virtue is commended in the poem. Without it one could not be "perfet within." When good angels fight, "Leader seemd / Each Warriour single" (6.232–33). Eve has heard through Raphael the speech of God to Abdiel:

> Servant of God, well done, well hast thou fought
> The better fight, who single hast maintained
> Against revolted multitudes the Cause
> Of Truth, in word mightier than they in Armes.
> [6.29–32]

Later, Michael will commend Enoch for "daring single to be just" (11.703). The questions remain, however, whether single virtue is possible for a woman and whether it is appropriate within a marriage.

As for the first, tradition tends against it, largely because "Adam was not deceived, but the woman being deceived was in the transgression" (1 Tim. 2:14). But that is *ex post facto,* and, in any case, it concerns the husband's authority, in which Eve concurs, although it is not until after her sin that she is told "hee over thee shall rule" (10.196; Genesis 3:16). On the whole, scripture does not exempt "weaker vessels" from separate obedience, but on the contrary singles them out for it, be they younger sons of women. Mary accepts the task announced by Gabriel alone. Esther and Susanna risk all for justice. Peter teaches that wives whose husbands "obey not the word" may win them to God by their "chaste conversation" (1 Peter 3:1–2): may, in other words, not only obey God without their husbands' support but may support and convert unbelieving husbands. Even the woman taken in adultery is told—and perhaps trusted—to go and sin no more (John 8:11).

Whether single virtue is appropriate within a marriage may be considered in two contexts: the marriage itself and the church it epitomizes.

Within the marriage, Eve's proposal is an affirmation that "unfeign'd / Union of Mind" (8.603–4), not the "outward formality" that

Milton says in *Tetrachordon* is "no way acceptable to God" (4:126), is
the essence of wedlock, which Milton identifies as "conjunction of
minde . . . not necessarily conjunction of body" (4:104). Adam has
called her "an individual solace dear" and wants "to have thee by my
side" (4.485–86); and his tenderness wins her to "Conjugal embraces"
and

> Those graceful acts,
> Those thousand decencies that daily flow
> From all her words and actions mixt with Love
> And sweet compliance, which declare unfeign'd
> Union of Mind, or in us both one Soule.
> [8.600–604]

But it is to preserve, not to negate, this kind of alliance that Eve re-
sists formal indivisibility from Adam's side.[59] For her, as for Britomart, love thrives on endeavor;[60] like Donne's "trepidation of the
speares" and Milton's "eccentricall equation" in the dance of the
blessed, Eve's eliptical path, potentially, "is innocent."[61]

The unity of mind that Adam and Eve enjoy represents also the
unity of the church. Milton was writing at a time when its unhappy
divisions were a source of much woe, yet also when the work of reformation was in danger of solidifying into formula. It would be a
mistake to see sectarian separatism in Eve's departure or prelatical
coercion of conscience in Adam's desire for her stay; the mutual responsiveness of their colloquy, rather, unveils the processes of matrimonial and congregational accommodation. They are working out
the kind of harmony that Milton argued for in the church, which was
composed of concord in things essential to salvation and a congruous
variety in everything else. "The house of God," he wrote in *Areopagitica,* cannot be built without "many dissections made in the quarry
and in the timber . . . neither can every peece of the building be of
one form; nay rather the perfection consists in this, that out of many
moderat varieties and brotherly dissimilitudes that are not vastly
disproportionall arises the goodly and the graceful symmetry that
commends the whole pile and structure. Let us therefore be more
considerat builders, more wise in spirituall architecture" (4:343).
Eve, considering the formation of a godly community, which is what
they are about, is concerned to avoid the slavish conformity under
whose yoke no true church can be wrought, and so implies to Adam
what Milton, quoting the prayer book, says of the church: "Those

neighboring differences, or rather indifferences . . . need not interrupt the *unity of Spirit* if we [will] but find among us *the bond of peace*" (4:349–50).

But Eve's concern bears on a matter that goes beyond church discipline to the heart of doctrine. Everything that Milton wrote springs from his belief that the true temple of God's Spirit is "th'upright heart and pure" (1:18); this is not only the stated premise of the poem but the condition of writing the poem, since Milton in his nightly solitude becomes the instrument of the Spirit he invokes by just such inward readiness as Eve desires. Within the church, unhampered responsiveness to the Spirit is a requirement for unity, since it is the Spirit who unifies. According to Pauline doctrine the church is one body (like a marriage) with diverse members having different gifts, "but all these worketh that one and the selfsame Spirit, dividing severally as he will" (1 Corinthians 12:11). Milton argues for freedom for those regenerated in God's image just as Eve argues for it for those generated in God's image, because "narrow circuit" prescribed by foe or prelate is presumption against the Spirit. Unfallen Eve prefigures the regenerate response which, Michael predicts, the "Wolves" of a secularized church will try to circumscribe:

> themselves appropriating
> The Spirit of God, promised alike and giv'n
> To all Beleevers; and from that pretense
> Spiritual Lawes by carnal power shall force
> On every conscience; Laws which none shall finde
> Left them inrould, or what the Spirit within
> Shall on the heart engrave. What will they then
> But force the Spirit of Grace it self, and binde
> His Consort Libertie; what, but unbuild
> His living Temples, built by Faith to stand,
> Thir own Faith not anothers: for on Earth
> Who against Faith and Conscience can be heard
> Infallible?
>
> [12. 518–30]

If Adam's perfectly justified anxiety led the pair to enact laws that were not of God, either "left them inrould" as explicit commandments or engraved on the heart, they would have bound the liberty to which grace is wedded and granted Satan the victory of "carnal power" over "living Temples, built by Faith to stand."[62]

The choices of Adam and Eve in Paradise will resound to the whole human family. That is true of all moral choice in a world where spiritual powers are active, but it is especially true for the parents of mankind, whose choices will affect the conditions of all choice. They have been warned of Satan's apostasy "lest the like befall / In Paradise to *Adam* or his Race" (7.44–45); the "or" extends the hazards and opportunities of Paradise into the racial future. Adam and Eve are discussing the crucial question whether human society is to be founded on fear and restraint or education and trust. Eve's "narrow circuit" is not only less space to roam; it signifies the result of allowing the Enemy to define and circumscribe their opportunities. That is God's prerogative, who except for "One easie prohibition" has given "Free leave so large to all things else" (4.432–33). It is fitting that Eve should be the advocate of free responsiveness, since she represents those whose liberty would be most bound in a defensive community. A policy of physical contingence (as distinguished from union of mind) implies the carnal dependence Milton fought. One must stand on "his own Faith, not anothers"; the person who gives up his faith into the care of another, censor or prelate or divine, "makes the very person of that man his religion; esteems his associating with him a sufficient evidence and commendatory of his own piety. So that a man may say his religion is now no more within himself, but is become a dividuall movable, and goes and comes neer him, according as that good man frequents the house" (*Areopagitica,* 4:334). To depend on Adam for her piety would be in Eve a kind of idolatry, so that to preserve "religion . . . within" she has to be a kind of "dividual movable" herself.

Eve argues reasonably, and Adam decides not to bind his consort. Both are right. That is not to say, however, that Eve needed to fight "singly" at the time of the temptation. On the contrary, Satan's attempt to shred their voluntary union of heart could have increased it. When he began to throw her faith in doubt, she should have sought help from God and Adam at once.

How are we happie, still in fear or harm? Eve's question echoes, perhaps, Augustine's "Whether man had . . . perturbations in Paradise, before his fall": "Who can be directly happy that either feares or sorrowes?"[63] But Milton's idea (and Eve's) of the peace of Paradise, whether shared or "within," is not freedom from perturbation (after all, Satan is *there*) but the tranquillity of heart that comes from "answerable deeds"—Eve's "peace within." "Still" invites Adam to consider the long-term effects of a policy of constraint. "If we think to regulat Printing," Milton wrote (substitute "gardening," or whatever art you will), "thereby to rectify manners, we must regulate all recreations and pastimes, all that is delightfull to man. [So, "How are we happy?"] No musick must be heard. . . . There must be licencing dancers. . . . Who shall regulat all the mixt conversation of our youth, male and female together, as is the fashion of this Country, who shall still ["still"] appoint what shall be discours'd, what presum'd, and no furder? Lastly, who shall forbid and sequester all idle resort, all evill company? . . . To sequester out of the world [even the unfallen world, which Satan is allowed to roam, an opportunity for merit] into *Atlantick* and *Eutopian* polities, which can never be drawn into use, will not mend our condition ["our condition"]; but to ordain wisely as in this world of evill, in the midd'st whereof God hath plac's us unavoidably": again, Eve would have to alter only the last clause, to, perhaps, "in this world of good wherein God hath plac't us, allowing liberty even to evil for the sake of our growth and perfection." To ordain wisely, Milton continues, is not to ordain by laws that "will make us all both ridiculous and weary, and yet frustrat," but by those "unconstraining laws of vertuous education, religious and civill nurture" (4:318). Can Adam and Eve protect their progeny by letting the Enemy dictate a life of anxiety and constraint, or will they have to teach and trust? Having considered Eve's question, Adam will choose "vertuous education."

But harm precedes not sin: because, as Socrates tells the men of Athens who have condemned him, "to a good man there can come no evil," since the only evil is to do evil; "nor are his affairs a matter of indifference to [God];"[64] and because "those actions which enter into a man, rather than issue out of him . . . defile not" (4:310).

On the principles of *Areopagitica,* and the rest of Milton's prose as well, Eve is right: if they allow the enemy to narrow the scope of goodness, he will have won a major victory. And that these principles apply to unfallen as well as regenerate life Milton makes clear in the tract itself:

> If every action . . . were to be under pittance, and prescription, and compulsion, what were vertue but a name, what praise could be then

due to well-doing, what grammercy to be sober, just, or continent?
many there be that complain of divin Providence for suffering *Adam* to
transgresse, foolish tongues! when God gave him reason, he gave him
freedom to choose, for reason is but choosing; he had bin else a meer
artificiall *Adam,* such an *Adam* as he is in the motions. We ourselves
esteem not of that obedience or love, or gift, which is of force: God
therefore left him free, set before him a provoking object, ever almost
in his eyes; herein consisted his merit, herein the right of his reward,
the praise of his abstinence. [4:319]

Eve next addresses these very points:

> . . . his foul esteeme
> Sticks no dishonour on our Front, but turns
> Foul on himself; then wherefore shund or feard
> By us? who rather double honour gaine
> From his surmise prov'd false, find peace within,
> Favour from Heav'n, our witness from th' event.
> And what is Faith, Love, Vertue unassaid
> Alone, without exterior help sustaind?

"Exterior help" echoes Raphael's "no outward aid require" and opposes "peace within." Would faith, love, and virtue not be "of force,"
and freedom lost, if they were not "within" and "assaid"? And if Eve
as well as Adam were not free to give obedience and love, if her actions were "under pittance, and prescription," would she not be a
"meer artificiall" Eve?

Later, of course, as the Serpent perverts Eve's hope of single virtue
to hope of single sapience, she will reject not only "exterior help" but
the inwardly digested help of Adam's counsel and God's word, and
at that moment both sin and harm will enter. But Eve does not yet
forget God, or think his providence "exterior help," for she continues,

> Let us not then suspect our happie State
> Left so imperfet by the Maker wise,
> As not secure to single or combin'd.
> Fraile is our happiness, if this be so,
> And *Eden* were no *Eden* thus expos'd.

This speech is itself imperfect, and spurs Adam to some of his best
thought. In her open-hearted innocence, Eve lacks a sufficient sense
of the reality of evil, which her dream has begun and Adam now continues to supply. Eden, he realizes, is indeed exposed, and a false

sense of security might be their worst danger. But that in itself becomes a reason to approve Eve's argument that active virtue is better than defensive withdrawal. Before the full impact of his own reasoning reaches him, however, Adam does exactly what some of Milton's fictive opponents do in *Areopagitica*. "'Tis next alleg'd we must not expose our selves to temptations without necessity, and next to that, not imploy our time in vain things" (4:315). Adam alleges only the first: "Seek not temptation then."[65] He does not consider Eve's desire vain, as her critics do, to "studie houshold good, / And good workes in her Husband to promote." "To both these objections," *Areopagitica* continues, "one answer will serve, . . . that to all men such books are not temptations, nor vanities; but useful drugs and materialls wherewith to temper and compose effective and strong med'cins, which mans life cannot want." For "books," "drugs," and "med'cins," read (for example) "works," "trials," and "virtues." The point is, though Eve in her innocence cannot express it quite this way, that the materials of sin and the materials of obedience are the same materials, faithfully or unfaithfully used. Remove the opportunity for doing wrong and you remove the opportunity for choosing to do right. *Mutatis mutandis,* the arguments of *Areopagitica* support Eve's position throughout.

Moreover, as Adam is about to realize, Eve is not seeking temptation—as, for example, Loredano's Eve does; she is seeking free obedience not "strait'nd by a Foe." She perceives that one does not resist evil by a crabbed and defensive exclusion but by open integrity and clarity of life. What she argues for is an open community:[66] a commonwealth that is not a stagnant pool of outward conformity and fixity of mind, but a perpetual fountain of charity and truth. What she argues against is the forced withdrawal, following the letter but not the spirit of God's behests, that was the worst effect of puritan separatism. She is careful not to blame God for their condition. Except that at this point she underestimates the Foe, she accepts the Pauline doctrine that God does not exempt his people from temptation but rather enables them to bear and outgrow it. She trusts that God has made them sufficient to stand, for if he were to expose them to evil without empowering them for good, Eden would be a kind of lie. The "peace within" that she hopes to find by active obedience prefigures the "Paradise within" that Michael tells Adam they can achieve by "answerable deeds" in spite of or in response to temptations and

frustrations. She "cannot praise a fugitive and cloister'd vertue, un-
exercis'd & unbreath'd, that never sallies out and sees her adversary"
(4:311) because "Faith, Love, Vertue" are not just states or feelings
but activities; they are but names unless they grow and bear fruit.[67]

Eve's argument, then, is Milton's argument for Christian liberty,
translated into prelapsarian terms. However, it is incomplete. It
needs the addition of Adam's argument, similarly translated, for
Christian responsibility. At first the two are disparate, but Adam's
peroration conjoins them. Thus, by speaking their minds with conjugal honesty, and I think too with "civill fellowship of love and amity," Adam and Eve have given each other what Milton in *Tetrachordon*
says matrimony should above all provide, "a mutuall help to piety"
(4:88).

Just as Adam's response to Eve's first argument echoes her pique,
so his reply to her better argument grapples more productively with
the difficulties she raises. He agrees that God's "creating hand / Nothing imperfet or deficient left / Of all that he Created, much less Man"
(including Woman). But, just as Eve has said that virtue dwells
within, Adam now points out that danger lies within, "yet lies within
[Man's] power: / Against his will he can receave no harme." He
agrees with Eve that inward virtue is necessary for obedience, but he
adds a warning that inward virtue can be betrayed and undone unless it adheres vigilantly to God's word.

> But God left free the Will, for what obeyes
> Reason, is free, and Reason he made right,
> But bid her well beware, and still erect,
> Least by some faire appeering good surpris'd
> She dictate false, and misinforme the Will
> To do what God expressly hath forbid.

This is, alas, exactly what will happen. But there is nothing in the
dialogue or in Eve's going that "God expressly hath forbid," and
"harm precedes not sin"; the combination of her own inward virtue,
Adam's counsel, and the word and providence of God render Eve
"sufficient to stand" whether or not she does, in fact, stand; and it
preserves the liberty without which love and virtue are not themselves. Adam's speech provides essential additions and corrections
for Eve's but does not invalidate, instead incorporates, her conviction that virtue must be free to act. It is because he makes this inte-

gration, not because he loses his nerve, that Adam's final speech changes direction when, having told Eve to "approve / First thy obedience," he adds, "But if thou think, trial unsought may finde / Us both securer than thus warnd thou seemst, / Go . . . ." Rather—poet-like, I think—he finds in his own word "obedience" illumination for his rapidly working mind and comprehends what true obedience is: as revealed by Raphael, by Eve's desire for uncloistered virtue, and by what he himself has just said about the inward operations of right reason and free will. And so he sends Eve forth in innocence exactly as Milton would send his reader forth in regeneracy, with an admonition whose rhythms are the heartbeat of the poem:

> Go in thy native innocence, relie
> On what thou hast of vertue, summon all,
> For God towards thee hath done his part, do thine

Notes

1. Some commentators disagree. The English translation of the authorized Dutch Bible of 1637 annotates Genesis 3:6, *"She gave also to her husband with her;* [or, *being with,* or, *by her.*] *and he did eat.* [*viz.* being inticed to it by the woman . . . .]"; *The Dutch Annotations Upon the Whole Bible,* trans. Theodore Haak (London, 1657). William Hunnis thinks that "Adam was with Eve when she did eate of the fruit forbidden," in *A Hyue Fulle of Honye: Conteyning the First Booke of Moses, called Genesis. Turned into English Meetre* (London, 1578). John Yates argues that "it is probable, that *Adam* stood by all the time of the disputation, and therefore his sinne was the greater, that he rebuked not the Serpent, and rescued his wife from all such suggestions: or if he was absent, (whereof the text makes not mention) then should he shew himselfe a weaker vessel then his wife, who had all the bad Angels (in one crafty beast) to set vpon her; whereas hee had onely one weake woman in his purest integrity to ouer-throw him . . .": *A Modell of Divinitie, Catechistically composed* (London, 1623), p. 178. A number of modern scholars have taken the use of the plural "ye" and "we" in the dialogue and "her husband with her" in Genesis 3:6 as proof of Adam's physical presence during the temptation: see Phyllis Trible, *God and the Rhetoric of Sexuality,* pp. 112–15 and p. 142, no. 38. However, for Milton and most Reformation commentators, Adam's silent collusion at such a crux was incompatible with original righteousness.

Although few commentaries attempt to explain Eve's separateness, two that allude to it are worth mentioning for what they do not say. Gibbens, answering the question "How could it be that the woman, hauing such excellent gifts by creation, could so easilie be seduced," replies, "Partlie by laying her selfe open vnto his assaults. His craftines appeareth, in that he incountreth with her, in the absence of her husband . . . ;" that is, he specifically does not put Eve's being alone in the category of "laying her selfe open vnto his assaults," which occurs in the ensuing dialogue: *Qvestions* (1602), pp. 113–14. Salkeld says nothing about the physical separation, but finds evidence in Eve's first reply to the Serpent that Adam and Eve enjoy what Milton calls "union of mind": "Though this precept was principally giuen to *Adam,* yet was it to be obserued of *Eue,* for as they were conioyned in nature, so were they not to be separated in regard of their precept and grace" (*A Treatise of Paradise,* p. 147). He does not say that they ought never to be physically separated, and indeed a physical dependence on Adam would cast doubt on Eve's inclusion in grace.

2. According to Joanne Lewis Cocklereas, "The iconography of the Fall never shows scenes to explain the cause for Adam and Eve's separation"; "Iconography and Eve," p. 145.

3. Waldock, *"Paradise Lost" and Its Critics* (Cambridge, England, 1947), p. 34; Rajan, *"Paradise Lost" and the Seventeenth-Century Reader* (London, 1947), p. 66; Tillyard, *Studies in Milton* (London, 1951), p. 13; Bell, "The Fallacy of the Fall in *Paradise Lost,"* *PMLA* 68 (1953): 874–75; Day, "Adam and Eve in *Paradise Lost,* IV," *TSLL* 3 (1961): 378; Bowers, "Adam, Eve, and the Fall in *Paradise Lost,"* *PMLA* 84 (1969): 266–71; Babb, *The Moral Cosmos of "Paradise Lost"* (Michigan State University Press, 1970), p. 49; Le Compte, *A Milton Dictionary* (New York, 1969), p. 237. Cf. Maurice Kelley, *This Great Argument* (Princeton, 1941), p. 149, n. 21; B. E. Gross, "Free Will and Free Love in Paradise Lost," *SEL* 7 (1967): 106; Davis P. Harding, *The Club of Hercules* (Urbana, 1962), p. 73; and innumerable others.

4. Burden, *The Logical Epic* (Cambridge, Mass., 1967); pp. 83–91; Gilbert, "Milton on the Position of Women," *MLR* 15 (1920): 250; Stein, *Answerable Style* (Minneapolis, 1953), p. 102; Ogden, "The Crisis of *Paradise Lost* Reconsidered," *PQ* 36 (1957): 1–19, repr. Barker, *Modern Essays,* p. 320; Parker, *Milton: A Biography* I (Oxford, 1968): 512; Lewalski, "Innocence and Experience in Milton's Eden," in *New Essays on "Paradise Lost",* ed. Thomas Kranidas (Berkeley, 1971), p. 100; Evans, *"Paradise Lost" and the Genesis Tradition* (Oxford, 1968), p. 280. See also Dan S. Collins, "The Buoyant Mind in Milton's Eden," *MiltonS* 5 (1973): 245–46, and Anthony Low, "The Parting in the Garden," *PQ* 47 (1968): 30–35.

In *The Art of Presence: The Poet and "Paradise Lost"* (Berkeley, 1977), Arnold Stein sees a balance of suggestivity and possibility until the separation but attributes (though conditionally) Eve's "abrupt dissatisfaction" to her dream and Adam's "giving in" to his passion (p. 111). I think the reverse is equally possible: Eve sees the need to temper passion and is not abruptly dissatisfied but concerned to preserve the opportunities Satan threatens; and Adam does not "give in" but remembers his own insights about true obedience developed in response to Eve's dream. Stein continues, "It is clear that Adam's not withholding permission is a personal fault, an error of will and judgment to be deplored and understood, but by that queer audience which is composed of admiring connoisseurs of stories, to be applauded" (p. 120). Clearly, I do not think either that Adam's action should be deplored or that Milton would have us applaud bad actions because they make good stories. I find no such break between art and truth in Milton's poem.

The theological difficulty raised by these interpretations is that for Eve to begin falling before encountering the Serpent requires either that God created Eve defective, that he allowed Satan to corrupt her in her sleep, a position that violates the doctrine of free will that Milton consistently adhered to, or that Eve was "self-tempted, self-depraved," which Milton's God declares she was not: the rebellious angels fell "by thir own suggestion" but "Man falls deceiv'd [by Satan] first: Man therefore shall find grace, / The other none" (3.129–32). That Eve is included in Man, as is customary in contemporary usage, is clear not only because she *is* deceived and does find grace but also because Adam individually, though he rationalizes, is "not deceav'd" (9.998; cf. 1 Tim. 2:14).

5. Summers, *The Muse's Method,* pp. 150 and 173–74; Patrick, "A Reconsideration of the Fall of Eve," *Études Anglaises* 28 (1975): 19–21; Shumaker, "The Fallacy of the Fall in *Paradise Lost,*" *PMLA* 70 (1955): 1186–87 and 1201; Samuel, "*Paradise Lost,*" in *Critical Approaches to Six Major English Works: "Beowulf" through "Paradise Lost"*, eds. R. M. Lumiansky and Herschel Baker (Philadelphia, 1968), pp. 237–43 (for other passages on prelapsarian growth see "*Purgatorio* and the Dream of Eve," *JEGP* 68 (1964): 441–49, and "*Paradise Lost* as Mimesis," in *Approaches to "Paradise Lost,"* ed. C. A. Patrides [Toronto, 1968]); Blackburn, "'Uncloistered Virtue': Adam and Eve in Milton's Paradise," *MiltonS* 3 (1971): 131–34; Revard, "Eve and the Doctrine of Responsibility in *Paradise Lost,*" *PMLA* 88 (1973): 72–73; Fish, "Discovery as Form in *Paradise Lost,*" in *New Essays,* ed. Kranidas, p. 8 (cf. *Surprised by Sin* [London, 1967], p. 231 n.]. Other mixed but mainly charitable views may be found in Eric Smith, *Some Versions of the Fall: The Myth of the Fall of Man in English Literature* (Pittsburgh, 1973), p. 33, and Louis L. Martz, *Poet of Exile: A Study of Milton's Poetry,* chapter 7. An early contribution to this group is Joseph Addison's: "The Dispute . . . proceeds from a Difference of Judgment, not of Passion, and is managed with Reason, not with Heat: It is such a Dispute as we may suppose might have happened in *Paradise,* had Man continued happy and innocent. There is a great Delicacy in the Moralities which are interspersed in *Adam's* Discourse. . . . " Like other critics, he says nothing of the "moralities" of Eve's. *Spectator* 351, in *A Familiar Explanation of the Poetical Works of Milton* . . . preface by Dodd (London, 1762), p. 111.

6. Barker, "Structural and Doctrinal Pattern," p. 190, and "The Relevance of Regeneration," p. 63. O. B. Hardison has given some support for this view in "'Hee for God Only, Shee for God in Him,'" a lecture delivered at the Folger Shakespeare Library, November, 1975.

7. George Buchanan (1506–82), *The Chameleon,* in *Miscellanea Scotica* (London, 1710), p. 99; quoted in *OED* 12:266.

8. "The Books of Adam and Eve," trans. L. S. A. Wells, in R. H. Charles, ed., *Apocrypha and Pseudepigrapha of the Old Testament* (Oxford, 1913), 2:142.

9. Charles, *Pseudepigrapha,* 2:146.

10. John Lightfoot, *The Harmony, Chronicle and Order of the Old Testament* (London, 1647), p. 4.

11. In Charles W. Kennedy, *Early English Christian Poetry, Translated into Alliterative Verse* (London, 1952), p. 60.

12. Avitus, *Poematum de Mosaice Historiae Gestis Libri Quinque* (A.D. 507), *PL* 59:332–33; trans. Kirkconnell, *The Celestial Cycle,* p. 11.

13. Prudentius, *Liber Cathemerinion,* 3:111–15, in *Prudentius,* trans. H. J. Thomson (London, 1949).

14. Norwich Text A, *The Story of the Creation of Eve, with the expellyng of Adam and Eve out of Paradyce,* 11.49–54, in *The Non-Cycle Mystery Plays,* ed. Osborn Waterhouse, *EETS* Extra Series 104 (London, 1909).

15. *Towneley Plays,* ed. George England and Alfred W. Pollard, *EETS* 70 (London, 1897), 11. 234–39.

16. *Ludus Coventriae or The Plaie Called Corpus Christi,* ed. K. S. Block, *EETS* Extra Series 120 (London, 1922), ll. 156–68.

17. Peyton (1620, 1623), stanza 271; in Kirkconnell, *The Celestial Cycle,* p. 269.

18. Vondel (1664) Kirkconnell's translation, in *The Celestial Cycle,* p. 462.

19. As J. M. Evans has pointed out, Milton "could not afford to admit any suggestion of tragic coincidence into the story. . . . If they were to part, they had to be shown doing so fully aware of the dangers to which they were thus exposing them-

selves." Unaccountably, Evans then adds the comment, "This decision, moreover, had to be presented as a wrong one *per se,* not merely *ex post facto*" (*"Paradise Lost"* and *The Genesis Tradition,'* p. 273). Like most critics, Evans seems to assume that the separation, though it shows them fully aware, is nevertheless a cause of the Fall, and shows them also wrong. I can see no evidence for this premise in the poem. Only the Fall is wrong per se, and the ex post facto appearance of wrongness attached to the separation depends on an assumption Milton never made, that the Fall was inevitable once the separation had taken place.

20. Salkeld, *A Treatise of Paradise,* p. 145.

21. Henoch Clapham, *Bibliotheca Theologica . . . drawn for the vse off yonge Christians . . . vnable to purchase Variety of holy-men theyr wrytings* (Amsterdam, 1597), pp. 8 and 8v.

22. David Pareus, *In Genesim Mosis Commentarius* (Geneva, 1614), p. 339.

23. *PL* 174:325.

24. Vergil, *The Aeneid,* trans. Frank O. Copley (Indianapolis, 1965), 4.569–70.

25. Ambrose, Epistle XX, trans. H. DeRomestin, in *SLNPNF,* Second Series, 10:425.

26. Chrysostom, *Homilies on First Corinthians,* p. 222.

27. Ed. James de Rothschild (Paris, 1878), ll. 1054–57; Societe des Anciens Textes Francais, 99.

28. *The Miroure of Mans Saluacionne: A Fifteenth Century Translation into English . . .* (London, 1888), p. 12.

29. Du Bartas, *Deuine Weekes and Workes,* p. 243.

30. Purchas, *Microcosmvs, or the Historie of Man* (London, 1619), p. 481.

31. Beaumont, *Psyche: or Loves Mysterie in XX. Canto's: Displaying the Intercourse Betwixt CHRIST, and the SOULE* (London, 1648), stanza 271.

32. Grotius, trans. Kirkconnell, p. 159. Cf. Torquato Tasso, *Le Sette Giornate del Mondo Creato* 7.938–41, in *Opere* (Milan, 1964): Femina fu cagion di tanta colpa, di tanti mali e de l'istessa morte. Femina a disprezzar l'alto divieto del Re celeste lusingando il mosse.

33. John Trapp, *Annotations upon the Old and New Testament* (London, 1662), p. 21.

34. Lancetta, (Venice, 1644), Act 2, scene 4.

35. Sachs, in *Bibliothek des Litterarischen Vereins in Stuttgart,* 102 (Tubingen, 1870): 34–35.

36. Ralegh, *History,* p. 70.

37. Publ. Willem Noomen (Paris, 1971), p. 32, ll. 141–85, and p. 36, ll. 500–505.

38. Martin Luther, *Lectures on Genesis,* ed. Jaroslaw Pelikan, in *Luther's Works* 1 (St. Louis, 1958): 151.

39. *PL* 34:445; Evans's translation, p. 97.

40. Evans, *"Paradise Lost"* and the Genesis Tradition, p. 97.

41. St. Thomas Aquinas, *Summa Theologiae, Secunda Secundae,* 163.2, trans. Thomas Gilby O.P. (New York, 1964), 44: 153.

42. Salkeld, *A Treatise of Paradise,* pp. 241, 274–75.

43. Kirkconnell, pp. 242, 43. Jun Harada points out that soliloquy, "uttered only by fallen characters," is a "closed form in which one pursues oneself," in "Self and Language in the Fall," *MiltonS* (1973): 215; Beverley Sherry that monologue is "a characteristically fallen mode of utterance in *Paradise Lost,*" signalling the disintegration of Adam and Eve "just prior to the eating of the fruit," in "Speech in *Paradise Lost,*" *MiltonS* 8 (1975): 259; and Janet Adelman that soliloquy is a fallen and narcissistic form in "Creation and the Place of the Poet in *Paradise Lost,*" in *The Author in His Work,* eds. Louis L. Martz and Aubrey Williams (New Haven, 1978).

44. Serafino della Salandra, *Adam Caduto*, (Casenza, 1647); verse excerpts quoted here are from Kirkconnell's translation, pp. 290–349, and prose excerpts are from a typescript translation of the entire play by Sister Mary Louis Towner, available in the Rare Book Room of the Library of the University of Illinois, Urbana-Champaign.

45. Trans. Towner, Act 2, scene 5.

46. Kirkconnell, p. 298; Towner, Act 2, scene 6.

47. Joseph Fletcher, *History of the Perfect-Cursed-Blessed Man*, (London, 1628), p. 26.

48. *The Poetical Works of Chaucer*, ed. F. N. Robinson (Cambridge, Mass., 1933), p. 97 (Prologue, l. 519).

49. Chester, ll. 185–86; Grotius, in Kirkconnell, p. 111.

50. Gasparo Murtola, "Della creatione del mondo" (Venice, 1608), in Kirkconnell, p. 590.

51. *The Fall of Adam and Eve: Being a Clear, Rational and Impartial Exposition, How our First Parents were Seduc'd in Paradise . . . Written Originally by an Eminent Divine in Amsterdam. Translated into English* (London, 1702), pp. 5–22. August Dillman discusses the temptation as a natural serpent suggesting evil thoughts in Eve in *Genesis Critically and Exegetically Expounded*, trans William B. Stevenson (Edinburgh, 1897), 1:149–50.

52. Giovanno Francesco Loredano, *The Life of Adam: A Facsimile Reproduction of the English Translation of 1659*, intro. Roy C. Flannagan with John Arthos (Gainesville, 1967), pp. 23–24.

53. Trapp, *Annotations*, p. 22.

54. For a complete account of the toleration controversies and Milton's part in them, see Barker, *Milton and the Puritan Dilemma*. Quotations are from chapter II, "The One Right Discipline," pp. 18 and 21.

55. J. Richardson, father and son, *Explanatory Notes and Remarks on Milton's "Paradise Lost"* (London, 1734), p. 406.

56. John Bunyan, *The Pilgrim's Progress*, intro. Louis L. Martz (New York, 1967), p. 168.

57. Sherry, "Speech in *Paradise Lost*," pp. 259–60 and passim.

58. Some readers think Eve's listening "as in a shadie nook I stood behind" is also "shadie." Before, she has "sat retir'd in sight" (8.41). Was it curiosity or courtesy that kept her from interrupting the intense dialogue she returned to? We can be sure that she is not prying into secrets: Adam has none from her "who sees when thou art seen least wise" (8:578); nor does she harbor any, since she tells Adam about her presence when the subject arises. Again, these nuances may tell us more about ourselves than about Eve, whose mind is "pure of evil thought."

59. In *Tetrachordon* Milton excludes both "individuality" and "indivisibility" from the essence of marriage (4:103–4) because, I think, he felt that the "due benevolences of bed and board," the refusal or impropriety of which constituted the only legal grounds of divorce, though attributes of marriage, are not its essence, which is the harmony of soul that furthers its primary purpose, "mutual help to piety."

60. Aubrey De Vere remarks that Britomart "loves as ardently as Amoret, but . . . cannot, like her, love only; her life must be a life of arduous action and sustained endeavor, and while these are with her she is contented alike in the presence or absence of her lover" (Spenser, Variorum Edition, 3:382). For both Britomart and Eve, endeavor is an enrichment, not an impediment, of love.

61. Donne, "A Valediction forbidding mourning," in Shawcross, pp. 87–88.

62. Louis L. Martz writes, "They are not confined to a narrow circuit; they can go anywhere together. And this idea that they are made, or ought to be made, to meet temptation singly—this represents, as Milton's whole poem before this has

made clear, a misunderstanding of the nature of the universe, where nothing stands alone, but everything lives best in the linked universe of love, with respect for those above and care for those below": *Poet of Exile,* p. 133. But Eve is not going forth primarily to meet temptation; she is going forth to do her work and to keep love linked with the rest of creation and free of "carnal dependence." Her mistake is in not using what she knows, recognizing her confusion, and seeking help from God and Adam when the Serpent's words begin to sound plausible to her.

63. Augustine, *The Citie of God* 14.10, trans. J. H[ealy], p. 511.

64. Plato, *Apology,* in *Plato on the Trial and Death of Socrates,* trans. Lane Cooper (Ithaca, 1967), p. 77.

65. Jerome, one of the Fathers least compatible with Milton, is quoted in *The Lady's Rhetorick* (London, 1707), "*There is nothing . . . so mischievous* as to be always obliged to exercise our Virtue. It is a greater satisfaction to be out of danger, than not to perish in the midst of it. In the first we enjoy security, but in the other we must labour continually, and strive for Safety. In the first we fear not to be lost, but in the other we endeavor to escape." This rather supine view was challenged by spirits more congenial to Milton who believed with Robert Crofts, for example, that "for a man not to be ill, where he hath no provocation therunto, is lesse commendable, and deserving, then to be good in the midst of dangers" (*The Terrestriall Paradise* [London, 1639], p. 53).

66. In *Interfaces of the Word: Studies in the Evolution of Consciousness and Culture* (Ithaca, 1977), Walter J. Ong writes: "In the world of living, sentient organisms, communication exists at its peak among human beings. The reason is that communication requires closure, or unification and distinctiveness of a being, maximum interiority, organization from within, like that of a system, and openness, or access to whatever is outside the closure. Human beings are both closed and opened to the maximum. . . . Paradoxically, communication demands isolation. Unless a being is somehow closed in on itself, self-possessed from within, able to say 'I' and to know in the saying that this 'I' is completely and indestructibly unique . . . there is no sharing to be done, no communication possible. I can only share what I have control of. If I do not lay hold of myself by reflection, do not know the 'taste of self, more distinctive than ale or alum' (in Gerard Manley Hopkins' words), I cannot give myself to another or to others. I have nothing to give—for I have no self, no person, to give" (pp. 335–36). In words suggested by Father Ong, Eve is opting for an open system, or for open-field thinking and accessibility, while trying to preserve the "open closure" (p. 337) of her own consciousness.

Cf. also U. Milo Kaufmann, *Paradise in the Age of Milton* (Victoria, B. C., 1978), p. 7: "Felicity comes to be inseparable from openness and change."

67. Compare, for example, the speech of Duke Vincentio in *Measure for Measure* I.1:

>   Thyself and thy belongings
> Are not thine own so proper as to waste
> Thyself upon thy virtues, they on thee.
> Heaven doth with us as we with torches do,
> Not light them for themselves; for if our virtues
> Did not go forth of us, 'twere all alike
> As if we had them not. Spirits are not finely touched
> But to fine issues, nor Nature never lends
> The smallest scruple of her excellence
> But, like a thrifty goddess, she determines
> Herself the glory of a creditor,
> Both thanks and use.

VI

"Fatal Bruise":
Mortal Food and Promised Seed

Supposing, then, that Eve however vulnerable is indeed "yet sin-less" and sufficient to stand halfway through the book in which the poet turns his notes to tragic; that Adam and Eve were indeed origi-nally righteous and are spiritedly engaged in the process of perfection until the moments of their respective falls; and that Eve is not only not wrong, but positively right in her quest for inward faith and vir-tue and the free procession of charity and truth: the question remains with which Milton, in astonishment and pain, begins his poem:

> what cause
> Mov'd our Grand Parents in that happy State,
> Favour'd of Heav'n so highly, to fall off
> From thir Creator, and transgress his will
> For one restraint, Lords of the World besides?
> [1.28–33]

The immediate answer is "th'infernal Serpent." But he can pro-vide only temptation, which can be good or bad depending on the re-sponse of the tempted; and sin is the conjunction of temptation and consent. How does Milton explain Eve's consent?

One of the answers is promptly provided on one of those occasions when even the Father of Lies speaks true:

> If then [God's] Providence
> Out of our evil seek to bring forth good,
> Our labour must be to pervert that end,
> And out of good still to find means of evil.
> [1.162–65]

187

Satan's corruption of Eve and her subsequent seduction of Adam do not manifest original improbity in their victims but do something much more hateful: they pervert the good in them and make their very virtues instruments of destruction. Let no one sentimentally suppose that Eve's fall is a kind of liberation or Adam's a kind of gallantry. In both, the rich covenant of trust is usurped and spoiled, and glorious goodness is twisted and debased.

"Eve Yet Sinless"

The beautiful, sleek serpent in whose body Satan woos Eve, his loveliness surpassing that of the serpents into which Jove transformed himself for his amours (9.506–10), his towering folds, his wanton wreaths, his elevated crest, and his manner of a courtly lover worshipping his lady, all suggest seduction. Combined with his intellectual pretensions and his contempt of food and sex (9.573–74), they suggest spiritual seduction. When "hope elevates, and joy / Brightens his Crest," his hope is in destruction and his joy in malice.

Like sexual seduction, the spiritual seduction subverts Eve's purity by posing a false dilemma that pretends an opposition between divine and human good, while at the same time alleging that God and his laws are not really divine at all. Thus Angelo in *Measure for Measure* tempts Isabella when he asks if there might not be charity in sin. Satan's version of the pattern is to suggest to Eve that "petty Trespass" might be means of "dauntless vertue." At the same time he changes from the singular "thee" and "thou" of his previous addresses to the plural: "ye shall not die . . . ye shall be as Gods . . . Man should thus attain to know . . . your need," in order to give Eve the impression that her "dauntless vertue" will be good for the whole race. Later, but no longer truly, Eve will allege to Adam that she sought godhead chiefly for him (9.877–78). In other words, Satan subverts her purity by falsely opposing it to charity: a personal version of the puritan dilemma.

For Milton, the choice between *caritas* and *castitas* is a false dilemma: one can only choose between neither and both, because the loss of one disables the other. *Castitas* is faithfulness of body, mind, and heart. *Caritas* is the outward-reaching love that cherishes the immortal well-being of every person. Charity is the highest of virtues, but chastity is its meet and necessary help. In the fallen world, on the sexual level, chastity is often regarded (or disregarded) as a merely carnal and prudential virtue, protecting legitimacy, social order, and emotional balance. In the unfallen and regenerate worlds of Milton's Paradise and the household of faith it figures forth, "the Sun-clad power of Chastity"[1] includes far more: it is a radiant clarity and wholeness that both discloses and repels evil and empowers for good, by fitting the "living Temples" of the Spirit to be conduits of grace.

When Satan spies his prey, "her Heav'nly forme / Angelic," her "graceful Innocence, her every Aire / Of gesture or lest action over-awd / His Malice"; rapt by her sweetness,

> That space the Evil one abstracted stood
> From his own evil, and for the time remain
> Stupidly good, of enmitie disarm'd,
> Of guile, of hate, of envie, of revenge.
> [9.457–66]

At this pause in the confrontation of evil with goodness, the pressure of the poem's theme of growth toward perfection, its insistence that virtue is goodness in action, and its faith that God is "Mercifull over all his works, with good / Still overcoming evil, and by small / Accomplishing great things" (12.565–67), suggests the possibility of an outcome far different from the perverse event. That is: if Eve had exercised her sun-clad powers, she might have done more than stand. She might have been a conduit of grace to others confronted by Satan—perhaps even to Satan himself. That might have become the mission on which, in responding to her calling in that prime season, Eve went forth.

There is considerable evidence, of course, that Satan would not have responded to such grace. Against it is "the hot Hell that alwayes in him burnes" (9.467) and the despair with which he has hardened his heart against repentance earlier (4.79–113). Further, God the Father has said that Satan and his followers

> by thir own suggestion fell,
> Self-tempted, self-deprav'd: Man falls deceiv'd
> By the other first: Man therefore shall find grace,
> The other none.
> [3.129–32]

I think, however, that these words are prophecy, not decree, and that the "therefore" of Satan's reprobation includes the deception of Man. What God will not do is "revoke the high Decree / Unchangeable, Eternal, which ordain's / Thir freedom"; they are "Authors to themselves in all" and trespass

> without least impulse or shadow of Fate,
> Or aught by me immutablie foreseen . . . for so
> I formd them free, and free they must remain,
> Till they enthrall themselves.
>
> [3.120–28]

What, then, if Satan and his army — the decree of freedom still un-revoked — had chosen to cease being self-deceived and self-enslaved instead of deceiving man? Might the Hell within have been extinguished?[2] Perhaps Satan's response to grace channelled through Eve would have continued to be what it is when her mere presence abstracts him from his evil — "Fierce hate he recollects" (9.471). But his position is in reality far frailer than hers, for he has only "that word / Disdain" and his reputation to keep him going, and that his boasts are vain even he knows (4.82–87). If to the loveliness and graceful gesture that temporarily bereave him of evil Eve had added a joyous faithfulness to God and Adam and repelled his attempts with radiant goodness, she would at least have done her utmost for him.

Satan and his party have already enthralled themselves; yet Satan's soul-searching at the beginning of Book 4 and his momentary rapture now suggest that he has consciously to reject every shred of lingering goodness in himself and commit the malicious act of corrupting innocent beings before he completes the work of damning himself utterly. His corruption of Eve is more purely malicious than his seduction of his troops. He has lied to them and misled them, but in spite of Abdiel's brave example they have chosen to rebel against God of their own accord, and rejected opportunities for obedience and repentance. They are not deceived; they prefer Satan's hate to Abdiel's love; they approve Satan's plan to destroy harmless creatures who have made no claim to power. It is with the success of this plan that their case becomes hopeless. Now, Satan is about to deface and corrupt two lovely, gentle beings by whom he cannot even imagine himself to be "impaired," though he resents angel wings being bidden to their service, and whose lives are vibrant with the gladsome service he disdains. He is about to vandalize the new creation out of mere envy of a blessedness he has had every opportunity to share. He has willfully cast out every ray of grace and goodness from his own nature in order to destroy, and so has chosen despair.

If Eve had prevented his putting his plan into action, he might have tried again and again, against beings better and better prepared to resist through grace and virtue following the precedents of their parents; that is, he might have continued to choose damnation. But his success with Eve ensures it. It cuts off his opportunity *not* to sin by corrupting innocence. When one gives in to temptation one sins against the tempter—as Adam, too, is about to do.

Eve neglects her opportunity to be a conduit of grace. Instead, she falls, and we are left to ask with stricken Adam, "How art thou lost, how on a sudden lost?" But she does not fall at once, and her resistance deserves attention as well as her failure.

Milton's definition of sin and its consequences and of the moment of its entry into the world is stated explicitly in *De Doctrina Christiana* (15: 179 ff.). Sin is "the transgression of the law." The law is "in the first place, that rule of conscience which is innate, and engraven upon the mind of man; secondly, the special command which proceeded out of the mouth of God," just as Eve tells the Serpent (9.651 54). Sin is of two kinds: "THAT WHICH IS COMMON TO ALL MEN, and THE PERSONAL SIN OF EACH INDIVIDUAL," which, Milton shows for the sake of justifying God's ways, each individual in fact performs. "THE SIN WHICH IS COMMON TO ALL MEN IS THAT WHICH OUR FIRST PARENTS, AND IN THEM ALL THEIR POSTERITY COMMITTED, WHEN, CASTING OFF THEIR OBEDIENCE TO GOD, THEY TASTED THE FRUIT OF THE FORBIDDEN TREE." Both kinds of sin consist of two parts. The first is "evil concupiscence," of which Adam and Eve become guilty "immediately upon their fall" (but, Milton argues, not before) and "transmitted to their posterity, as sharers in the primary transgression, in the shape of an innate propensity to sin." (The human race is conceived as an organic whole, present in the loins of Adam and hence sharers in his fall; but Milton is also at pains to show that each also sins on his own.) The second is "the crime itself, or the act of sinning, which is commonly called Actual Sin. This may be incurred, not only by actions commonly so called, but also by words and thoughts, and even by the omission of good actions. It is called Actual Sin, not that sin is properly an action, for in reality is implies defect; but because it commonly consists in some act."

The immediate effects of sin, which Milton shows in the poem, are "guiltiness . . . terrors of conscience . . . the sensible forfeiture of the divine protection and favor; whence results a diminution of the majesty of the human countenance, and a conscious degradation of mind. . . . Hence the whole man becomes polluted . . . whence arises shame"; these are signs of "SPIRITUAL DEATH; by which is meant the loss of divine grace, and that of innate righteousness, wherein man in the beginning lived unto God. . . . And this death took place not only on the very day, but at the very moment of the fall. They who are delivered from it are said to be 'regenerated,' to be 'born again,' and to be 'created afresh'; which is the work of God alone."

The origins of sin are, first, "the instigation of the devil" and, second, "the liability to fall with which man was created, whereby he, as the devil had done before him, 'abode not in the truth.'" "Liability," as I have mentioned before, does not mean tendency, for God having made his rational creatures free and sufficient does not "touch with lightest moment of impulse" their free will, "to her own inclining left / In eevn scale" (10.45–47). It means a capability for which one is wholly answerable.

The ingredients of sin are manifold, displaying the doctrine that every sin includes every other.

> If the circumstances of this crime are duly considered, it will be acknowledged to have been a most heinous offence, and a transgression of the whole law. For what sin can be named, which was not included in this one act? It comprehended at once distrust in the divine veracity, and a proportionate credulity in the assurances of Satan; unbelief; ingratitude; disobedience; gluttony; in the man excessive uxoriousness, in the woman a want of proper regard for her husband, in both an insensibility to the welfare of their offspring, and that offspring the whole human race; parricide, theft, invasion of the rights of others, sacrilege, deceit, presumption in aspiring to divine attributes, fraud in the means employed to attain the object, pride, and arrogance.

All of these, Milton asks us to believe, were committed at the very moment when Adam and Eve, "CASTING OFF THEIR OBEDIENCE TO GOD, . . . TASTED THE FRUIT OF THE FORBIDDEN TREE." The moment of the fall, for each, is the moment of that "casting off"; as the commentators often remarked, citing 1 John 2:14, "had Gods Word abidden in [Eve], she had overcome that wicked one."[3]

As a mimesis of the temptations of everyday life writ large, the temptation of Eve recapitulates experience in thoroughly practical ways. Satan's instrument is not an obviously evil being nor, on the other hand, "some faire appearing good" of an exotic and arresting kind, but a very attractive yet comfortably ordinary and endearingly familiar snake. His medium is that by which in the Renaissance mind God most clearly presents himself to men and men to one another: the word. His materials are Eve's best qualities: her openness, her compassion, her good faith, her trust, her desire to learn and grow, her courage—the very qualities, of course, that disobeying God destroys. Because Satan by his lies perverts these goods to evil, and because Eve does not use her "liability to fall" as an opportunity to exercise these virtues in resisting and overcoming his fraud and to trust "the divine veracity," Eve will be "Defac't, deflourd, and now to Death devote" (9.901). Until "the very moment" of her fall, Satan's attempt, like previous trials, is still potentially a "good temptation."

When and how does the temptation of Eve stop being potentially good and "the very moment" of her fall occur?

A "good temptation" is known by its fruits. A temptation is an attempt to elicit desire for something forbidden by God. (In Paradise only one thing has been forbidden, without which no happy trial could exercise their faith, since goodness is natural; and the tempter is external. In fallen and even in regenerate human nature temptation may also be internal.) A desire for any good thing, such as Eve's desire for wisdom, is not wrong in itself, but an ingredient of virtue to be rightly tempered. One can feel hunger and defer one's meal until wholesome food is at hand. A lawful hunger becomes a sinful concupiscence when one desires unlawful food or that which is offered by a godless giver. Only the good, as the Lady in the *Maske* knows (801–12), can give good things. When the desire for good is drawn toward a forbidden object or an unreliable source, creating a tension between "some faire appearing good" (9.354) and the solid good of keeping faith with God and others, Reason must, as Adam counsels, be "still erect." This tension is a "good temptation" as long as it is regarded as a trial or an affliction and successfully resisted, with the result that the effort of resistance strengthens the resister's will, self-knowledge, sense of God's grace, and loyalty to God-in-others.

James speaks of good trials or temptations (1.2-15, 4-7) when he writes "My brethren, count it all joy when ye fall into divers temptations; Knowing this, that the trying of your faith worketh patience. But let patience have her perfect work, that ye may be perfect and entire, wanting nothing." A temptation ceases to be good when the person being tempted succumbs to moral confusion, abandons her or his freedom, and begins to desire the object of the temptation more than she or he desires God's grace to resist, or to believe an unreliable source rather than God. At that point the temptation ceases to be felt as a test, or as a painful disruption of one's peace of heart, and becomes internalized as concupiscence, which is a sin in itself. As Adam tells fallen Eve, "onely coveting to Eye" the thing forbidden provokes peril (9.923-24). To avoid coveting, or mistaking something forbidden for something good, James teaches, one must pray wholeheartedly for guidance. "If any of you lack wisdom, let him ask of God, that giveth to all men liberally, and upbraideth not; and it shall be given him. But let him ask in faith, nothing wavering. For he that wavereth is like a wave of the sea driven with the wind and tossed. For let not that man think that he shall receive any thing of the Lord. A double minded man is unstable in all his ways." While Eve remains single-minded, as the simplicity of language in her first replies to the Serpent warrants her to be, she is still in a state of grace. After the Serpent's indignant oration (9.679-731) has confused her mind, she omits two crucial acts: to remember Adam's counsel and to seek wisdom and help from God. Then the channels of her senses are left undefended and her fancy, seduced from reason, receives the misinformation that there is wisdom in the fruit. Even then she might have directed her trust towards God rather than the Serpent and willed to resist the fruit and to seek Adam's present help. Instead, she turns to commend the tree. Until then, she still has the opportunity that she has rightly and eloquently defended — to do her part, and win James's benediction: "Blessed is the man that endureth temptation: for when he is tried, he shall receive the crown of life, which the Lord hath promised to them that love him."

The sin of omission in Eve's turning is prefigured in reverse, but not contained, in the narrator's description of her, as Satan nears, gently upstaying flowers that are glowing, fragrant images of Eve herself, "mindless the while, / Her self, though fairest unsupported Flour, / From her best prop so farr, and storm so nigh" (9.431-33).

Her self-forgetful devotion to her charges is not a sin but a virtue
that will be preverted from attention to goodness to inattention (and
then excessive attention) to badness. It is not surprising that Eve,
full of benevolence, could forget Satan's "fierce hate" if he himself,
though full of "the hot Hell that alwayes in him burnes" could forget
it, "overawd" by her least action, in the presence of her innocence.
Such is the power of goodness that even he is self-forgetful for a time
and has to recollect his hate. So Eve, though "unwary," might have
recollected her charge. This recollection, as the writers on temptation agree, must start as soon as one begins to be enticed to do what
God has forbidden. For, as James continues, "Let no may say when
he is tempted, I am tempted of God: for God cannot be tempted with
evil, neither tempteth he any man: But every man is tempted, when
he is drawn away of his own lust, and enticed. Then when lust hath
conceived, it bringeth forth sin: and sin, when it is finished, bringeth
forth death. Do not err, my beloved brethren. . . . Resist the devil
and he will flee from you." Since there can have been no evil concupiscence in Eve until the moment of her fall, the fall must occur
when her desire for the fruit draws her away from God.

Peter teaches a similar doctrine of temptation (1 Peter 6–7, 4–12),
and includes the stern warnings with which Adam has equipped
Eve: "Be sober, be vigilant; because your adversary the devil, as a
roaring lion, walketh about, seeking whom he may devour. . . . The
Lord knoweth how to deliver the godly out of temptations. . . . Ye
therefore, beloved, seeing ye know these things before, beware lest
ye . . . being led away with the error of the wicked, fall from your
own steadfastness" (1 Peter 5:8; 2 Peter 2:9, 3:17.) There is only one
way in which the teachings of James and Peter do not apply to Adam
and Eve as to their descendants: they do not have to contend with
the "innate propensity to sin" that afflicts even the regenerate.[4] They
are not exempt from refining trials; they have perhaps even the opportunity for redemptive suffering; they are offered the great adventure of doing battle with evil itself, for their adversary "walketh
about, seeking whom he may devour"; and they could have won.
"Here you see," as Godfrey Goodman says, "a commission graunted,
and a power giuen vnto Satan to tempt man, and that in the time of
his innocencie, (for innocencie is best discouered by the triall of ten-
tation): thus Christ was likewise tempted in the wilderness. . . ."[5]

Even though the narrator comments, after the Serpent's first

speech, "Into the Heart of *Eve* his words made way" (9.550), Eve's
heart at first does not approve them. Like her dream, they still "may
come and go, so unapprov'd, and leave / No spot or blame behind";
otherwise she would not be "yet sinless" over a hundred lines later.
There is no evidence that Eve responds to the Serpent's flattery in
her first reply, and in her second she very sensibly rejects it. It is not
real praise but an attempt to confuse Eve's mind by divorcing language from actuality, or sign from what it pretends to signify, in
order finally to reverse the meaning of "that Tree, / The only sign of
our obedience left / Among so many signs of power and rule / Con-
ferrd upon us" (4.427–30). Satan uses flattery not to extoll goodness
but to debase it in two ways. First, in order to elevate Eve he degrades
everything else.

> Here
> In this enclosure wild, these Beasts among,
> Beholders rude, and shallow to discerne
> Half what in thee is fair, one man except,
> Who sees thee? (and what is one?)
> [9.542–46]

The *contemptus mundi* is preposterous, and Eve is too surprised to re-
join at once (if preposterousness deserves rejoinder). Love does not
need to bolster the beloved by denigrating all else. Second, although
it looks like flattery, the speech is really an attack on Eve's self-esteem.
Her husband, her work, her world are worthless; she should employ
numberless ravished spirits in the task of adoring her. The passage is
in fact so silly that it is quite proper for Eve to ignore it and get on to
the really interesting question of how the Serpent acquired the consummate gift of speech. That of course is what he wants her to do,
but if she had done it vigilantly, remembering Adam's warning and
all she has learned about God's ways, she might have penetrated his
disguise. She asks two questions: "How cam'st thou speakable of
mute," and "how / To me so friendly grown above the rest / Of brutal
kind, that daily are in sight?" In the latter, those who think her weak
will find a response to flattery; yet the words can carry a more complex tone: she is cautious, yet interested, as his proper governess,
and perhaps gaily and a bit patronizingly amused; she speaks skeptically, yet affectionately, with such courtly raillery as any great lady

might accord any courtier who has suddenly spoken with a familiarity above his station.

In reply to her first question, Satan invents for his snakehood a tale embellished with such plausible images, and works his disdain of food and sex, his arrogance toward other animals, and his supposed capacity for "speculations" so skillfully into his renewed attempt at flattery that even we, who know that none of what he says has really happened, may forget for a moment that the whole story is a fabrication. The remarkable thing is that Eve, who thinks him just a friendly serpent who has daily been in sight, is not entirely taken in. She is, the narrator says, "amaz'd" and "unwarie," but her mistake is not that she believes the flattery — she does not — but that she believes the story. That is not a sin unless her "Firm Faith and love / Can by his fraud be shak'n or seduc't" (9.286–87). She does not yet know which tree the Serpent claims to have eaten from, "For many are the Trees of God," and the Tree of Life is equally near. She does know, from Raphael and from her experience as a gardener, that all things improve with nurture. She is "unwary" to believe that any capacity might come through sudden and magical means, but she is very properly skeptical of the quality of the capacity, as her reply shows. For she does not merely reject the flattery but considers it a symptom of unsound reason: "Serpent, thy overpraising leaves in doubt / The vertue of that Fruit, in thee first prov'd."[6]

This deft parry is followed too soon by the question, "where grows the Tree," yet that is not exactly idle curiosity from one of the "Lords of all," and in the rest of the speech Eve is mindful of God and his bounty and of the generations to come. After the Adder's wily reply, still in Paradisal imagery, Eve speaks two words at which our hearts should plummet, yet a certain balance and decorum is still preserved, for though her act of speech subordinates her to the Serpent's guidance, it is still an imperial command: "Lead then."

As often happens, Milton now packs the viprous imagery other writers have falsely applied to the Garden or Eve into something else: here, an epic simile, comparing Satan's leading to "a wandring Fire" that "misleads th' amazed Night-wanderer" — too like in sad event. Eve, being led into fraud, is "our credulous Mother"; her trust, an essential quality of innocence that in the separation colloquy she wanted to preserve and to merit, is being exploited. Eve is still "mild as doves" but she is not "wise as serpents," as Adam has told her she must be, and the Serpent's wiliness and slyness, like the crooked path he leads her by, "seem strait" to her overtrusting innocence.

Her next speech, however, is still within the decorum of "Virgin Majesty" and "sanctitude severe and pure." She has not yet succumbed to flattery, nor does she succumb at once to curiosity, but comments drily, "Serpent, we might have spar'd our coming hither" and adds skeptically that even if what the Serpent has said is true its credit must rest with him; their errand is "fruitless" to her—a pun that works for us as ironic prefiguration of "fruitless hours" but for her, so far, as sober fact. We are reminded that "Fruit" brought "all our woe" and the poignancy of the last moments of innocence is increased by the knowledge that here, on the verge of the abyss, Eve is still, and could remain, simply right. Of that tree, she gravely explains, they may not taste nor touch:[7]

> God so commanded, and left that Command
> Sole Daughter of his voice; the rest, we live
> Law to our selves, our Reason is our Law.
>   [9.652–54]

The additions Milton makes to Eve's words in Genesis endow her with a succinct understanding of the nature of the Tree. It is God's signature on the work of creation, a visible sign of his evoking voice, signifying to Adam and Eve that a power higher than their own excellent human reason awaits their fruition "by degrees of merit," and giving them the opportunity to "see and know and yet abstain." Satan, the original plagiarist, has denied his Creator and claimed to be self-made. The Tree defends Adam and Eve from that mistake. In all other things, Adam and Eve need no law because their upright reason naturally seeks good and shuns evil.

To the Serpent's next guileful insinuations (9.656–58), Eve "yet sinless" replies with the simple diction of plain truth, except perhaps for the possibly wistful "fair." But the tree *is* fair. God has made it so. It is a good thing while rightly used as a pledge of faith, and after Satan turns it into a temptation Eve is not wrong to recognize that it is fair—it would not be a temptation otherwise—as long as she does not lust for it in her heart and so subvert her will. Eve still speaks with the simplicity of uncorrupted virtue. It is this simplicity, or integrity, that Satan now sets out to pervert.[8]

"How on a Sudden Lost?"

Satan's abuses of grammar, rhetoric, and logic have received a
great deal of expert scrutiny.[9] I shall focus my comments on his distortion, as perverse critic, of the naming of the sign that God, the
master Poet whose words call forth diverse responses from their
hearers according to their natures, has chosen to call

> the Tree whose operation brings
> Knowledge of good and ill, which I have set
> The Pledge of thy Obedience and thy Faith,
> Amid the Garden by the Tree of Life.
>
> [8.323–26]

"Operation" can mean either efficacy or use. "Brings" is in the present tense. Adam is free to consider what kind of knowledge might be
obtained by despoilment and what kind by using the Tree as pledge.

Satan's deconstruction of God's terms is a part of his strategy to
undermine Eve's faith, as he embeds his real thesis—"doe not believe"—in a web of lies. He proceeds by a pretense of altruistic zeal;
by idolatry of the "Sacred, Wise, and Wisdom-giving Plant" from
which he claims power to discern "Things in thir Causes" and the
"wayes / Of highest Agents" whom he belittles; by false epithets for
God, "the Threatner"; by a snobbish disparagement of Adam and
Eve as "low and ignorant," their eyes "but dim" (a description, in fact,
of what he wants them to become); by the imputation to God of his
own desire to hurt, as if it were an unjust deity and not their own
apostasy from goodness that could hurt them; by debasement and
trivialization of goodness; in short, by shattering the decalogue, the
law of love, and the bond between words and facts. At the center of
the web lies the bait:

> Who enclos'd
> Knowledge of Good and Evil in this Tree,
> That whoso eats thereof, forthwith attains
> Wisdom without their leave?

The primitive notion that one could acquire moral wisdom by vio-
lating a divine command was of course unthinkable to Renaissance
Christians who believed that "Reason is our Soules left hand, Faith
her right, / By these we reach divinity." Faith in the ways of God,
whose signposts are his commandments, was considered the only

source and preservative of true wisdom, and the pursuit of knowledge, so guided, was as Vives said "for every human mind the keen-
est of all pleasures."[10] Since God would not forbid knowledge, least
of all moral knowledge, interpreters explained the name of the Tree
in other ways. Metonymically, "from the event" as Milton's God
tersely says, it signifies "Good lost, and Evil got" (11.87). Ironically,
and proleptically, it derives from Satan's false promise; Milton's God
speaks in this mode when he says "like one of us Man is become / To
know both Good and Evil" (11.84–85), though what Adam and Eve
have fallen into is moral chaos. More directly, it denotes the sign,
pledge, or memorial of the obedience by which Adam and Eve did,
in fact, acquire moral knowledge until the Fall. The Tree exercises
free will and moral discrimination by providing an opportunity to
see and know and yet abstain; as the sole daughter of God's voice, it
stands sentinel over the steady and temperate development of every
kind of knowledge in which Adam and Eve are so delightedly engaged.

Milton's treatment of the forbidden Tree and its effects has behind
it a clear but complex body of commentary, all of which agrees that
eating the forbidden fruit resulted in the withering, not the enlarg-
ing, of understanding and of will. For Augustine, the Tree preserves
"free election of will, for if man once forsake Gods will, he cannot vse
himselfe, but to his owne destruction."[11] Purchas thought that "*Adam*
was without studie the greatest Philosopher . . . and the greatest Divine, (except the Second *Adam*) that euer the earth bare. . . . Nature
was his Schoolemaster; or . . . Gods Vsher, that taught him . . . all
the rules of divine Learning, of Politicall, Oeconomicall, and Moral
Wisdome," and the forbidden Tree was "a visible rule, whereby good
and euill should be knowne."[12] Gibbens, who documents sources co-
piously in his marginal gloss, writes,

> It is vntrulie supposed by the Hebrue Doctors, that the tree had ver-
> tue in it to giue sharpeness of wit to him that did eate thereof: which
> conceit gaue to Iulian to cauill at the Scripture, as though God had
> pleasure to haue deteined men in ignorance. . . . But [rather] was it
> called the tree of knowledge of good and euill; because it was made a
> rule for man to know, what was good, and what was euill, so soone as
> it was inioyned man by precept not to eate thereof.

What it taught man was "to measure good and euill, not by his owne will, but by the will and work of God . . . because the will of God is the fountaine of iustice and of goodnes."[13] Ralegh's explication uses the gloss from the *Testamenti Veteris Biblia Sacra* of Immanuel Tremellius and Francisco Junius (1596) to which Ross, Holland, Ainsworth, and Milton also probably allude:

> Now, as touching the sense of this tree of Knowledge of good and euill, and what operation the fruit thereof had, and as touching the propertie of the Tree it selfe, *Moses Bar-cephas* an ancient *Syrian* Doctor . . . giueth this iudgment: That the fruit of this Tree had no such vertue or qualitie, as that by tasting thereof, there was any such knowledge created in *Adam,* as if he had beene ignorant before; but as *Iunius* also noteth: . . . *The Tree of Knowledge of good and euill (that is) the experience of euill by the euent.* For thus much we can conceiue, that *Adam* being made . . . by the workmanship of Gods owne hand, in greater perfection then euer any man was produced by generation . . . he could not . . . be ignorant, that the disobaying of Gods Commandment was the fearfullest euill, and the obseruation of his precepts the happiest good.

He continues that just as a healthy man can conceive of sickness, "yet in no such degree of torment, as by the suffering and experience," so Adam, though not ignorant of the effects of disobedience before the Fall, "feelingly knew" after it the immeasurable good he had lost and the inexpressible evil he had bought. "He then saw himselfe naked both in bodie and minde; that is, depriued of Gods grace and former felicitie: and therefore was this tree called the tree of Knowledge."[14]

Milton agrees with these commentators that eating the forbidden fruit caused the loss, not the increase of knowledge and freedom. He does not agree with the more severe puritans who thought that the Tree taught "absolute subiection to God,"[15] since subjection is not the point; Adam and Eve were being "by degrees of merit raised," and the Tree gives opportunity for a degree of merit. He does not think that Adam had "perfect knowledge" "without studie," but that both Adam and Eve enjoyed learning. He does not agree that the presence of the Tree actually taught moral discrimination, since "man was made in the image of God, and had the whole law of nature so implanted and innate in him, that he needed no precept to enforce its observance" (15:115).[16] However, disobedience destroys moral discrimination; after they have eaten, Adam and Eve can no longer tell good and evil apart. He calls it not a rule but a "sign," a "pledge," and a "memorial" of obedience; it is an opportunity to choose the love of God freely and demonstrably, to be visible saints and form a visible church, and to exercise their freedom. He agrees that the Tree was named "from the event" and goes a step further: "for since Adam tasted it, we not only know evil, but we know good only by means of evil" (15:115); this is perhaps "that doom which *Adam* fell into" (4:311).

In *Paradise Lost,* unfallen Adam and Eve are "Reaping immortal fruits of joy and love" (3.67). Until they eat the forbidden fruit, they are making such rapid progress as natural philosophers that their archangelic teacher warns them, "knowledge is as food, and needs no less / Her Temperance over Appetite, to know / In measure what the mind may well contain;" yet nothing will be withheld, he assures them, that may serve God's glory and their happiness.[17] Similarly, the Tree by offering one restraint teaches them the temperance that keeps them free from self-enthrallment. It exalts them by invoking obedience to nothing less than God; and by giving them a service that is not inferred by reason, but is wholly voluntary, it distinguishes their wills. Nor are they forbidden any moral knowledge. God has sent Raphael, and indeed denominated one tree, to teach them what evil is, has permitted Satan to reveal himself in Eve's dream, and has given them "minds that can wander beyond all limit and satiety" (4:320). Yet after the Fall, God says that man would have been happier "had it suffic'd him to have known / Good by it self, and Evil not at all" (11.88–89). The knowledge of evil they would have been better off without, then, is not *cognitio,* or *doctrina,* or *sapientia,* or any kind of knowledge of evil by which virtue shines (15:115), but *scientia,* or subtle skill, as the Latin name (*Arbor scientiae boni et mali*) implies, and *experientia,* or "feeling knowledge," of the effects of evil. Adam and Eve could obtain usable knowledge from the Tree in only one way; they could increase and refine their moral powers by abstaining from it. As the contrast between the effects of obedience and the effects of the Fall clearly show, moral growth and discernment progress by resisting temptation and doing good. When they have fallen, Adam and Eve are reduced to petty spitefulness; they are unable to think in moral terms at all. Until the Fall, their zestful though tempered intellectual and moral growth displays the truth with which Milton begins his *Christian Doctrine:* "Obedience and love are always the best guides to knowledge" (14:25).

Satan, the perverse critic who has already unfitted himself to understand anything important, gets it all wrong. Self-deceived, whether in sheer impercipience or in ironic musings preparatory to his campaign, he soliloquizes upon first hearing of the command:

> One fatal Tree there stands of Knowledge call'd,
> Forbidden them to taste: Knowledge forbidd'n?
> Suspicious, reasonless. Why should thir Lord
> Envie them that? can it be sin to know,
> Can it be death? and do they onely stand
> By Ignorance, is that thir happie state,
> The proof of thir obedience and thir faith?
> O fair foundation laid whereon to build
> Thir ruine! Hence I will excite thir minds
> With more desire to know, and to reject
> Envious commands, invented with designe
> To keep them low whom knowledge might exalt
> Equal with Gods; aspiring to be such,
> They taste and die.
>
> [4.514–27]

The speech recapitulates Julian the Apostate, and it does something more: it demonstrates the habit of the self-willed mind that modern psychologists call "projection." As Trapp comments on Genesis 3:5, "It is remarkable, that the devil here chargeth God with envy, which is his own proper disease. . . . There is nothing more usual with the wicked, then *to muse as they use,* and to suppose that evil to be in others, that they find in themselves. *Caligula . . .* would not believe there was any chaste person upon earth."[18] So, apparently, Satan almost believes the lie himself when he tells Eve,

> Why then was this forbid? Why but to awe,
> Why but to keep ye low and ignorant,
> His worshippers.
>
> [9.703–5]

Moreover, the truths she knows about nurture and growth make it just credible that she could believe Satan's parody of them. Even so, if she had let "the credit" of the tree's supposed operation rest with Satan, as she intended, there would have been no sin. His lies corrupt her only when she conceives concupiscence and consents to disobey.[19]

Satan extracts this consent by perverting and debasing the virtues Eve has been developing and tempering in the previous scenes. His underlying method is to paganize God ("the Threat'ner") and then "demythologize" the spiteful deity of his own invention ("And what are Gods?"). Listening courteously and trustingly to the Snake's pretense of friendly interest, Eve heeds the pretended candor and neglects the insidious malice; guileless herself, she fails to rebuff the slander against God and accepts the perversions of truth that godlessness allows. Detached from God, "things fall apart," Eve's sense of the harmony of the cosmos is broken, and her virtues become parodic distortions, reductions, or excesses of themselves. Faith dwindles to superstition, trust to misplaced credulity, freedom to rebellion, wisdom to self-conceit; she exchanges "*spirituall Dignity* for carnall *Precedence*" (3:12), love for the desire to possess and command, and the right wish to "be like [God], as we may the neerest by possessing our souls of true vertue . . . united to the heavenly grace of faith" (4:277) for lust after godlike power bereft of virtue and grace. These "narrow circuits" are perverse trivializations of the love-in-freedom established at the lake, developed in the honest intimacy of the response of Adam and Eve to her dream, and kept open and vital in the separation scene; forgetting her bond with God and hence all bonds, Eve descends to the banal pettiness of soul-destroying egotism.

The material of Satan's conquest, then, is not in Eve's "feminine" weaknesses, which might still have been repaired; not in lack of virtue or education; but in her failure to "summon all." Goodness is a matter of action, not just innocence; of rightly and faithfully exercising all one's virtues and abilities in response to God's grace in the moment of trial. She should have, and might have (for all we have seen until now) answered with "cold horror"—Adam has even suggested that rage would not be sinful in such a confrontation—and prayed, and admonished, and turned on her heel and fetched Adam; the separation dialogue and everything else in her life up to now should have taught her that. Had she done so, she would have richly justified her own arguments for uncloistered virtue. As it is, the "event perverse" charges the reader with greater efforts and reliance on God in his or her own trials. But Eve, the fairest unsupported flower (but until now undrooping) goes slack, like the roses Adam is about to bring.

After Satan's words "replete with guile / Into her heart too easie entrance won," after all the channels of her senses are usurped and appetite awakened, Eve pauses to reflect, and in this pause, while even yet she might have recalled God's word and by a supreme effort of will besought grace to refuse the fruit, at this last moment of possible return, she falls. The "very moment" of her fall, and the proof of her responsibility for it, is the monologue during which she joins her consent to the Serpent's guile. Idolatrously, hugging the lie, "to her self she mus'd" (9.744).[20]

Milton, acknowledging the Paracletan muse at the beginning of Book 9, has said that his poem will fail "if all be mine, / Not Hers who brings it nightly to my ear" (9.46–47). Eve's monologue and the meditation on the Tree that follows her fall demonstrate the perversion of language that is the abuse of poesie. Now all *is* Eve's. Even the Serpent slinks away unnoticed. Her circuit has been straitened to the narrow compass of greedy self, and self itself to infant appetite as, drained of God, "intent now wholly on her taste," she "ingorg'd without restraint, / And knew not eating Death."

"Fruitless Hours"

Some readers feel that the Fall in *Paradise Lost* issues from a choice between reason and passionate feeling, between innocence and mature knowledge, or between love of God and love of humankind. But, as I hope this reading has helped to show, all of these are good things that Milton wholly integrates in the prelapsarian scenes, and the Fall brings the loss of them all. The fusion of "Sanctitude severe and pure" with "Beauties powerful glance" that Adam and Eve are in the process of achieving until the Fall is the essence of Paradise. Now the poet calls us to view with terror and compassion their separation and loss.

In the parody of meditation[21] that follows her fall—pitiably petty and self-exultant—Eve breaks, like Satan, what will become both tables of the law, casting off both love of God and love of Adam. She puts the god of self above God, bows down before a spurious icon, violates the peace of Paradise, commits "parricide" by killing, in fact, the parents of the whole race, decides that Adam should die with her, commits adultery by breaking the spiritual bond that Milton thought the essence of marriage, steals a sacred object, proposes to bear false witness to Adam, and covets Adam and his very nature as her own possession.

Her solitary speech is marked by altered style. Heretofore, Eve's utterance has been multifoliate, rich in suggestion, metaphor, image and beauty of sound. Her periodic cadences have reached out to embrace the whole of life, whatever her concern of the moment. If it is her love for Adam, then she sings of her pleasure in morn and evening, fragrant earth and solemn bird, sun, moon, and the "Gemms of Heaven," when he is with her (4.639–56). In her first difference of opinion with Adam she takes cognizance of the range of being, calling Adam "Offspring of Heav'n and all Earth's Lord" and remembering "Enemie . . . Angel . . . Flours . . . God . . . thee." From this copiousness derives the figurative propriety of her description of the effects of evil: "narrow circuit strait'nd by a Foe." For Milton, evil is "defect," which implies both privation of good and perversion from good. "Narrow circuit" is an oxymoron which the pun of "strait'nd" further perplexes. By collapsing the outriding circularity of "circuit" into the linearity of "narrow" Eve has composed the perfect mixed metaphor for what evil does: it both narrows and confuses. The metaphor does the violence to one's sensibilities that the evil she is characterizing would do.

After the temptation has begun, this richness and concinnity of figure and form continues. Eve's first reply preserves the capaciousness that "narrow circuit" opposes.

> For many are the Trees of God that grow
> In Paradise, and various, yet unknown
> To us, in such aboundance lies our choice,
> As leaves a greater store of Fruit untoucht,
> Still hanging uncorruptible, till men
> Grow up to thir provision, and more hands
> Help to disburden Nature of her Bearth.
> [9.618–24]

The very plainness of speech of her last sinless answer (9.659–63) fits the simplicity of truth. But when she turns to muse idolatrously upon the forbidden tree, her eloquence itself is reduced to narrow circuit, circuitous but starved of imagery. The formerly embracing cadences are now broken into jerking phrases. Her sense of a far reaching cosmos replete with diverse life and eloquent of divinity is narrowed to the circuit of "this Fruit divine," and her generous thoughts to mean calculation in financial and arithmetical metaphors, begun in her first monologue with "what profits . . . ?" and carried through her inward debate whether to share with Adam: " . . . in what sort / Shall I appear? shall I to him make known . . . and give him to partake . . . or rather not, / But keep the odds . . . to add what wants . . . but what if God have seen . . . And *Adam* wedded to another *Eve*, / Shall live . . ." (9.816–29). Finally, she abandons the lively images of her songs and reasoning thoughts and tempts Adam with a list of abstractions about herself: "opener mine Eyes . . . dilated Spirits . . . ampler Heart, / and growing up to Godhead" (9.875–77), followed by the afterthought "which for thee / Chiefly I sought," an echo of Satan's earlier perversion of her charity now used as an excuse for offering Adam, perhaps, death.

Adam, too, resorts to monologue at his fall, and he too—himself no longer a "true poem" (3:303)—dwindles from eloquence to limping verse. But before he decides irrevocably to eat the fruit, he finds the perfect metaphors for Eve's loss: "Defac't, deflourd, and now to Death devote." "Deflourd" catches up the whole delicate, chaste ardor and soul-nourishing beauty of Eve, her art, the Garden she has nurtured and adorned, their life's work of flowering toward fruition, now blighted—the Paradise being lost. "Defac't" catches up the motif of "the human face divine" (3.44), expressing those "looks Divine" in which "the image of thir glorous Maker shon," and the radiant, lucent visage of Eve whose "looks . . . infus'd / Sweetness into my heart," Adam says, when "Grace was in all her steps, Heav'n in her Eye, / In every gesture dignity and love" (8.474–75, 488–89). Now, Eve has returned with "Countnance blithe" but distempered cheek (9.885–87), and when both have fallen they cast "lascivious Eyes" that "darted contagious Fire" which, indulged, leaves them disrobed of honor, and they find "thir Eyes how op'nd, and thir minds / How dark'nd" (9.1053–54); there has been "a diminution of the majesty of the human countenance, and a conscious degradation of the mind." To be defaced is to be unselved.

Even while lamenting the loss, however, Adam follows in Eve's steps and again allows virtue to be discountenanced. Instead of trusting God for a remedy he joins Eve in sin and casts away not only love of God but his opportunity for true love of Eve.[22] Instead of raising her up, he casts himself down, and all their progeny within him. It is very "human" of Adam in the fallen, diminished sense of the word, to fall with his beloved instead of standing with God and becoming a channel of grace to her. His speech arouses compassion as well as anguish. But by withdrawing from God for love's sake he withdraws from the source of love, and human love at once becomes so debased that Adam consents to a love-triangle with death: "If Death / Consort with thee, Death is to mee as Life" (9.953–54). The lovely progression toward full union with a whole and growing person is broken and love becomes a greedy ingorging. Eve is no longer "dearer half" or "my other self" but merely "my own . . . my own . . . mine" (9.956–57).

What follows is self-absorbed lust, "terrors of conscience," recrimination, moral insensibility, irritability, triviality of mind, "high Passions, Anger, Hate, / Mistrust, Suspicion, Discord" (9.1123–24). Adam and Eve have lost both "looks divine" and "Beauties powerful glance" and are "discount'nanc't":

> Love was not in thir looks, either to God
> Or to each other, but apparent guilt,
> And shame, and perturbation, and despaire,
> Anger, and obstinancie, and hate, and guile.
> [10.109–14]

Adam, in whom now "Understanding rul'd not" (9.1127) understands one thing:

>   our Eyes
> Op'nd we find indeed, and find we know
> Both Good and Evil, Good lost, and Evil got,
> Bad Fruit of Knowledge, if this be to know,
> Which leaves us naked thus, of Honour void,
> Of Innocence, of Faith, of Puritie
> Our wonted Ornaments now soild and staind,
> And in our Faces evident the signes
> Of foul concupiscence. . . .
> [9.1070–78]

Both their "looks divine" and their eloquence have been despoiled, and they speak "estrang'd in look and alterd stile" (9.1132).

The Fall, then, is not the exploitation of weakness but the perversion of virtue. Satan has perverted simplicity to credulity, trust to corruptibility, "dauntless vertue" to willful overreaching, courage to rashness, hope to discontent, right reason to false logic, love to the hunger to possess and exceed. Eve's desire for wisdom is right, but she cannot achieve godly ends by godless means. Her desire for freedom and inward virtue is right, but Satan uses it to enslave, daunt, and enfeeble by seducing her from the source of wisdom, freedom, and virtue. Adam's loyalty to the bond of nature is right, but that can be preserved only by the bond of grace. The lesson is much more strenuous, and much more apt to speak to our condition, than it would be if Eve were merely weak and Adam merely uxorious. If prevenient depravity were necessary for the Fall, what Paradise would have been lost? Because Adam and Eve are truly images of God endowed with the capacity to love and to grow through the vigilant use of all their faculties, their fall is far more tragic than the errings of weak beings would be. At the same time, God's chastening is more justified and more efficacious, having worthier materials to work on. Most important, their regeneration is the renewal of much more ability and the possibility of future goodness is far more promising. It is because true Paradise was truly lost that true Paradise can be, by one greater Man, truly regained.

"The Seed of Woman"

"I do not know of any thing more worthy to take up the whole passion of pitty, on the one side, and joy on the other," Milton says in *Of Reformation*, "then to consider first the foule and sudden corruption, and then after many a tedious age, the long-deferr'd, but much more wonderful and happy reformation of the *Church* in these latter days" (3:1). In his account of the Fall, Milton invites us to consider with pity the foul and sudden corruption of Eve, through her of Adam, and through him of the whole world for many a tedious age. In the final books, beginning with Eve's plea for reconciliation (10.914–36), he calls us to witness with the whole passion of joy the first fruits of the regeneration begun in their hearts by God's prevenient grace. Eve, prostrate and weeping, remains "Immoveable till peace obtain'd from fault / Acknowledg'd and deplor'd," and Adam, moved to commiseration, "with peaceful words uprais[es] her soon" (10.938–39, 946). Adam's response to Eve's contrition is to seek God's will anew, and their mutual penitent tears lead to new faith and hope in the Redeemer they know of only by the mysterious name of the Seed of Woman.

Eve's part as the first to repent and seek reconciliation is the one act for which she is generally given her due, if not more. Her openness to "godly motions" is the renewal of that receptiveness to the Spirit that she seeks to preserve in the separation scene; a remnant of her supple prelapsarian nature remains for prevenient grace to work on. The beginning of her resumption of responsibility is marked by lines that echo Adam's creation for no less than "God only" and hers for no less than "God in him": "both have sin'd, but thou / Against God onely, I against God and thee" (10.930–31). However, she makes a number of false steps that betray lack of faith in God's providence. She calls the Serpent "a Foe by doom express assign'd us," feels "vehement despair," and suggests barrenness or suicide as remedies for woe. It is in rectifying these mistakes that Adam—at first merely, and equally wrongly, thinking to escape God's "vengeful ire" —stumbles upon his great moment of illumination:

> Then let us seek
> Som safer resolution, which methinks
> I have in view, calling to minde with heed
> Parts of our Sentence, that thy Seed shall bruise
> The Serpents head; piteous amends, unless
> Be meant, whom I conjecture, our grand Foe
> *Satan,* who in the Serpent hath contriv'd
> Against us this deceit: to crush his head
> Would be revenge indeed; which will be lost
> By death brought on ourselves, or childless days
> Resolv'd, as thou proposest.
>
> [10.1028–38]

Even though initially Adam's thoughts are prudential and vengeful, his recollection of the Judgment leads him to recognition of God's mercy and thence to prayer. As Georgia Christopher has pointed out,[23] it is with Adam's comprehension of the *protevangelium* uttered at the Judgment that regenerate life begins.

Although *Paradise Lost* is generally regarded as the story of the Fall of Man, Milton devotes very little time to fallen Adam and Eve. Sin, being defect, is basically uninteresting, though its effects are ruinous. The Judgment gives opportunity to repair the ruins in two related ways. First, it restores their original callings, the responsibilities toward nature, toward their children, and toward each other that they have failed in falling; and while it restores them under more difficult conditions caused by the brokenness of their bonds with God and nature, these very difficulties of toil and child-bearing are means of exercising and purgatively restoring the virtues and faculties deranged by sin. Second, it promises a Redeemer and give him a part, through those renewed callings, in his coming. That Eve is now to be ruled by Adam is typologically fitting, since apprenticeship to the Law will prepare God's people for the freedom that the "Seed of Woman" will restore. Yet Eve is never demeaned by coercion or loss of mutuality. While earnestly instructing her to resume her responsibilities, Adam begins to discover the meaning of the promise that the Seed of Woman shall overcome the Foe. They repent mutually; and they depart from the Garden "hand in hand."

One of the frauds of Satan with which Milton designedly permits his Adversary to tempt his reader early in poem — apparently with some risk of success — is the illusion that wickedness is more interesting than goodness. Once an attentive reading of the poem has unmasked Satan's deception, however, subsequent readings show what a tiresome trick it is. Goodness and blessedness bring forth endless diversity and vitality; the history of sin is the history of defect and a shrivelling of life. Satan grows less perceptive, more cliché-ridden, more narrowly self-obsessed, and more bloatedly vacuous with each episode and each rereading. Adam and Eve are drastically diminished by the Fall. Before it, their lives teem with interest. They are delighted lovers with engagingly and perplexingly distinct personalities, involved in all the textures and discoveries of human interchange; they do thoroughly interesting work as rulers and promoters of a lovely and various creation that their heightened senses keenly enjoy; they expect children whom God will endow with souls as richly distinct as their own; they have passionate feelings and searching intellects to develop, temper, and refine; they are gardeners, artists, natural historians, moral philosophers, and poets; they converse with God, with angels, and, through endlessly unfolding pleasures of linguistic discovery, with each other; and they confront challenges that give scope for growth to every faculty, virtue, and talent, including the exacting task of identifying and resisting a powerful adversary capable of innumerable attractive disguises whose opposition might have provided occasions for further flowerings of goodness and truth. The Fall robs them of individuality, vitality, eloquence, charity, intelligence, and all the deep and lasting pleasures of honesty, love, and trust. Their fallen quarrels and Satan's petty malice display the unspeakable tedium of sin, as the sinner winds himself into narrower and narrower circuits of vainglory, self-justification, projection of blame, mockery, trivialization, negation, isolation, and destruction. After the Judgment, however painfully, however hampered by the wounds of sin, they begin, starting with Eve's plea for forgiveness, to resume with wavering feet the path that unfallen they freely strode, now with a new responsibility and a new kind of hope. If Adam and Eve had not fallen, everything in the prelapsarian scenes could have been seen as prefiguring the act of faith of refusing Satan's lures; they could then have continued their growth toward perfection strengthened by a temptation to which they did not succumb. Since they did fall, everything in the prelapsarin scenes may be seen as preparation for their renewed responses to their callings, now in woe, yet with the hope that they can still do their parts in them and in the most awesome responsibility of all: that of preparing the way of the Lord.

There is nothing fortunate about the Fall. It calls forth the whole passion of pity and issues, as Adam under Michael's tutelage pityingly foresees, in agony, hatred, corruption, and death. Nevertheless, the grace of redemption and repentance, sown by God and bearing fruits of contrite prayer in two frail beings weeping wordlessly at the beginning of Book 11, call forth the "whole passion of joy." Their heartfelt sighs and prayers, the Son says to the Father, "sprung from thy implanted Grace in Man," are

> Fruits of more pleasing savour from thy seed
> Sow'n with contrition in his heart, then those
> Which his own hand manuring all the Trees
> Of Paradise could have produc't, ere fall'n
> From innocence.
>
> [11.23–30]

The pattern is that of Luke 15:7, "I say unto you, that likewise joy shall be in heaven over one sinner that repenteth, more than over ninety and nine just persons"; these are not commendations of a *felix culpa* but examples of divine and angelic magnanimity that needs no paradoxes but, in the sheer procession of goodness, uses every occasion for the increase of charity. It comes fittingly from the Son, who in his compassionate humility will suffer mockery and death and has already called himself, though Creator of all, the Seed of Woman. It is not the "foul corruption" but the "happy reformation" that he commends; yet man's repentance "from thy seed" is more pleasing to God than all the works of "his own hand." The reciprocity of grace and response is being renewed, now under the shadow of death, yet with the promise that however Satan tries to pervert good to evil, thanks not to sin but to love, God uses every means, even evil itself, to bring forth good. The heartsore contrition of Adam and Eve is more pleasing to God than their righteous works because without it they and all mankind in them would have been lost; and in his utter love he would have none lost.

The rhythm of calling and response that characterized prelapsarian experience is re-established in the last books though sung in a new mode. God makes "new flesh / Regenerate grow" in their hearts (11.4–5); Adam and Eve respond with "sighs . . . / Unutterable"; their Intercessor offers their mute prayers to the Father and renews his offer of himself in propitiation; the Father sends Michael both to expel them from the Garden and to give guidance and hope; Adam and Eve respond with the faith that follows repentance[24] and undertake the responsibilities of the life of labor, renewed love, and cleansing woe that lies before them until they are released by death into "joy and bliss" (11.43).

As Michael begins his instruction of Adam by vision and narrative,[25] he puts Eve in a position that, once more, subordinates in order to exalt:

> Ascend
> This Hill; let *Eve* (for I have drencht her eyes)
> Here sleep below while thou to foresight wak'st,
> As once thou slepst, while Shee to life was formd.
> [11.366–69]

The comparison, alluding to the creation and regeneration of both the individual and the Church, summons a host of associations. As Eve was created during Adam's sleep, Adam is, in a sense, recreated during hers; not from her side but by her Seed. Out of the symbolic death of sleep comes, for Eve, resurgent life. In her creation, Adam gave a part of himself for her. Now, Eve has offered to "importune

Heaven, that all / The sentence from thy head remov'd may light / On me," and although she is not a sufficient sacrifice herself, her cries are answered with amazing and unimaginable grace as she receives the information that out of the matter and matrix of generation that a woman proceeding from her would, alone, provide, the perfect sacrifice would be made Man. As God made Eve from Adam's flesh and bone, so after many a tedious age the Seed of Woman would be brought forth from *"Marie, second Eve"* (5.387). Meanwhile, as Adam has beheld divine visions during her creation, Eve beholds them now, and although Michael instructs Adam to inform her of what he has learned, "Chiefly what may concern her faith to know, / The great deliverance by her Seed to come" (12.599–600), she wakes already informed of this essential truth and resolved to do her part.

What does Eve dream? The images of her vision are not vouchsafed to us — perhaps because we are to provide them from the meditations of our own hearts. Her dream is one of those passages that the poet leaves open for the progression of truth within the reader. However, we may remember that the poem is such a dream, as Milton tells us when he invokes the Heavenly Muse: "thou / Visit'st my slumbers Nightly" (7.28–29). This is not a dream in any ordinary sense, but one granted to a mind prepared by "industrious and select reading, steddy observation, insight into all seemly and generous arts and affaires," as Eve has prepared for hers by her whole prelapsarian life, and one not "to be obtained of dame memory and her siren daughters, but by devout prayer to that eternal Spirit, who can enrich with all utterance and knowledge, and sends out his seraphim, with the hallowed fire of his altar, to touch and purify the lips of whom he pleases" (*Reason of Church-Government* 3:241). And we may remember that the poet's meditations upon the message given to Eve in her dream provide a whole new poem: *Paradise Regained*.

Many guides to our interpretation of Eve's regenerate dream are present in *Paradise Lost*. One such guide is its proleptic parody, the demonic dream in which Satan travesties, by false exaltation and spurious knowledge, the true knowledge and exaltation of the later dream; and Eve's unfallen response prepares for her regenerate response to this one: both combine humility with readiness for answerable deeds. Another guide is Michael's description of his part in providing this latter dream; yet Michael is God's instrument, and God

does more good through him than he knows. He says after his revelations to Adam,

> go, waken *Eve;*
> Her also I with gentle Dreams have calm'd
> Portending good, and all her spirits compos'd
> To meek submission: thou at season fit
> Let her with thee partake what thou hast heard,
> Chiefly what may concern her Faith to know,
> The great deliverance by her Seed to come
> (For by the Womans Seed) on all Mankind.
> That ye may live, which will be many dayes,
> Both in one Faith unanimous though sad,
> With cause for evils past, yet much more cheer'd
> With meditation on the happie end.
>   [12.594–605]

Michael's speech recapitulates the content and the decorum of the
last books. Adam and Eve will live "sad, / With cause," but "much
more cheer'd." The prime purpose of marriage, "one Faith unanimous," is being restored. Adam is to let Eve partake, as always, of his
knowledge, and their mutual meditations will strengthen both their
understanding of the promise and the bond between them. Michael's
parenthetic emphasis, "For by the Womans Seed," encapsulates the
miracle and roundly answers Adam's tendency to exclaim that Man's
woe stems from Woman, not by extenuating Eve's sin but by turning
attention to her renewed capacity for goodness as a forebearer of
grace.

   But, as she is about to say, Eve already knows what most concerns
her faith. What Adam will have to tell her, then, that was not included in "gentle Dreams . . . portending good," is the revelation of
the effects of sin that those dreams will enable her to bear. For she
will know, if not by Adam's relation then by her own experience, the
sharpest of sorrows, that of witnessing the fruits of disobedience in
their own offspring; as she has said, "miserable it is / To be to others
cause of misery" (10.981–82). Adam's knowledge of the history of
human suffering and of the persecution of the just will make her
"sad, / With cause," and the pain of childbirth will be slight compared to the pain of seeing one son murder another. That murder, as
a type of the Crucifixion, will be sufficient reminder that the process

of redemption involves anguish, though its issue is deliverance and bliss. As Michael unfolds to Adam the miseries to come, above all the pitiable condition of those who do evil, the losses are far more numerous than the gains until the long-deferred "happie end." Yet, in each age, one just man bears grace through the mess and pain of human history—frail, at hazard, yet sufficient—as precursor of the Promised Seed.

Finally, we learn about Eve's vision from her own response (11. 610–23). As Lee M. Johnson has pointed out, this "blank verse sonnet" results from a mode of perception that "approximates angelic intuition"; she has received "an annunciation of the Word" and "the musicality of her utterance may be . . . Milton's way of indicating that she is now in harmony with heaven."[26] Eve's supernal apperception goes beyond Adam's rational thought concerning the hope given at the Judgment (10.1028–40), and beyond his momentary doubt "Whether I should repent me now of sin . . . or rejoyce / Much more" (12.474–76); she does both unstintingly, and she embraces her transformed calling with a tranquil resolution that is the speaking picture of the peace of God and the Paradise within. That peace is not rest but the readiness of a conscience embarked on a pilgrimage fraught with every sort of difficulty and sorrow, yet prepared to respond to God's call with answerable deeds.

Adam, running to her, finds her awake, informed, and ready: "Whence thou returnst, and whither wentst, I know." As he has learned that, geographically, God is everywhere, she has learned that he is in "rousing motions"[27] rightly perceived: "For God is also in sleep, and Dreams advise." These have presaged "some great good"; since she knows the essence of that good, her "some" leaves space for Adam's instruction and for the reader's response, but it also suggests that her consolation is not only the intellectual belief that even the unregenerate may have, but the complete trust of saving faith.[28] She has fallen asleep "with sorrow and hearts distress" for failure and loss and arises ready to relinquish the Garden and undertake new and harder labors: "But now lead on; In mee is no delay." She accepts submission to her husband, which is the chastisement of being perversely beguiled and beguiling, with generosity and promptitude; gracefully varying Adam's theme, "thy stay, not free, absents thee more," she vows that her stay (with him) and her going (from the Garden) are, though enjoined, yet free through the joining of her own desire; "With thee to goe, / Is to stay here; without thee here to stay, / Is to go hence unwilling." To her renewed seriousness of purpose, she adds the sweetness of her first love song to Adam (4.639–54), in which all the joys of Paradise derived from him; now, "thou to mee / Art all things under Heav'n, all places thou, / Who for my wilful crime art banisht hence." She does not now "forget all time," however, but combines with her renewed love for Adam the sense of responsibility revealed by her unfallen acts and by her present sober acknowledgment of her crime. And she ends with wonder that God has still chosen her to do her part in the work of redemption. Her response answers exactly to Adam's resolution to learn henceforth

> that to obey is best,
> And love with fear the onely God, to walk
> As in his presence, ever to observe
> His providence, and on him sole depend,
> Mercifull over all his works, with good
> Still overcoming evil, and by small
> Accomplishing great things, by things deemd weak
> Subverting worldly strong, and worldly wise
> By simply meek;

and she will no doubt learn

> that suffering for Truths sake
> Is fortitude to highest victorie,
> And to the faithful Death the Gate of Life;
> Taught this by his example whom I now
> Acknowledge my Redeemer ever blest.
> [12:561–73]

But it is Eve who has the last word in the poem, as she concludes with solemn joy,

> This further consolation yet secure
> I carry hence; though all by mee is lost,
> Such favour I unworthie am voutsaft,
> By mee the Promis'd Seed shall all restore.

The last books of *Paradise Lost* are a perspective glass for the reader as for Adam and Eve that, by open-endedly promoting a holy rage against fallenness and a rectified receptivity to holy desires, invites the reader to engage "all the faculties of his mind," renewed and exercised by the poem, to do in life what Milton has done in harmonious numbers: to apply the scriptural typology with the full strength of reason, will, imagination, and affection to the process of re-sanctification and the regaining of paradise made possible by "one greater Man" and guided by that "Spirit that do[th] prefer / Before all Temples th'upright heart and pure." Adam's instruction by vision and narration and Eve's by dream, and the response of both in heart and in will, exemplify this process in all the faculties, and their entire prelapsarian lives have prepared them, and us, for this response. Milton's Eve is not a vain creature who fell inevitably, but the work of a provident Creator, and in all her unfallen responses to her callings a heartening portrayal of fresh, unpredictable, glad, unstinted goodness. Her "foul and sudden corruption" is far more worthy of sorrow and her "wonderful and happy reformation" far more hopeful for the possibilities of regeneration in the ever-present "us" Milton incorporates into his poem than they would be if Milton had passed on to us the weak and foolish being tradition made her. All of Eve's prelapsarian acts, as well as Adam's, prefigure her regeneration and promote the reader's. She is, as well as we, justly convicted of "wilful crime," not hapless frailty, in her fall, since she is a fully responsible person; but for the same reason she is, as well as we, capable of regeneration in all her faculties, by God's grace and Adam's help, as he with hers. They go forth to the dust and heat of a more difficult life hand in hand, with "Providence thir guide," knowing that God again has done his part and ready to do theirs; and because Milton has justified God's ways to Eve as well as Adam, and has given our imaginations a paradisal habitation worth answerable deeds, he sends his regenerate and responsive reader forth from the poem to the arduous and joyful task of choosing and restoring goodness sped by the poem's integral promise and thrust:

> For God towards thee hath done his part, do thine.

Notes

1. Milton, *A Mask*, line 781. Eve's chastity is not to be confused with "the sage / And serious doctrine of Virginity" (lines 785–86), since she does not refuse "the Rites / Mysterious of connubial Love . . . Our Maker bids increase" (4.742–48), and her ardent looks are far different from the "rigid looks of Chast austerity" which the Elder Brother compares to the Gorgon shield wherewith Minerva, "unconquer'd Vir-

gin, . . . freez'd her foes to congeal'd stone" (lines 447–49). Eve's chastity is, rather, "wedded Love . . . Loyal, Just, and Pure" (4.750–55) and the "Virgin Majestie" of her pellucid purity. On the interrelations of chastity, art, and love, see *An Apology*, 3: 303–7.

2. Milton discusses the fate of the evil angels in *De Doctrina Christiana* 1.9 (15:107–12); they are "reserved for punishment" and await judgment; and "they utterly despair of their salvation." Despair, of course, is the ultimate sin, since it denies the power of God's grace. At the time of the temptation of Eve, not yet having effected the Fall nor been defeated by the Incarnate Son, Satan and his cohorts are still in the process of choosing and spreading despair. Since the Fall, Milton explains, and even since the second defeat, they have been permitted "to wander throughout the whole earth, the air, and heaven itself, to execute the judgments of God. They are even admitted into the presence of God. Their proper place, however, is the bottomless pit." Throughout the poem, however, and even in the tractate, Milton insists that misery is always *chosen*. On Satan's "calling" and refusals, see Barker, "Structural and Doctrinal Pattern," p. 186; and cf. Louis L. Martz, *Poet of Exile: A Study of Milton's Poetry* (New Haven, 1980), p. 107.

3. Trapp, *Annotations*, p. 20. As Stanley Fish comments, as Eve "yet sinless" considers the Serpent's arguments, "the distance between her and sin is measured, as always, by the strength of her will, which is, as always, sufficient, just as the reader's will is sufficient to *his* task, which is to keep in mind, always, her sufficiency" (p. 236).

4. "Guiltiness is taken away in those who are regenerate, while original sin remains" (15:197); that is, the guilt of "evil concupiscence" is removed by the atonement even though sinful desires remain to be borne and overcome.

5. Godfrey Goodman, *The Fall of Man, or the Corruption of Natvre, prooved by the light of our naturall Reason* (London, 1616), p. 428. Goodman, however, speculates in a totally un-Miltonic way that Eve "might be ignorant of Gods commaund, for the precept was not giuen vnto her" (p. 430). On the right uses of temptation see also Richard Rolle, *The remedy ayenst the troubles of temtatyons* (STC 21262) and Richard Capel, *Tentations: Their Nature, Danger, Cure* (London, 1633). Capel argues that "Eve had no sin: yet [Satan's] tentations went beyond her, and her first listening to him and his Syren song, was a sinne in her; his first tempting her to the first sinne could not possibly presuppose a former sinne in her to worke with and upon" (p. 31).

6. Some readers, such as John Peter (*A Critique of "Paradise Lost"* [New York, 1960], p. 122), think that Eve means overpraising the forbidden fruit. But if the fruit had done what the Serpent claims, he could scarcely overpraise it, and Eve would be saying that his praise of its virtue casts doubt on its virtue. The obvious overpraising is of her.

7. Cheryl H. Fresch gives an excellent account of this passage in "Milton's Eve and the Problem of the Additions to the Command," *MiltonQ* 12 (1978): 83–90.

8. Cf. 2 Corinthians 11:3, "But I fear, lest by any means, as the serpent beguiled Eve through his subtilty, so your minds should be corrupted from the simplicity that is in Christ." Simplicity here means not simple-mindedness but clearness and wholeness. In 4.312–18 the poet says that "simplicity and spotless innocence" are "man's happiest life."

9. See especially Lee A. Jacobus, *Sudden Apprehension: Aspects of Knowledge in "Paradise Lost"* (The Hague, 1976), pp. 149–65; Irene Samuel, *Plato and Milton* (Ithaca, 1947), pp. 101–29; John M. Steadman, *Milton's Epic Characters: Image and Idol* (Chapel Hill, 1968), pp. 139–73. On the whole question of forbidden knowledge see Howard Schultz, *Milton and Forbidden Knowledge* (New York, 1955), which includes discus-

sions of the inviolability of mysteries, intellectual temperance, and the virtues of learning and reason when well used.

10. Vives, *De tradendis disciplinis,* quoted in Hogrefe, *The Sir Thomas More Circle,* p. 38.

11. Augustine, *Of the Citie of God,* p. 488.

12. *Purchas his Pilgrimage, or Relations of the World* . . . (London, 1613), pp. 11, 16, 17. See also *The Mirrour of the World,* trans. William Caxton (1480), ed. Oliver H. Prior, *EETS,* Extra Series, 110 (London, 1913): 153; Alexander Ross, *An Exposition on the fovrteene first chapters of Genesis* (London, 1626), p. 43; and Henry Holland, *The Historie of Adam* (London, 1606), p. 8.

13. Gibbens, *Qvestions and Dispvtations,* pp. 71–73. In *Areopagitica* Milton calls "*Julian* the Apostate" the "suttlest enemy to our faith" (4:307).

14. Ralegh, *History,* pp. 69–70. Milton refers to Junius' translation, e.g. 15:133 of which the gloss reads,

> arbor scientiae boni & mali: sive experientiae boni & mali. Sic metonymicè ab eventu dicitur, quia homo post esum illius vetitum a Domino . . . sciturus & experturus erat quantum bonum amisisset, & in quantum ruisset malum per suam ipsius. . . . His itaque duobus signis, uno imperato, altero vetito, informabatur homo tum de mutabili natura sua, ut sibi a se metueret, tum de immutabili constantia Dei, ut studiosissimè adhaeret Deo, seǵue in fide & obsequio illius contineret (*Testamenti veteris Biblia Sacra* [Hanover, 1596]).

Christopher Cartwright sums up the history of interpretation this way:

> *Et arborem scientiae boni & mali.*] Dicit (inquit Lyra) Josephus, quod fructus illius arboris habe at virtutem accelerandi & acuendi usum rationis: sed hoc est falsum; quia ad hoc non se extendit virtus corporalis. Et ideo dicunt Doctores Catholici, quòd dictum est lignum scientiae boni & mali ex eventu consequenti, quia per esum illius ligni homo experimentaliter cognovit quanta esset distantia inter bonum obedientiae, & malum inobedientiae. (*Electa Thargumico-Rabbinica; sive, Annotationes in Genesim* [London, 1648], p. 26.)

15. Whately, *Prototypes,* p. 4. I believe that it is the more strident Calvinist commentary about the command, and not the command itself, that Milton softens in Eve's phrase "Sole daughter of his voice," which is in keeping with the process of calling and response that for Milton is true obedience.

16. John Diodati says that the Tree was given that man might "know by experience, his true happinesse, if he persisted in innocency, or his unhappinesse, if he disobeyed this commandment of tryall, joyned to the perfect law of righteousnesse, which God had imprinted in his soule": *Pious Annotations Vpon the Holy Bible* (London, 1648), p. 2.

17. Don Parry Norford, in "The Separation of the World Parents in *Paradise Lost,*" *MiltonS* 12 (1979), says, "It is not without reason that in Christianity the Tree of Knowledge would be the root of all sin, for to ask questions, to want to know, endangers the established order" (p. 6). I do not know of any Christian interpreters who suppose that genuine knowledge is forbidden, although certain prelates of whom Milton disapproved denounced certain kinds of scientific inquiry. Norford also comments,"true growth and maturity come about, not merely through conceptual knowledge, but by acting and experience—that is, by eating of the forbidden fruit" (p. 23, n. 12). Raphael's speech on the temperate acquisition of knowledge also stresses the point that conceptual knowledge is usable only insofar as it is integrated into experience. However, the eating of the forbidden fruit is not acting, in Milton's terms, since sin is not "properly an action, for in reality it implies defect."

After they have eaten it, Adam and Eve find their capacity for action and experience much diminished. This is a natural result of their apostasy, since they have tried to acquire wisdom and love not by action, as they do before the Fall, but by consumption of food for which fraudulent claims have been made.

18. Trapp, *Annotations,* p. 20.

19. A. B. Chambers discusses contemporary views of the psychology and theology of sin in "The Falls of Adam and Eve in *Paradise Lost,*" in Kranidas, *New Essays on "Paradise Lost",* pp. 118–30.

20. Eve's musing demonstrates what Henry Lawrence writes about the difference between temptation and sin and the responsibility of the tempted for the sin: "However immediately or properly the Divell may concurre in the point of temptation, yet hee ever concurres remotely, in respect of the sin committed, for between the temptation of the Divell, and sin, there ever mediates . . . cogitation or thought, in which the temptation properly and formally lyes, so as hee may be an effectual cause of temptation but not of sin, for hee may necessitate a man to feel temptation, but not to consent to it": *An History of Angells* (London, 1650), p. 73. On soliloquy as a sign of the Fall see the essays of Harada, Sherry, and Adelman cited in n. 43 to Chapter VIII above. J. Max Patrick discusses the passage as a demonstration of Eve's capacity for "cool, careful, intricate, independent reasoning" and of her failure to make "good use of her faculties" in "A Reconsideration of the Fall of Eve," p. 20.

21. Eve's meditation parodies the steps of composition of place, of understanding, and of will explained by Louis L. Martz in *The Poetry of Meditation: A Study of English Religious Literature* (New Haven, 1962).

22. On Adam's lost opportunity through failure of trust, see Irene Samuel, "The Dialogue in Heaven," in Barker, *Modern Essays,* pp. 242–43; Barker, "Structural and Doctrinal Pattern," pp. 190–91; and Fish, *Surprised by Sin* (London, 1967), pp. 264–65. Aquinas replies to the question whether Adam's sin might be attributed not to despair but to the presumption of sinning while counting on God's mercy (*Summa Theologiae* 2a2ae163.4, 44:161).

23. Georgia Christopher, "The Verbal Gate to Paradise: Adam's 'Literary Experience' in Book X of *Paradise Lost,*" *PMLA* 70 (1975): 69–76.

24. In *De Doctrina Christiana* Milton writes, "The effects of regeneration are REPENTANCE and FAITH. REPENTANCE . . . is THE GIFT OF GOD, WHEREBY THE REGENERATE MAN PERCEIVING WITH SORROW THAT HE HAS OFFENDED GOD BY SIN, DETESTS AND AVOIDS IT, HUMBLY TURNING TO GOD THROUGH A SENSE OF THE DIVINE MERCY, AND HEARTILY STRIVING TO FOLLOW RIGHTEOUSNESS (15:379) . . . Repentance, in regenerate man, is prior to faith. Chastisement is often the instrumental cause of repentance" (15:387).

25. This process and the reader's involvement in it are discussed by Joseph H. Summers in *The Muse's Method,* chapter VIII: "The Final Vision."

26. Lee M. Johnson, "Milton's Blank Verse Sonnets," *MiltonS* 5 (1973): 143–44.

27. The phrase is from *Samson Agonistes,* l. 1382.

28. Milton distinguishes among intellectual persuasion, blind assent, and saving faith in 15:393–409 and states: "SAVING FAITH IS A FULL PERSUASION OPERATED IN US THROUGH THE GIFT OF GOD, WHEREBY WE BELIEVE, ON THE SOLE AUTHORITY OF THE PROMISE ITSELF, THAT WHATSOEVER THINGS HE HAS PROMISED IN CHRIST ARE OURS, AND ESPECIALLY THE GRACE OF ETERNAL LIFE" (15:393).

Index

Note on the Author

Diane Kelsey McColley, author of several articles on Milton and *Paradise Lost,* is an assistant professor of English at Rutgers University, Camden College of Arts and Sciences. She received a bachelor's degree from the University of California at Berkeley in 1957 and a Ph.D. degree from the University of Illinois at Urbana-Champaign in 1974.